Withdrawn from
Davidson College Library

Library of
Davidson College

Redefining Comparative Politics

Volume 173 Sage Library of Social Research

RECENT VOLUMES IN . . .
SAGE LIBRARY OF SOCIAL RESEARCH

13 Gelles **The Violent Home, Updated Edition**
78 Matthews **The Social World of Old Women**
84 Gelles **Family Violence, 2nd Edition**
96 Rutman **Planning Useful Evaluations**
119 LaRossa/LaRossa **Transition to Parenthood**
126 McPhail **Electronic Colonialism, 2nd Edition**
135 House **The Art of Public Policy Analysis**
139 Druckman/Rozelle/Baxter **Nonverbal Communication**
141 Quinney **Social Existence**
142 Toch/Grant **Reforming Human Services**
145 Rondinelli **Secondary Cities in Developing Countries**
150 Frey **Survey Research by Telephone, 2nd Edition**
152 Estes/Newcomer/and Assoc. **Fiscal Austerity and Aging**
153 Leary **Understanding Social Anxiety**
154 Hallman **Neighborhoods**
155 Russell **Sexual Exploitation**
156 Catanese **The Politics of Planning and Development**
157 Harrington/Newcomer/Estes/and Assoc. **Long Term Care of the Elderly**
158 Altheide **Media Power**
159 Douglas **Creative Interviewing**
160 Rubin **Behind the Black Robes**
161 Matthews **Friendships Through the Life Course**
162 Gottdiener **The Decline of Urban Politics**
163 Markides/Mindel **Aging and Ethnicity**
164 Zisk **Money, Media, and the Grass Roots**
165 Arterton **Teledemocracy**
166 Steinmetz **Duty Bound: Elder Abuse and Family Care**
167 Teune **Growth**
168 Blakely **Planning Local Economic Development**
169 Mathews **Strategic Intervention in Organizations**
170 Scanzoni **The Sexual Bond**
171 Prus **Pursuing Customers: An Ethnography of Marketing Activities**
172 Prus **Making Sales: Influence As Interpersonal Accomplishment**
173 Mayer **Redefining Comparative Politics: Promise Versus Performance**
174 Vannoy-Hiller **Equal Partners**
175 Brewer/Hunter **Multimethod Research in the Social Sciences**
176 Chafetz **Gender Equity**

Redefining Comparative Politics

Promise Versus Performance

Lawrence C. Mayer

Volume 173
SAGE LIBRARY OF
SOCIAL RESEARCH

SAGE PUBLICATIONS
The Publishers of Professional Social Science
Newbury Park   London   New Delhi

Copyright © 1989 by Sage Publications, Inc.

All rights reserved. No part of this book may be reproduced or utilized in any form or by any means, electronic or mechanical, including photocopying, recording, or by any information storage and retrieval system, without permission in writing from the publisher.

For information address:

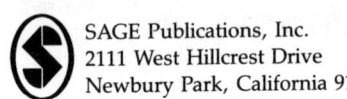
SAGE Publications, Inc.
2111 West Hillcrest Drive
Newbury Park, California 91320

SAGE Publications Ltd.
28 Banner Street
London EC1Y 8QE
England

SAGE Publications India Pvt. Ltd.
M-32 Market
Greater Kailash I
New Delhi 110 048 India

Printed in the United States of America

Library of Congress Cataloging-in-Publication Data
Mayer, Lawrence C.
    Redefining comparative politics : promise versus performance / by Lawrence C. Mayer.
      p.   cm.—(Sage library of social research ; v. 173)
    Bibliography: p.
    Includes index.
    ISBN 0-8039-3463-7.—ISBN 0-8039-3464-5 (pbk.)
      1. Comparative government.   I. Title. II. Series.
JF51.M444   1989
320.3—dc20   89-34765
                                                                         CIP

FIRST PRINTING 1989

Contents

Preface 7

1. Introduction: Revolutions and Thermidorean
   Reactions 11
   The Revolution in Comparative Politics 14
   The Impact of the Revolution on Political Research 17
   A Stalled Revolution 20
   The State of the Field: The Plan of the Book 24

2. The Epistemology of Social Science and the
   Comparative Method 28
   A Science of Politics 29
   Actual Limits on the Explanation of Human Behavior 37
   *The Problem of Exogenous Variables: The Experimental and
      Statistical Methods* 38
   The Comparative Method 42
   Theory Building with the Comparative Method 44
   Comparison and the Problem of Measurement 51
   Conclusions 56

3. Development, Ethnocentrism, and Dependency:
   Theory and Polemic 60
   Conceptualizing Political Development 64
   Explaining Underdevelopment 75
   Marxism, Leninism, and Underdevelopment 79
   Dependency Theory as an Explanation of Underdevelopment 83
   Conclusions 95

4. Industrial Democracies 101
   Conceptualizing Industrial Democracy 102
   Accountability as the Basic Democratic Value 110
   The Structure of Accountability and the Problem of Power 116
   Specialization and the Problem of Power 118
   Representative Bureaucracy 122
   Neo-Corporatism 124
   Democracy and the Crisis of Legitimacy 129

5. Parties and Political Behavior 141
   The Relevance of Parties 143
   Party Systems, Political Stability, and Electoral Systems 149
   Party Ideology or Program and Party System Performance ... 158
   Political Cleavage and Partisan Alignments 165
   Conclusions 172

6. Micro-Level Analysis: Culture, Violence, and
   Personality 178
   The Concept of Political Culture 181
   The Cultural Requisites of Democracy 192
   Cultural Change in the Postindustrial World 202
   The Cultural Basis of Modernization 206
   Explaining Authoritarianism in Psychological Terms 214
   Psychological Explanations of Violence 220
   Conclusions: Micro-Level Research and Psychoanalytic Theory ... 224

7. Kremlinology, Autocracies, and Comparative Politics 234
   Data Problems in the Analysis of Autocracies 235
   Conceptualization: Totalitarianism 239
   The Analysis of Trends in the Soviet Dictatorship: Glasnost and
     Perestroika 252
   Political Parties in Industrialized Autocracies 260
   Conclusions: Kremlinology Joins the Field? 263

8. Conclusions: Whither Comparative Politics? 272
   What Needs to Be Done to Build Explanatory Theory? 276
   The Integration of Theory and Data 278
   Explanation versus Exhortation: The Normative Dimension ... 285
   Where Do We Go from Here? The Relevance of Kuhn's Model
     for Political Science 289
   Equivalent Measurement as a Key Priority 291

   Index 297
   About the Author 303

Preface

Revolutions are ushered in with unbounded optimism that a new millenium will follow the dismantling of the old order. Yet, the hopes and promises of those who promulgate and lead revolutions are never completely realized. The concept of a revolution may provide a useful analogy to the trends in the field of comparative politics over nearly the past four decades. The premise of this book is that in the early 1950s, the leading scholars in comparative politics declared a fundamental transformation of that field with respect to its values, its underlying purposes, and its methods of analysis, a transformation that would so affect the essence of that field that the term *revolution* seems appropriate. The theme of the book is that this revolution, as with its sociopolitical counterparts, fell short of achieving its millenium. The widespread dissatisfaction with the "overstated claims" and "unfilled expectations" of the heady optimism of the 1960s had led to a breakdown of the consensus on the nature and purposes of the field (Wiarda, 1985). Although many political scientists now reject the premises of that revolution, most of the leading figures in the field still give lip service to its goals. The questions that the book seeks to explore are: To what extent, in what ways, and why was this intellectual revolution incompletely successful in achieving its millenium?

Not since that period of unbridled optimism, the period of clarion calls for the revolution in comparative politics extending from the early 1950s to the late 1970s, has there been an attempt at a systematic and evaluative look at the field as a whole and where it is headed. Nearly four decades after the clarion calls were issued, a systematic look at the corpus of literature issued in response to those calls seems in order, especially since data from research by this author and others seem to confirm that the revolution has incompletely penetrated the field and has imperfectly been reflected in the way its practitioners teach and do research (Sigelman and Gadbois, 1983; Mayer, 1983).

The criteria for this analysis of the field emanate from another underlying premise of this book, that the essence of the putative revolution in comparative politics has been to transform the field of comparative political analysis from a field defined by its geographic focus to a method that is useful and perhaps necessary in the construction of explanatory theory. The relationship between the comparative method and social science epistemology is explored in depth in Chapter 2. Thus, the *raison d'être* of the new comparative politics has become a method of accounting for exogenous contextual variables in a process of the cumulative building of explanatory theory. The thesis of this book is that this task has been very imperfectly fulfilled for three recurring reasons.

The first is that comparative scholars, in their quest for theory that is applicable to the growing variety of political contexts, have ignored the fact that generality and empiricism tend to be conflicting values. In elevating the general applicability of theory to a nearly absolute value, the imperative of specifying precise empirical indicators is frequently overlooked.

Secondly, the conceptualization in much of the literature remains too imprecise to afford consensual understanding of terms, let alone to permit consensus on the assignment of such precise empirical indicators. This fuzzy conceptualization will be shown to exacerbate the question about the validity of the measures used.

Thirdly, the putative explanatory purpose of modern comparative politics frequently becomes subordinated to more or less thinly disguised polemical or normative purposes. For example, it will be argued in the third chapter, on development, that the increasingly influential dependency literature, far from being an epistemologically respectable explanation of the existing inequality among nations with respect to material well-being, generally takes the form of a polemic whose principal purpose is the assignment of blame for the perceived evils of the world to Western industrial nations in general and to those authors' perception of capitalism in particular.

Furthermore, it will be argued that, with all of the breast beating about the revolution in the focus of comparative politics, a significant portion of the teaching and research in the field does not reflect the imperatives of that revolution, in part because many ostensible comparativists do not fully understand those imperatives and the essence of social science explanation itself, in part because old habits are hard to break, and in large part because country by country description is less demanding than the effort to build comparative explanatory theory.

Thus, while the format of the book is a survey of much of the literature in the field, the common theme of the book is a critical analysis of the direction that the field as a whole has been taking, an analysis that is both methodological and also directed at some of the substantive trends that are discussed in the literature. Important areas of the literature are surveyed and critiqued to illustrate these perceived trends. This survey is not intended as anything like a complete survey of all of the literature or even of all the important areas or topics in that literature. Topics and literature were selected according to the criterion of epitomizing or effectively illustrating the trends, strengths, or weaknesses being discussed. For example, comparative public policy, one of the growth fields in the discipline, is given short shrift in this book. Moreover, many important works are not discussed, and many of the outstanding scholars in the discipline will not find their names in the index. This should not be read, nor is it intended, as a negative statement about their importance to the field or the direction it is taking. The completeness or comprehensiveness of a survey of the literature may be an appropriate criterion by which to judge a textbook designed to inform the uninitiated about the content of the field. Since the present volume does not claim that purpose, the criterion of comprehensive coverage is not appropriate. Rather, this volume should be judged on the accuracy of the criticisms of the trends that are discussed and on the usefulness of the suggestions for the future directions and research agendas of the field.

REFERENCES

Mayer, Lawrence. 1983. "Practicing What We Preach: Comparative Politics in the 1980s." *Comparative Political Studies* 16(2, July):173–194.

Sigelman, Lee and George Gadbois. 1983. "Contemporary Comparative Politics: An Inventory and Assessment." *Comparative Political Studies* 16(3, Oct.):275–307.

Wiarda, Howard. 1985. "Comparative Politics Past and Present." In *New Directions in Comparative Politics*, edited by Howard J. Wiarda. Boulder, CO: Westview Press.

CHAPTER ONE

Introduction: Revolutions and Thermidorean Reactions

Since the 1950s, a revolution is supposed to have taken place in the field of comparative politics. Yet, three decades later, the expectations of this so-called revolution have, for the most part, not been realized. The purpose of this book is to assess and evaluate the state of and trends in comparative politics in the 1980s. A survey and critique have been made of selected major literature in the most heavily researched topics in the field, and assessment and evaluation have taken place from the perspective of this question: Why did the so-called revolution fail to materialize completely?

There is no claim to have considered every important piece of research, every notable scholar, or even every significant research topic or area. Such a goal would seem beyond the scope of any tome of reasonable length, and it is certainly beyond the scope of the present volume. Rather, the aim is to be selective with respect to the literature considered. Selectivity, however, raises the question of the criteria for inclusion.

The criteria for choosing topics and literature to be considered are as follows: (1) The author strives to consider the topics of research areas that, in his judgment, have produced the greatest volume of literature or are among the most pervasive with respect to inclusion in comparative politics courses. It would be difficult to imagine, for example, a course in general comparative politics that did not include the topic of political development or the topic of Western industrial democracy. Yet, even though some scholars consider it a "hot" topic, the topic of political economy has not yet become so pervasive. (2) The author has chosen topics and pieces of literature that, in his judgment, best illustrate the point he is trying to make about patterns and trends in the field. The studies selected may not be the best scholarship available on a given subject, especially if they are used to illustrate a shortcoming in the work on that topic. (3) No one has complete command of the entire range of literature in a field as vast and diversified as comparative politics. It may be, therefore, understandable that the author has selected literature, *ceteris paribus*, with which he is most familiar.

While there are ideal definitions of the field confining it to its explanatory purposes, generally any work concerned with governments outside the United States are assigned to the field of comparative politics. In other words, comparative politics is usually defined by the geography of its objects of study rather than as a method. This book will consider literature as comparative by its geographic definition but will use comparative analysis as a method to derive criteria for evaluating the literature.

The criteria for these evaluations are delineated in the first two chapters. Chapter 1 discusses the so-called revolution in comparative politics from the traditional legalistic, institution-oriented study of foreign governments to the role of comparative politics in constructing scientifically acceptable explanations of political phenomena.

Clearly, as this chapter will demonstrate, this revolution in the goals and values of the field was not consensually accepted. A diminishing but still significant number of respected scholars in the field overtly reject the premise of the so-called revolution that the field can and should adopt the building of empirically falsifiable, explanatory theory as its goal. Other scholars support or advocate the revolution in theory but teach their classes and conduct their scholarship according to prerevolutionary criteria. This point is emphasized in the studies by Sigelman, Gadbois, and this author cited below. Even Roy Macridis, whose now-famous critique of traditional comparative politics constituted the most frequently cited clarion call to the revolution in the field, conducted his substantive scholarship in a very traditional manner.[1]

Therefore, the literature and teaching in the field still reflect a tremendous methodological pluralism among the field's practitioners. This volume is not intended to disparage the work of scholars who eschew the premises of that revolution. Rather, the intent is to focus on the worth of that substantial and influential segment of the scholars who proclaim their intent to contribute to the goals of the "new" or "modern" comparative politics as defined by the theoreticians of this revolution. The so-called revolution did, in fact, assume a leading role in the scholarship and literature in comparative politics for several decades. Many of the leading scholars in the field have proclaimed their work to be a significant contribution to the goals of the new comparative politics. Thus, while the revolution in comparative politics did not define the arena of legitimate scholarship, it has assumed such rhetorical importance in the writing of so many of the field's leading scholars that it seems fair to examine the achievements of that revolution and to analyze the reasons why expectations were not realized.

It may, in fact, be true that the scholars who proclaimed the goal of a scientific comparative politics did not "practice what they preached." It may also be true that the expectations of this so-called revolution were unrealistic. Yet, the fact that so many of our most prominent scholars proclaimed these unrealistic goals raises the legitimate question of how and why goals that apparently seemed attainable to the most prominent scholars in our field have proven so elusive in practice.

Therefore, the book takes the vigorously stated intentions of these scholars at face value. The book asks whether the field has, in fact, become more of an explanatory enterprise according to the criterion of scientific epistemology because most of our most prominent scholars declared that was where the field ought to go or that was where the field was headed.

Since the stated goals of the new comparative politics involve making scholarship in the field more scientific, the principles of scientific explanation constitute appropriate criteria by which to judge the research of these advocates of the new comparative field. Accordingly, Chapter 2 discusses the integral role of comparison as a method in the philosophy of science and the attributes that research must possess in order to contribute to the explanatory purpose of the new comparative politics.

Several attributes of the comparative literature may detract from this explanatory purpose. One, of course, is the noncomparative, descriptive, legalistic orientation so vigorously attacked by the early critics of traditional comparative politics. Secondly, however, there is an error in the opposite direction. In reaction to the focus on the idiosyncratic facts of particular countries that characterized the traditional approach, some scholars formulated logical systems of such excessive generality that these systems lacked empirical content.[2] Thirdly, it will be argued that a more recent trend is to confuse explanatory theory with subtle polemics, to politicize the literature, as it were. While value-laden assumptions necessarily underlie any writing about politics and government, an explanatory purpose may still be distinguished from the attempt to persuade, to inculcate a point of view. The latter, of course, is entirely legitimate in its place; however, it should be recognized as such and not confused with the heart of the academic enterprise—explanation.

THE REVOLUTION IN COMPARATIVE POLITICS

It is now well known that the field of comparative politics extensively underwent a conceptual and methodological revolution in the early 1950s, a revolution that accompanied and, in many respects, led a similar revolution in political science as a whole. This revolution aimed at changing the very purpose of the field from the description of the institutions of foreign governments to the explanation of political behavior. This new purpose entailed the standard of being more comparative—that is, generalizing about more settings or systems using fewer variables—than configurative—describing the interaction of a wide variety of variables in a single system. While the comparative approach assumes that a single variable can be extracted and analyzed in isolation from the rest of the system, the configurative approach assumes any given aspect of a system makes sense only in the context of the system as a whole. For example, the configurative approach would hold that one cannot understand the fragmentation of the French party system except as a product of the interaction of French history, culture, and geography. The comparativist would assert that it makes sense to relate the party-system-fragmentation variable in a number of systems to some other single variable in those systems. The shift in emphasis from the configurative approach—the approach that characterized the more traditional comparative politics—to the comparative approach—the approach that characterizes the new comparative politics—reflects a change in the very purpose, orientation, and reason for being of the field.

Henceforth, the description of facts is, according to the criteria of the new comparative politics, not to be valued as an end in itself but rather as a means to the goal of explanation. The facts so gathered are considered useful to the extent that they can be integrated in explanatory theory. This explanatory purpose provides a criterion of relevance, a standard for deciding what facts are worth gathering. According to the new comparative politics, the value of single-country studies is a function of whether such studies entail generalizations that could logically apply to other national settings. According to this new perspective, we no longer seek to understand a place or nation as such but to use nations as settings or groups of contextual variables in seeking to explain processes and generic patterns of behavior. The field has moved from the goal of *understanding*, a term that generally refers to an intuitive feeling that one knows why phenomena occur, to *explanation*, the ability to demonstrate why phenomena occur and the ability to predict future occurrences with a known probability of success.

From the 1950s onward, a plethora of literature was produced exhorting and celebrating this revolution in comparative politics, literature that seemed to assume a growing consensus that the new comparative politics was the wave of the future, even while this literature was often less than precise about the nature of the new comparative politics.[3] History, however, has shown a penchant for moving in a nonlinear fashion. As Crane Brinton has shown, revolutions of the left, far from ushering in an egalitarian millenium, have a way of coming full circle to a new authoritarianism or, to use the term from the classic French case, *Thermidorean reaction* (Brinton, 1952). Thus, while rhetoric may reflect revolutionary ideals, realities frequently revert to the *status quo ante*. It is not self-evident, for example, that Napoleon's directorate was appreciably less authoritarian than the monarchy of Louis XVI or that the Soviet worker has a more meaningful political input than did the subjects of the Tsar.

The rhetoric in the leading comparative politics literature generally reflects the ideals of the aforementioned revolution. The ideals of science, theory, generality, and empiricism have frequently been extolled. Portions of this literature leave one with the impression that the nature and purpose of the field are now settled issues, that a consensus has been reached on the new comparative politics. This impression of a consensus is clearly misleading. As noted above and again below, the field remains highly pluralistic with respect to approach, methods, and focus. However, the rhetoric of scientific aspirations still pervades the literature from many of the most visible scholars in the field. This literature states or implies that the description of phenomena in one or more countries is no longer justified as an end in itself but only insofar as such description contributes to the goal of cross-nationally applicable explanatory theory (Almond and Powell, 1966). Such assertions about the success of the revolution, however, do not determine its factual success. Whether the field has, in fact, been transformed by this revolution, or to what extent it has been transformed, is an empirical question susceptible to data analysis, an analysis that has been undertaken.

THE IMPACT OF THE REVOLUTION ON POLITICAL RESEARCH

One might be led to expect from such "state-of-the-field" literature that the research, the textbook writing, and even the university teaching in comparative politics will reflect the new scientific ideals. Country studies should increasingly be supplanted in the journals with broadly comparative, theoretically oriented studies. Such country studies as continue to appear would be expected to strongly imply an explanation of political phenomena that is applicable to a number of other nations. Description would be expected to be rigorously related to a theoretic purpose. Any pretense of pursuing science must necessarily entail a movement toward the testing of stochastic theory and explanation against hard data, an empirical standard for truth claims as opposed to the metaphysical generalizations that all too frequently have characterized traditional political philosophy.[4]

Intellectual revolutions, like their political counterparts, cannot be accomplished in a violent, cataclysmic effort. Intellectual revolutions entail the retooling of the minds of individuals—a fundamental shift in the way one views phenomena, asks questions and assesses truth claims—or the widespread replacement of existing scholars with a new generation of intellectuals with the new epistemological and ontological orientations. Intellectuals do not change their fundamental orientation toward the world of ideas easily; the clarion calls for such a shift by a few "rebels" in the field may well have an imperfect impact on the mass of practicing scholars in the field. Such scholars may well be tempted to conduct research and to teach in the ways in which they were trained. Many may lack the time, energy, and incentive to relearn their trades in midcareer. This reluctance is especially prevalent with respect to the use of increasingly sophisticated mathematical tools in modern political analysis. It is indeed probable that a number of scholars in the past were motivated to pursue careers in the social sciences partly out of fear of and aversion to the mathematical requirements of the so-called hard sciences. Furthermore, the process of retooling does not directly lead to publications and, under the pressure of justifying a publication list each year for the purposes of tenure, promotion, and salary increases, it may be more professionally rewarding to spend scarce time and resources in writing more of the same old thing than to study new methods or to attend institutes to relearn one's field in midcareer and middle age.

The foregoing considerations cast doubt on the easy assumption that most work in comparative politics actually conforms to the imperatives of the aforementioned revolution. Hence, it is well to inquire into the actual impact of the new comparative politics on the research, textbook writing, and teaching in the field.

Data have been collected that indicate the revolution in comparative politics has penetrated the field to a significant but highly imperfect extent. These data raise the question of why this reorientation and redefinition of the field, which seemed so obviously appealing to so many of the best minds of the field, has had such an imperfect impact on the way in which work in the field is conducted. It is to this question that this book tries to suggest answers. These data are specifically concerned with the question of a comparative or explanatory purpose as opposed to a single-country organization and/or descriptive purpose for research, textbooks, and teaching in the field.

Lee Sigelman and George Gadbois surveyed the published research in the two major journals devoted exclusively to the field of comparative politics. Their research, covering a period of almost thirteen years, coded each article as comparative or noncomparative in orientation according to shifting criteria (Sigelman and Gadbois, 1983). By a definition of comparative politics suggested by this author some years ago (Mayer, 1972), a comparative study is one that attempts to generalize about similarities and differences with respect to politically relevant phenomena between two or more nation states. By the criterion, Sigelman and Gadbois find that 62% of the 444 studies surveyed in the two journals would be noncomparative—that is, focusing on a single nation (Sigelman and Gadbois, 1983). Thus, only a little more than a third of the published research in the two major organs of the field meet the minimal standards that Roy Macridis set forth in his now-famous exhortation for a new comparative politics some thirty years ago. Even when the definition of comparative politics is expanded to its broadest conceivable limits to include single-country studies that suggest explanations possibly applicable to other nations, 36.7%, or well over a third of the surveyed research, remains noncomparative. Moreover, insofar as any trend is discernible to these two authors, it is that the traditional, single-country study is increasingly dominant.[5] It is clear that a substantial and increasing portion, if not a majority, of the published research in comparative politics remains essentially noncomparative some thirty years after Macridis, Eckstein, and others announced the great revolution.

Data gathered by the present author on patterns in the organization and content of textbooks in comparative politics and of comparative politics courses themselves yield similar results, a picture of the revolution in comparative politics having imperfectly penetrated the field (Mayer, 1983). Although the data reveal that a slim majority of all textbooks are at least partially, if not completely, organized in a comparative format, nearly half of the comparative politics textbooks are still essentially presented in a country-by-country format that eschews an emphasis on generalizing across system boundaries. Textbooks in subfields of comparative politics that are defined geographically (e.g., governments of Western Europe) are more likely to be organized on a country-by-country basis than books that are topically defined (e.g., books on the comparative study of violence or parties). Textbooks are now more likely to include theoretical material than was the case twenty-five years ago. It seems fair to conclude that the revolution in comparative politics has had a highly imperfect impact on the textbooks, a finding of some import, since textbooks are a major means by which scholars in a field define and communicate its essence to their potential successors.

Similarly, the revolution has had a significant but highly imperfect impact on the organization and content of courses taught in the field of comparative politics. The manner in which courses are taught is obviously important because teaching is the other major means by which the field is defined and by which new recruits to the field are socialized as to its nature. In a mail survey of scholars listing comparative politics as their speciality in the American Political Science Association 1980 Biographical Directory, the present author found that a significant minority (41%) of the courses taught in comparative politics are still taught in a traditional country-by-country format (Mayer, 1983). Moreover, it is likely that these data underestimate the resilience and strength of the traditional orientation, since the sampling universe, members of the association, are more likely than nonmembers to be discipline-oriented scholars aware of and in agreement with modern trends in the field.

A STALLED REVOLUTION

The data on the nature and direction of research, teaching, and textbook content seem to indicate an uncertain state and direction for a field that remains badly divided as to its nature and purpose. On the one hand, there is a substantial segment of the field's practitioners proclaiming and exhorting a revolution in the field's methods and very *raison d'être*. On the other hand, it is evident that the work in both teaching and research of almost half the people in the field, including some of the prophets of the revolution, fail to reflect the imperatives of that revolution. Clearly, it is one thing to proclaim a revolution; it is quite another thing to implement it. This revolution appears to have penetrated the work of the practitioners of the field to a highly imperfect extent.

Part of the resistance to the comparative, explanatory orientation in comparative politics is due to the widespread suspicion that the study of politics and government may not appropriately utilize the scientific method or, alternatively, that there are several distinct scientific methods. This last position holds that the social sciences entail distinct epistemological imperatives from the natural sciences; however, this difference does not render the former disciplines any less scientific. Chapter 2 will argue that this pluralism-of-scientific-methods position robs the concept of scientific method of any meaning or coherence, and the position that one cannot use scientific epistemology to explain social and political events stems from an important misunderstanding of that epistemology.

Another part of this resistance stems from a perception that, however possible it may be to apply scientific epistemology to the study of politics, much of the work that purports to do so falls short of that goal in design, execution, or both. This source of skepticism about the new comparative politics has considerable merit, as will be shown in the critical review of the literature in the substantive chapters that follow.

There is a third type of work that detracts in its own way from the effort to transform comparative politics into a scientific enterprise. Polemical literature, often in a pseudo-explanatory guise, has become a trend in certain aspects of the field.

In part, this trend has arisen out of a criticism that the research that seeks to be rigorously scientific is not relevant to resolving the critical social and political problems of our day.[6] There has been a widespread perception that substance has been sacrificed to method, that questions were chosen by their amenability to rigorous research techniques rather than by the importance of their answers to the critical problems of mankind, e.g., war, hunger, pollution, overpopulation, or inequality. The concern is that such great problems of mankind have become so pressing that solutions to them cannot wait for the slow process of cumulating knowledge through basic research. Professor Easton, one of the intellectual progenitors of the "post-behavioral revolution," claims that this revolution is different from a mere return to classicism and tradition, that it is "future oriented" rather than a return to some "golden age." It has, however, much in common with the traditional attack on the explanatory mode in political research. As do the classical theorists, post-behavioralists maintain that the function of political science is to prescribe the values that guide political behavior. Easton says that the task of political scientists is to "prescribe criteria" (Easton, 1971). In other words, such post-behavioralists claim that our job is not merely to describe and explain what was or to predict, given certain preconditions, what will probably be, but to prescribe what should be. The criteria for these prescriptions should essentially be humanistic values. But is not this prescriptive rather than explanatory role of political theory the very attribute of classical political science that Easton so effectively attacked in the original edition of his classic work, *The Political System* (Easton, 1953)?

One body of pseudoexplanatory literature presents a valued state of affairs as a scientific inevitability. Such literature claims to have discovered the impersonal forces of history, evolutionary laws moving inexorably in a linear direction. The postulation of such impersonal laws, putatively beyond the power of man to cancel or change, is what Karl Popper has called "historicism."[7] The knowledge of such laws is supposed to enable one to predict the destiny of man with certainty. These laws stipulate that the forces of history will evolve only to stop at some designated state of affairs; hence, historicism is chiliastic millenarianism. Once the millenium is reached, the historical forces will somehow cease to operate; however, it is usually not clarified as to why the movement of history should stop at any given point. Such laws are generally framed at such a level of generality that any conceivable human experience may be interpreted as consistent with them; accordingly, they cannot be refuted by such experience. (We will see in Chapter 2 that this attribute of refutability is a key element in what we mean by scientific epistemology.) The Hegelian dialectic constitutes one example of such historicism. For Hegel, history consists of the interaction of ideas. Every idea generates its own negation, and this conflict generates a synthesis of the two (or, as Hegel puts it, the negation of the negation).

Since, for Hegel, reality exists not in the world of the senses but in the world of ideas, his terms are empty of sensory content; consequently, Hegel is unaccountable to the observations of others for his assertions of truth, assertions that are far from self-evident to all reasonable men. He asserts, for example, that "the state is the Divine idea as it exists on earth. . . . We must therefore worship the state. . . ."[8]

It is not surprising that the millenium envisaged by historicists is generally a state of affairs that they value. Popper shows that Hegel had ulterior motives in his millenium of a triumphant Prussian nationalism. It will be shown that other historicists in literature of the developing areas see history moving toward the final end of Western industrial democracy.

Stage theorists such as Walt Whitman Rostow and Kenneth Organski (1965) typify this phenomenon. Rostow, in fact, conceived of his theory of history as a capitalist's answer to the Marxian dialectic. Both of these writers suggest a series of stages of development through which, they postulate, all nations must pass in a linear fashion. Deviations from the Western model are conceptualized as a lack of development, a normatively inferior type, as opposed to simply a different political and economic form determined by different historical, cultural, and physical contexts. Such grand theories of history usually are, to a large extent, normative exhortations in a thin guise of scientific objectivity.

A Marxist perspective is one of the best-known examples of such historicism. One activity that continually occupies the attention of contemporary Marxist theorists is the effort to rationalize a diverse array of phenomena and events as consistent with the logical entailments of Marxian theory. Examples of such phenomena that do not seem *prima facie* to be consistent with the theory include the failure of capitalism to collapse from within, the failure of the industrial class structure to polarize, the rise of the peasantry to the forefront of anti-Western revolutionary movements, and the increasingly bourgeois orientation of the industrial labor force. This perspective, we will see, informs the construction of the increasingly popular "dependency" theory in the development literature, a theory that is critically analyzed at some length in Chapter 3. It will be argued that although dependency theory purports to explain phenomena, there is disagreement as to whether it does so within the framework of rigorous epistemological criteria and that, in fact, dependency theory is largely concerned with implying moral judgments about past behaviors and existing states of affairs. The dependency literature identifies inequalities among nations in the use of natural resources and in levels of consumption as a problem, the causes of which must be explained and a correction for which must be found. Yet, there is no consensus among competent scholars that it is a function of political scientists to explain inequality and, more importantly, to engineer equality. The growing concern in much of the development literature with material inequality among nations exemplifies the growing normative character of contemporary political theory.

THE STATE OF THE FIELD: THE PLAN OF THE BOOK

It appears that the revolution in comparative politics is not only incomplete but, in some respects, it appears to be coming full circle and approaching the *status quo ante*. In other respects, comparative politics today does differ from the stereotype of traditional comparative politics painted by the aforementioned critics of that approach. It will be recalled that they characterized the traditional approach as noncomparative, legalistic, and descriptive in purpose. Of course, like all stereotypes, this one is imperfectly true. A number of "prerevolutionary" efforts lack one or more of these putative attributes. Some, in fact, are comparatively organized, a few suggested explanations of political phenomena, and a few utilized an interdisciplinary approach with such nonlegalistic concepts as "national character," a precursor of the more modern concept of political culture. What such works did lack almost without exception is testable explanations according to the rigorous criteria of scientific epistemology.

Whether such explanations pervade postrevolutionary comparative political analysis is one question that subsequent chapters will address.

This chapter sketches a putative revolution in comparative politics from its aforementioned traditional attributes to a discipline that utilizes the comparative method to construct empirically verifiable explanatory theory. Comparison as a method enables the scholar to determine the impact of the myriad of contextual variables that otherwise would have had to remain as a residual of unexplained variation. This point is fully discussed in the next chapter. This revolution, this transformation of comparative politics into a method that renders the scientific explanation of complex social and political events feasible, is the promise of the new comparative politics.

The question that this book is attempting to address is the extent to which the performance of comparative politics, the actual teaching and substantive research by scholars practicing in the field, lives up to that promise. The bottom line of this inquiry is the extent to which the work of these scholars lives up to the imperatives of the goal of constructing scientifically acceptable explanations of political phenomena.

These imperatives of scientific explanation and their relationship to the comparative method have been extensively developed elsewhere. These works, including one by the present author, are concentrated on the explication of the comparative method and scientific epistemology. Only incidental and illustrative attempts were made to examine the application of those imperatives to the range of the substantive literature in the field.

This book emphasizes and concentrates on looking at that substantive literature with respect to the question of whether the promise of the revolution is being fulfilled. This chapter has raised some questions about that fulfillment by looking at the field in the aggregate. The chapters that follow examine specific examples of the literature throughout the field.

Inasmuch as the comparative method is the foundation of the criteria of this examination, a concise synthesis, consolidation, and interpretation of the vast, complex, and scattered literature on the comparative method seem in order. This task will be accomplished in chapter 2.

NOTES

1. The most famous of these critiques is Macridis (1955). See also Macridis and Brown (1960).
2. For a discussion of this practice, see LaPalombara (1970).
3. Among the famous exhortations in this regard is Macridis (1955). Perhaps the standard statement of "scientific" comparative politics is Przeworski and Teune (1970). For other assumptions of the triumph of the new comparative politics, see Eckstein (1963), Bill and Hargrave (1973), and Mayer (1972).
4. For the classic discussion of the metaphysical character of traditional philosophy, see Ayer (1952).
5. For instance, Macridis (1978); Wesson (1981); Deutsch, Dominguez, and Helco (1981); Beer and Ulam (1973); Dragnitch and Rasmussen (1982).
6. For an extensive discussion of the "post-behavioral revolution," see Easton (1971).
7. This is the technique that Karl Popper has called "historicism." See his classic attack on this mode of analysis in Popper (1945 and 1962).
8. This is quoted from page 31 of Popper (1945 and 1962).

REFERENCES

Almond, Gabriel and Bingham Powell. 1966. *Comparative Politics: A Developmental Approach*. Boston: Little, Brown.
Ayer, A. J. 1952. *Language, Truth and Logic*. New York: Dover Publications.
Beer, Samuel and Adam Ulam. 1973. *Patterns of Government*, 3rd ed. New York: Random House.
Bill, James and Robert Hargrave. 1972. *Comparative Politics: The Quest for Theory*. Columbus, OH: Charles Merrill.
Brinton, Crane. 1952. *The Anatomy of a Revolution*. Englewood Cliffs, NJ: Prentice Hall.
Deutsch, Karl, Jorge Dominguez, and Hugh Helco. 1981. *Comparative Government: Politics of Industrialized and Developing Nations*. Boston: Houghton Mifflin.
Dragnitch, Alex and Jorgen Rasmussen. 1982. *Major European Governments*, 6th ed. Homewood, IL: The Dorsey Press.
Easton, David. 1953. *The Political System*, 1st ed. New York: Knopf.
Easton, David. 1971. *The Political System*, 2nd ed. New York: Knopf.
Eckstein, Harry. 1963. "A Perspective on Comparative Politics, Past and Pres-

ent." In *Comparative Politics: A Reader,* edited by Eckstein and David Apter. New York: The Free Press.

LaPalombara, Joseph. 1970. "Parsimony and Empiricism in Corporate Politics: An Anti-Scholastic View." In *The Methodology of Comparative Research,* edited by Robert T. Holt and John E. Turner. New York: The Free Press.

Macridis, Roy. 1955. *The Study of Comparative Government.* New York: Random House.

Macridis, Roy and Bernard Brown. 1960. *The DeGaulle Republic.* Homewood, IL, NJ: The Dorsey Press.

Macridis, Roy. 1978. *Modern Political System: Europe,* 4th ed. Englewood Cliffs, NJ: Prentice Hall.

Mayer, Lawrence. 1972. *Comparative Political Inquiry.* Homewood, IL: The Dorsey Press.

Mayer, Lawrence. 1983. "Practicing What We Preach: Comparative Politics in the 1980s." *Comparative Political Studies* 16(2, July):173–194.

Organski, Kenneth. 1965. *The Stages of Political Development.* New York: Knopf.

Popper, Karl. 1945, 1962. *The Open Society and its Enemies.* New York: Harper and Row.

Przeworski, Adam and Henry Teune. 1970. *The Logic of Comparative Social Inquiry.* New York: John Wiley.

Rostow, Walt W. 1960. *The Stages of Economic Growth.* London: Cambridge University Press.

Sigelman, Lee and George Gadbois. 1983. "Contemporary Comparative Politics: An Inventory and Assessment." *Comparative Political Studies* 16(3, Oct.):275–307.

Wesson, Robert. 1981. *Modern Governments: Three Worlds of Politics.* Englewood Cliffs, NJ: Prentice Hall.

CHAPTER TWO

The Epistemology of Social Science and the Comparative Method

The revolution in comparative politics discussed in the introductory chapter was part of a broader revolution in the field of political science itself. This broader revolution was clearly intended by its progenitors to bring political science in line with what they perceived to be the attributes of other respected academic disciplines, especially the natural sciences. Specifically, the architects of the revolution in political science endeavored to transform the field from an essentially descriptive enterprise that emphasized the idiographic attributes of social and political phenomena to an enterprise that could explain and predict such phenomena through the formulation of general laws. Comparative political analysis should, in this view, be seen as a method that, if not coterminous with the effort to build a science of politics, is at least one of the useful tools in this effort. This reconceptualization of the comparative field from a geographical focus on foreign government to a method of building a science of politics presumes that such a science is a possible and desirable goal. While this presumption is increasingly widely accepted among political scientists, it is by no means universally accepted.

Hence, it is the task of this chapter to show that there is a scientific method, that it can and should be applied to social and political phenomena, and that comparative analysis is one method that contributes to the process of formulating scientifically acceptable explanations of political phenomena. Furthermore, it will be argued that comparison is, in one sense, virtually synonymous with the scientific process and that cross-national comparison is an indispensible tool for constructing many explanatory theories.

Since the new comparative politics receives its principal *raison d'être* from its contribution to building a science of politics, that contribution provides a major criterion for evaluating the significance of each piece of literature in the field. In turn, the contribution of any piece of literature to building a science of politics is a function of how one conceptualizes such a science. Accordingly, this chapter will begin by briefly delineating the essential attributes of a science of politics as that concept is used in this volume. The chapter will go on to analyze the contribution of comparative analysis to building such a science.

A SCIENCE OF POLITICS

Despite pockets of resistance, there is a widespread consensus entrenched in the natural sciences and growing in the social and behavioral sciences that a scientific method exists to explain the phenomena with which that discipline is concerned. Description or narratives have a valuable role to play in the data collection enterprise; however, they do not constitute ends in themselves. Description and narration are of value to the extent that they contribute to the explanatory process.

Explanations in the social or behavioral sciences differ from those in the natural sciences with respect to their completeness and to the accuracy of the predictions they generate. However, the structure of scientific explanation remains the same regardless of the subject matter. The standards of what does or does not constitute a scientifically adequate explanation does not vary with the subject matter.

A scientific explanation consists of a principle, a general statement of a relationship among two or more concepts, that logically entails either the certainty or the probability of the specific phenomenon to be explained such that if the principle were true, then the phenomenon to be explained, the *explicandum*, should occur, given the stipulated preconditions. An explanatory principle is more than a statement of an empirical relationship; it further implies why the relationship should exist. This principle thus becomes a theory that itself accounts for the observed relationship.

For instance, in the violence literature, it was shown that there is a correlation between indices of want formation in relation to indices of want satisfaction on the one hand and a composite index of violent political behavior on the other, or between indices of economic and political discrimination and political separatism on the one hand and measures of civil strife on the other. The correlations obtained have the status of scientific propositions (the probabilistic social science counterpart to scientific laws). However, the question of why these relationships should be observed is answered by a theoretic principle that the psychological states of frustration, anger, or "relative deprivation"—the relationship between what one thinks he or she deserves and what one expects to be able to obtain—lead to aggression. One does not directly observe the psychological states, of course. However, if the theory were true, the observed relation logically should be observed in stipulated circumstances. A theory is thus only indirectly testable.

Theory thus compromises the epistemological criteria of crude positivism which hold that we only know that which is directly observable. B. F. Skinner, for instance, advocates the eschewal of all inner-man or personality constructs as a reversion to metaphysics. It is enough to know that certain behaviors do recur when reinforced by certain stimuli, he claims; the inference of causation is unnecessary. By definition, theoretical constructs, as well as any inference, involve a measure of subjectivity. Skinner and other positivists implicitly raise the question of why it is useful to infer a theoretic construct to logically account for observed patterns and thus interject an element of subjectivity into scientific analysis. Knowing that directly observed patterns of behavior do occur will afford the ability to predict and, in some measure, to control such behavior; hence, it is unnecessary to speculate on why such patterns exist.

Scientific theory is not true or false. Rather, it is more or less useful with respect to the number and variety of empirical relationships for which it can account and the extent to which empirical relationships can be derived from it, thereby expanding our knowledge.

In a deterministic science (such as physics), we may say that if the principle were true the explicandum must follow. In the behavioral sciences, we are only able to say that it is more likely to follow than if the preconditions did not exist. The precise probability of the occurrence of the explicandum can frequently be stipulated through the statistical method. Thus, the explicandum must be shown to be a specific case of a more generic concept that is systematically related to another concept. Therefore, explanation is, by definition, a generalizing activity that inexorably involves the method of comparison.

While a scientific explanation consists of a principle that entails the explicandum, such an explanation also implies that the relationship between the explicandum and the factor that putatively accounts for the explicandum, the *explicans*, is causal in nature. When we predict that an observed relationship will continue to exist, the only logical basis for making such a prediction is the assumption that some causal factor is operating.

However, the mere fact of any imperfect relationship does not necessarily entail causation. A conclusion of causation always involves inference, the process of moving from a body of data to a conclusion with a certain amount of interpretation. The imperatives for the necessary conclusion that a given relationship is causal have been listed by Ernest Nagel as follows: (1) The relationship is invariable. (2) The explicans is both a necessary and a sufficient condition for the explicandum although, rather than list all the sufficient conditions, the practice is to list the event that completes the sufficient conditions. (3) The relationship is between phenomena that are specially contiguous. (4) The explicandum follows the explicans in an invariable temporal sequence, and this relationship is asymmetrical (Nagel, 1962). These conditions are never encountered in the social sciences; therefore, one of the major tasks of social inquiry is causal inference, the attempt to distinguish on an empirical basis which relationships are causal in nature and which ones are not.

This task is rendered difficult in social inquiry by the fact that our explanations imply some but not all of the causes of the explicandum. To this extent, our explanations are incomplete (Brodbeck, 1968; Hempel, 1968). The consequence of this incompleteness is that the explicandum does not invariably follow from the presence of the putatively causal variable, the explicans. It will be shown below that social research has as one of its major concerns the task of rendering explanations relatively more complete and that the comparative method is one major method in accomplishing this task.

Przeworski and Teune cite a famous example of an incomplete explanation, one to which we shall return. M. Rouget, a 24-year-old worker in a large factory, has voted Communist (Przeworski and Teune, 1970). Why did he do so? We know that young, male, industrial workers tend to vote for left-wing parties. M Rouget's attributes fit the first set of concepts; his vote is a particular instance of left voting, implying that there is something about being young, male, and a worker in a large factory that causes one to vote for left-wing parties. Why did he vote that way? In part, because of the aforementioned attributes.

Of course, knowledge of these attributes does not enable us to predict M. Rouget's vote with certainty. We can only say that of the aggregate of people with those attributes, a significantly greater portion will vote left than the aggregate of people without those attributes. We can predict probabilistically but not with certainty. Why not? Our predictions can only be probabilistic because there are more factors that can and do influence individual votes than any single analysis can encompass. The foregoing analysis, for instance, omits the influence of church affiliation, church attendance, family, peers, and all combinations and permutations of unique individual experiences. By identifying some but not all of the factors that influence the explicandum, our explanations remain incomplete.

Obviously, the more causal factors we can isolate and include in our analysis, the more complete, by definition, our explanation becomes and the more accurate our predictions will be. It is inconceivable that we could isolate and identify more of the causes of an explicandum without enhancing our ability to predict its occurrence. Predictability is not an either/or phenomenon in a probabilistic discipline; rather, the accuracy of predictions in such a discipline is a matter of degree. To the extent that a principle significantly enhances one's power to predict an explicandum over not having the principle, we say the principle affords explanatory power. Principles that appear to account for some phenomena under question without enhancing the ability to predict them possess what Anatol Rapoport has called "explanatory appeal" (Rapoport, 1968).[1] Abraham Kaplan has referred to this distinction in terms of "seeing an explanation" as opposed to "having" one. The former types of explanation, lacking explanatory or predictive power, are called by Kaplan "runic explanations."

Kaplan provides an example of such a "runic" explanation, the attribution of the problems of the Weimar Republic to Germany's Jewish population (Kaplan 1964). However, since nations with comparable Jewish populations did not experience comparable socioeconomic problems, that explanation afforded no predictive power, although it apparently satisfied a great many German citizens. Clearly, explanations that lack predictive power ought to be regarded with a good deal of suspicion.

The fit of the predictions generated by explanatory principles to actual occurrences provides a test of the utility of those principles and renders them accountable. Accountability, one of the major imperatives of scientific epistemology, means that truth claims must be demonstrated, not merely asserted. Scientific epistemology is not concerned with criteria for the formulation of such truth claims or explanatory principles; rather, it is concerned with criteria for the justification of such claims.

Truth claims that do not entail any predictions about the sensory or empirical world remain impressionistically true or false, depending upon the individual. Conclusions are subjective in the sense that they depend on the internal dispositions of each individual drawing them. By imposing criteria for the justification of truth claims in terms of sensory data, scientific epistemology seeks to render conclusions intersubjective—consistent from one subject to another despite their differing internal dispositions.

These criteria of justification demand that explanatory principles logically entail some expectations of what any observer would see under stipulated conditions. Unless such a precise set of expectations is generated, one has no means of assessing the compatibility of truth claims with reality. Truth claims that generate unrealized expectations must accordingly be rejected or revised so as to be compatible with sensory experience. In other words, scientific epistemology demands that truth claims or explanatory principles be stated in such a way that they are intersubjectively falsifiable, that there be some conceivable body of data that would cause one to reject or revise the truth claim.[2]

Statements that do not generate such expectations tell us nothing about the experiential world. Such statements may refer to phenomena outside of our experiential world, such as statements about the nature of heaven, hell, or purgatory. They may refer to events that occurred in the past on a one-time basis without any logical expectation that they would ever occur again under stipulated conditions, events such as the biblical account of creation. To say that such statements are not scientific is not to say that they are false; it is to say that their consistency or the lack thereof with the relevant evidence cannot be demonstrated. Such statements constitute what A. J. Ayer calls metaphysical statements (Ayer, 1952). He calls such statements meaningless in the sense that they tell us nothing about our world of experience.

There are those who assert that the concept of knowledge should extend to such metaphysical statements. Such scholars treat the concept of knowledge as a normative one and seem to resent the implication that their eschewal of the criteria of the scientific method renders their truth claims normatively inferior. For instance, Leo Strauss charges that scientific epistemology denies the status of knowledge to "prescientific knowledge", by which he presumably means such metaphysical statements as revealed religious truth and intuitive judgments, in other words, those conclusions of which he is subjectively certain (Strauss, 1957). However, what is self-evident to him is not necessarily self-evident to others.

Abraham Maslow similarly advocates humanistic and holistic conceptions of science ". . . in blunt contradiction to the classical, conventional philosophy of science still too widely prevalent and they offer a far better substitute for scientific work with persons" (Maslow, 1970, p.3).

"Pure science," he declares, "has no more intrinsic value than humanistic science" (Maslow, 1970, p.3). The difficulty is that the concept of knowledge is widely understood to refer to a given class of assertions, thereby distinguishing them from other assertions. That class of assertions may also present certain advantages over other assertions that give those assertions called *knowledge* a certain value. Being demonstrable, scientific propositions generate results that are intersubjectively discernible. By definition, the results of scientific knowledge are there for all to see, regardless of their internal dispositions. The power is generated and the lights go on, or the bomb goes off and it matters little whether the theories about nuclear reactions that formed the bases of these phenomena are essentially true.

When one refers to assertions as knowledge or science even though they do not possess the attributes of scientific propositions, one fails to give these other assertions those desired attributes and renders the concept of knowledge meaningless. If all assertions are knowledge, the terms *knowledge* and *assertion* become synonymous, and one of them becomes redundant.

It is clear, then, that those propositions that we regard as scientific must, by definition, be empirical in the sense of being falsifiable by sensory data. It is also clear, however, that this requirement could be met by probabilistic statements as well as by deterministic ones. It is not necessary to hold that a single deviant case entails the rejection of the theory. It is only necessary to specify in advance of testing a theory which or how many deviant cases would entail its rejection. Hence, the fact that human behavior is overdetermined and impossible to predict with certainty in individual cases does not render a science of such behavior impossible to construct.

The concept of free will is held by many to conflict with the attempt to build a science of human behavior. The concept of free will, a concept fundamental in the Judaic-Christian tradition, entails the human capacity to choose, to control one's behavior. To argue, as is implied by social science, that human behavior is caused, one seems to deny that capacity to choose and, perhaps more significantly, to deny the moral responsibility that presumes this capacity to choose. Hence, the entire enterprise of a science of human behavior seems to be in direct conflict with an important aspect of that Judaic-Christian tradition, the power to choose between right and wrong.

For this reason, B. F. Skinner entitles the book popularizing his theory of the causes of human behavior, *Beyond Freedom and Dignity* (1971). The latter two terms imply the freedom to choose to do right or wrong, the ability to disobey the "laws" of behavior. If one's behavior is determined by factors outside oneself, one cannot be blamed or praised for one's actions. The Judaic-Christian moral tradition presumes the capacity to defy causes, to resist the imperatives of one's environment, or to overcome temptation. Similarly, one does not seem as deserving of praise for good works that were caused by factors external to the actor in question.

The argument that people make choices that are completely autonomous of factors external to human will is subject to serious reservation. While it is clear that people do choose, the choices they make are constrained by experiences and by contextual variables. *Will* refers to human desire; *choice* refers to picking from among available alternatives. Clearly, one cannot will states that, because of contextual or other external factors, are not among the available alternatives.

The very fact that human behavior is so predictable supports the working assumption that, while people make choices, the choices are rendered more or less likely by factors external to the actor. While the resolution of the debate between the supporters of free will and the supporters of social causation can never be objectively determined, the working assumption that behavior is caused does, in fact, yield substantial predictive power about many important aspects of that behavior.

The attribution of any given behavior to the internal nature of the actor eschews the inquiry into how the actor acquired such a nature. When you answer the question, "Why did he do that evil thing?" with the explanation, "Because he is vicious," you not only avoid the question of how he became vicious, but you are, in effect, stating a tautology. You know he is vicious because of the behavior that the attribute *viciousness* is adduced to explain. The putative dispositional attribute of the actor, far from referring to any precise set of independently conceptualized phenomena, becomes an undefined repository of all those causes of behavior that cannot be identified and measured.

ACTUAL LIMITS ON THE EXPLANATION OF HUMAN BEHAVIOR

It should be clear from the foregoing that, while the probabilistic propositions of social science are structurally the same as those of natural science, an important difference remains between the two fields of inquiry. While in the natural sciences the variables under analysis can generally be isolated from exogenous variables that could affect the outcome to be explained, such outcomes in the social sciences are usually affected by a nearly limitless array of variables that cannot be effectively isolated one from the other. Hence, all feasible propositions in the social sciences must be qualified that they will hold true only to the extent that these unanalyzed or exogenous variables cancel one another out or, otherwise put, they hold true other things being equal (*ceteris paribus*). Of course, the other things never are equal; they act to produce unexpected outcomes that render social science propositions less than universally true. It is the ubiquitous existence of this *ceteris paribus* qualifier that distinguishes propositions in the social sciences from the deterministic propositions feasible in the natural sciences. The phenomena in which social scientists are interested are almost always overdetermined; simplistic propositions to the effect that X causes Y usually constitute a very imperfect description of reality. The outcome Y will not invariably follow the putative cause X, due to the presence or absence of these exogenous variables.

The inability to make deterministic predictions does not render such causal statements untrue. Such statements may well be partial truths, in the sense that they account for some but not all of the causes of the explicandum. It was noted above that most social or political phenomena are overdetermined, meaning that social phenomena are the product of an almost infinite myriad of factors, only a fraction of which can be identified in any manageable study. These unanalyzed factors in any given theory are exogenous to that theory. The impact of such exogenous factors on any given explicandum will generate results in some fraction of the observations that are not entailed by the theory; these factors are those "other things" that the *ceteris paribus* clause assumes will cancel one another out, but they never do so.

THE PROBLEM OF EXOGENOUS VARIABLES: THE EXPERIMENTAL AND STATISTICAL METHODS

A major problem of social research is to isolate putatively causal relationships from exogenous variables. Several methods are available for this purpose: the experimental method, the statistical method, and the comparative method.[3]

The experimental method best fits popularized notions of the way scientists actually proceed. This method attempts to effect the actual isolation of the exogenous factors under analysis from exogenous factors that may impact on the phenomenon in question by the consciously selective administration of the putatively causal stimulus to one group (the experimental group) but not to another group (the control group), with both groups selected so as to be as alike as possible in other salient respects. Each group is then measured or tested for the variable that constitutes the explicandum. Since no other relevant stimuli were introduced, it should then be possible to assess the actual impact of the explicandum. Some opportunities for this kind of analysis do exist in political research, for instance, simulations and game theory. However, the complex patterns of human behavior and interaction in which political scientists are interested can rarely be isolated from the context in which they occur; hence, one can rarely be certain that the experimental group (to which the putatively causal factor is administered) and the control group (to which that factor is not administered) are, in fact, alike in all other respects. Moreover, many of the putatively causal phenomena in which political scientists are interested cannot be selectively administered or withheld at will; consequently, the social scientist is forced into the role of a passive observer rather than the active creator of a situation implied by the experimental model. Such phenomena can only be imperfectly simulated in experimental research. Experiments are termed valid to the extent that their findings can be extrapolated from the experimental setting to social and political behavior in general. The artificiality of the experimental setting may impede the validity of experimental findings. Frequently, the putatively causal stimuli may involve hypothetical rather than actual situations. For example, the dispositional sets known as social alienation or frustration thought to generate civil violence cannot be reproduced at will in individuals; hence, experimental research utilizing these variables would have to take on a hypothetical mode.

For example, although they were using survey research rather than the experimental method, the small, parochial nature of their sample forced Grofman and Muller to construct a concept called "the potential for political violence" to represent the likelihood of engaging in actual violence (Grofman and Muller, 1973). This potential-for-violence variable was indicated by responses to a questionnaire constituting an approval-of-political-violence scale and an intention-to-engage-in-violence scale. However, it is one thing to approve of violence on paper; it is quite another thing to actually engage in violence. The empirical connection between the contrived and managed potential-for-violence variable in this study and the variable in which the authors are theoretically interested—violent behavior—remains an open question.

When one moves from the controlled and deliberate administration of artificial stimuli in the experimental situation to the passive observation of natural (i.e., uncontrolled) stimuli in the nonexperimental world, the impact of exogenous variables can no longer be excluded. The impact of such variables can, however, be assessed by one of two methods.

The statistical method can reveal what a stochastic relationship between two variables *would* be if all other relevant variables canceled one another out and thus had no aggregate impact on the explicandum. In the case of contingency relationships, tendencies toward the joint occurrence of the independent and dependent variables, the cases to be tested are divided into those that possess the exogenous variables to be controlled and those that do not. In this "elaboration model," it is then possible to ascertain whether the presence or absence of the control variable changes either the structure or magnitude of the relationship in question. If the putatively causal relationship disappears when the control variable is not present, it is reasonable to conclude that it was the control variable, rather than the independent or test variable, that had the direct causal impact. The control variable in such a case may either be the intervening variable or it may cause both the independent and dependent variables, depending on whether the control variable occurs before the independent variable.

In the case of correlation, the concept of a relationship in which one variable changes proportionally to change in another variable, it is also possible to assess the impact of one or more exogenous variables on the relationship in question. The technique of partial correlations is based upon the Pearsonian product moment correlation coefficient (r), a technique that measures

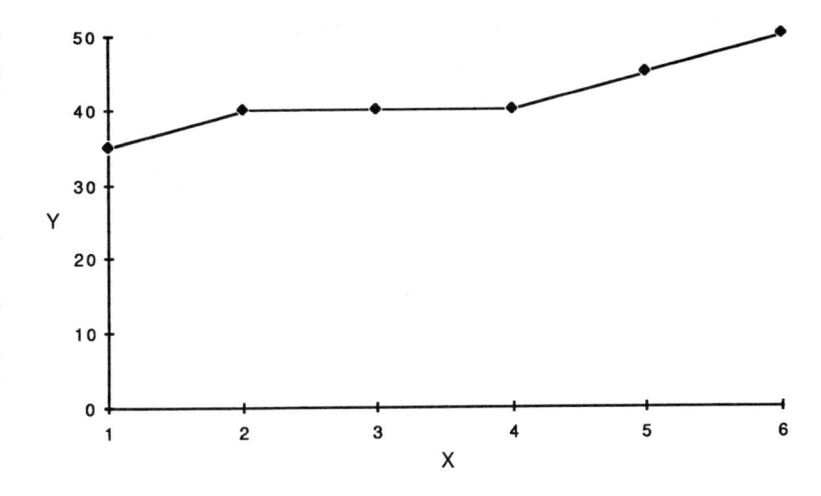

The Epistemology of Social Science and the Comparative Method 41

Figure 2.1. Hypothetical Regression

the extent to which the magnitude of the independent variable is predictable from the magnitude of the dependent variable (Blalock, 1964). The coefficient is based upon the square root of the mean squared deviation in the magnitude of the cases of the dependent variable about their mean. As such, it is sensitive to the extent that cases on the dependent variable fall into a linear pattern. It is not sensitive to the magnitude of change in that variable; hence, it does not measure the impact of the independent variable on the dependent variable. In Figure 2.1, the hypothetical data set indicates a high correlation between the variables although the magnitude of the dependent variable remains virtually unchanged, reflecting that changes in the magnitude of the independent variable have little impact on the magnitude of the dependent variable. Yet, because the magnitude of the dependent variable is highly predictable from knowledge of the magnitude of the independent variable, this hypothetical data set would also yield a very high correlation coefficient. Hence, an inference of causation from a high value of r can be misleading.

The discrepency between the predicted magnitude of the dependent variable and the actual magnitude of the dependent variable is known as the residual. A partial correlation involves correlating the independent and the dependent variables respectively with a control variable, then correlating the residuals with one another. Since those residuals reflect that part of the variation in the independent and dependent variables that is not predictable from the control variable, a partial correlation reflects what the value of r would be if the magnitude of the control variable did not vary, a valuable tool in the aforementioned task of distinguishing causal relationships from other forms of relationship.

THE COMPARATIVE METHOD

The third method of adjusting the imperatives of scientific inquiry to the ubiquitous reality of exogenous variables is the comparative method. Unlike the experimental method, the comparative method does not aspire to isolate the explanatory theory in question from the impact of exogenous variables; rather, like the statistical method, the comparative tries to identify and measure the impact of exogenous variables.

The unique role of the comparative method in building explanatory theory arises from the fact that one may identify two distinct types of objects for analysis: the attributes of individuals and the attributes of whole systems. Przeworski and Teune refer to them as levels of analysis (Przeworski and Teune, 1970). System-level attributes include such phenomena as a nation's political culture, historical experiences, geographical factors (e.g., permeable or insular borders), or demographic factors (e.g., the social stratification system). These system-level attributes constitute the context within which relationships exist among the characteristics of individuals or groups, a context that frequently will affect the magnitude or even the nature of such within system relationships. It is entirely conceivable, for example, that the relationship between some measure of economic or political deprivations and actual participation in civil violence would be stronger in a system with a history of "successful" violence than in a system in which such violence has been practically nonexistent. In the former class of systems, the experience of accomplishing political goals by violent means would likely render such means more legitimate. The foregoing remains a stochastic theory, however, until the impact of a nation's historical experience with violence on the original relationship is empirically investigated.

When a relationship between within-system concepts differs in structure or significantly in magnitude from one system to another, the reasonable inference is that some system level variable has a causal impact on the original explicandum. This situation constitutes "system level interference" in a within-system relationship (Przeworski and Teune, 1970). Conversely, as a within-system relationship holds true in a greater variety of contexts, one gains more confidence that the relationship is, in fact, causal.

Clearly, the only way that one can empirically determine whether such system level interference exists is by the application of the within-system relationship in as many different contexts as possible. This application of within-system relationships in different contexts constitutes the definition of comparative analysis as a method. This method of assessing the contextual impact on within-system explanatory generalizations is not necessarily cross-national. One may discern differing contexts within complex nations, or one may engage in comparative analysis within a nation in a diachronic sense. The important point is that the method permits one to empirically determine the impact of different contexts on any explanatory generalization.

If, for example, the relationship between economic or political deprivation and violent behavior held true to about the same extent in systems with a violent or revolutionary past and those systems with a history of peaceful evolution, one might reasonably conclude that the variable of a nation's history with respect to violence had little or no effect on the probability of violent behavior in the near future. Przeworski and Teune suggest that comparative analysis is only appropriate when system level interference is present; in the example just given, comparative analysis would be unnecessary. However, it is not possible to establish the absence of system level interference without comparative analysis. A putatively causal relationship among two or more concepts that is derived from data gathered in one context remains conjectural until it is tested against data from other contexts.

An example can be found in the frequent assertion that the economic strength of the United States is due to its particular economic system, a system that places relatively greater reliance on the market for the allocation of economic goods. However, as long as the data supporting this assertion are drawn from this one context, one cannot dismiss the possibility that the joint presence of the two concepts (of economic well-being and policies placing more reliance on the market) is spurious. When one finds that indicators of economic strength are strongly present in other systems with very different economic policies, one may reasonably suspect that the economic strength of the United States is due to other factors. Among the possible explicans are such system level variables as natural resources, population growth, or even insular borders that may have allowed during that nation's developmental years a concentration of resources on capital goods rather than on national defense.

THEORY BUILDING WITH THE COMPARATIVE METHOD

Knowledge is expanded in science by the discovery of deviant cases, by the falsification of explanatory propositions as they are stated. While finding that the data support existing propositions gives one more confidence that such propositions are, in fact, at least partially causal rather than spurious, the tentative confirmation of propositions still serves to consolidate that which is already known or suspected rather than expanding on that knowledge. It is in the process of accounting for disconfirming or anomolous data that one expands on what is already known.

In an illustration discussed earlier, M. Rouget's vote is explained in terms of age, occupation, and sex. Knowing one's age and occupation enables us to predict one's vote with a given probability (substantially above chance); however, knowledge of one's gender substantially improves our ability to predict voting behavior in France. We gain substantially more confidence in our theory as we apply it to a variety of other systems (e.g., Italy, Chile) and find that it still holds true. When we apply the theory to Norway, however, we find that gender difference in voting behavior disappears. Thus, we can now say that men are more likely than women to vote for a left-wing candidate except in Norway.

At this point, explanation ceases as Norway becomes a label for the repository of whatever unidentified factors cause it to be an exception to the theory. In this use of a label, the term *Norway* is a substitute for the analysis of potentially relevant exogenous variables; thus, the proper names of systems in comparative analysis are similar to the "inner man" concepts used by personality theorists to "explain" behavior. To the question, "Why did he do that?" the personality theorist might answer, "Because of his courage, his goodness, his anality," or some other personality concept. However, such concepts not only serve as repositories for the unexplained causes of the behaviors in question, but they constitute essentially tautological reasoning. Why did he risk his life? Because he is courageous. What is a courageous person? Among other things, it is someone who would risk his safety.

Moreover, a proper noun can never serve as the explicans in a scientifically adequate explanation because, referring to a finite phenomenon, such an explanation cannot logically entail any conclusions beyond that phenomenon. It was shown above that explanatory power necessarily entails predictive power, the capacity to logically extrapolate from those patterns directly observed to what would be expected in stipulated preconditions. This capacity becomes possible only when the concepts in the explanatory principle each refer to an infinite category of observations. When the concepts have a finite empirical content, the proposition becomes descriptive.

Thus, the fact that the proposition about sex and voting does not hold true in Norway does not entail any expectations about where else the proposition will not hold true. Our knowledge is not advanced beyond that which is directly observed. A field of inquiry that does not permit us to extrapolate from that which is seen to that which should logically be expected in stipulated circumstances is mere description.

This chapter has argued that it is through the finding of such deviant cases, the falsification of explanatory propositions, that knowledge is advanced. In the foregoing example of a deviant case being an idiosyncratic system identified by a proper noun, knowledge is advanced by the specification of those generic attributes of the system that putatively cause it to be an exception to the theory, or, as Przeworski and Teune put it, by translating the proper names of systems into common noun variables (Przeworski and Teune, 1970). Hence, one should not say that there is a sex difference in voting except in Norway; rather, one should say that there is a sex difference in voting except in those systems in which religion has a diminished political salience, of which Norway happens to be one case. One would then logically expect sex differences in voting also to disappear in other systems in which religion has a low political salience. The theory purporting to explain voting behavior has now become more complex with the addition of the salience-of-religion variable, more narrowly applicable (there are now fewer instances that would entail the prediction of particular vote) but more complete and more accurate with respect to the predictions derived from it.

The cumulative addition of relevant variables by accounting for deviant cases is what is meant by building theory. Theory building in this sense is not the product of a single, grand creative insight so much as the incremental process of cumulating knowledge bits over time. A major argument of this chapter is that the unique potential of comparative analysis lies in the cumulative and incremental addition of system-level attributes to existing explanatory theory, thereby making such theory progressively more complete.

Clearly, there are logistic constraints on the number and variety of contexts to which an explanatory theory may be applied in any given project. At today's prices, many thousands of dollars are required to execute cross-national surveys, and grant money for social research is becoming rather more scarce than in the past. As our knowledge of social reality expands, multivariate analysis is becoming the norm; hence, given the pressure to "complete" and publish a number of research projects within a given time frame, the trend is toward fewer cases with more variables.

Accordingly, the strengths of the comparative method would be best utilized if research were more truly cumulative, if more effort were directed to the testing of existing explanatory theory in a wider variety of settings. Unfortunately, the incentive structure (the kinds of manuscripts most likely to be published) serves to encourage the formulation of new explanatory principles and frequently to urge others to undertake the mundane task of submitting such principles to empirical tests. If such principles are tested, the testing usually occurs in a single setting or in very few settings (Sigelman and Gadbois, 1983). Clearly, more academic prestige is attached to the role of theorizer than to the role of replicator of existing theory.

Yet, at the current state of development of comparative politics, the replication function may be the most crucial one for expanding the corpus of what we can say that we know. The journals are replete with innovative theoretic insights that cry out for testing, falsification, and modification. It is through falsification that knowledge is expanded; yet, rarely does one find a published study in which the null hypothesis is accepted.

The literature in epistemology stresses the conflicting criteria of "parsimony" and accuracy for explanatory theory. However, the value of parsimony has frequently been extolled at the expense of the conflicting imperative of accuracy. *Parsimony,* in this sense, refers to the goal of having theories unencumbered with numerous qualifying variables. Obviously, there are advantages in the ability to explain much of the variation in any given phenomena with one or two factors. The more exogenous factors exist of which one need take account, the more difficult the research task becomes.

Rarely, however, do such "parsimonious" theories explain

much of the variation in the complex phenomena in which political scientists tend to be interested. Such phenomena are, as was noted above, nearly always overdetermined. Hence, parsimonious theories frequently generate inaccurate predictions because they are so incomplete. The value of parsimony needs to be balanced against the conflicting value of increasing a theory's predictive power. The value of parsimony has, in the social sciences, the impact of producing very large unexplained residuals. The task of more completely explaining and more accurately predicting reality is inexorably a task of rendering explanatory theories more complex through the addition and analysis of formerly exogenous variables. The more of the unexplained residuals that are specified and incorporated into one's theory, the more accurate will be the predictions deductively entailed by the theory. Theory building consists of the specification and analysis of factors that were part of the unexplained residuals in existing explanatory theory.

The identification of factors in the unexplained residual begins with the falsification of the theory as stated. When a theory that had been supported by the data in several other settings is falsified in a given system, the task at hand is to delineate in generic terms those attributes in which the deviant-case system differs from the systems in which the theory was supported, attributes that could logically account for the deviant-case results.

For example, shortly after the Second World War, a parsimonious theory that purported to explain the instability and collapse of parliamentary governments throughout Europe in the prewar years gained widespread credence. The complex phenomena of the instability and collapse of these parliamentary regimes was putatively traced to one institutional factor, the type of electoral system used by the nation in question. This explanation, most notably associated with the work of F. A. Hermans and Maurice Duverger (Hermans, 1951; Duverger, 1963),[4] suggested that a category of electoral systems collectively known as proportional representation (P.R.) promotes fragmented party systems which, in turn, enhance the probability of cabinet instability. This causal model would look like this: P.R. → party fragmentation → cabinet instability → system collapse. The proponents of this theory were able to offer both empirical and logical support for it. Empirically, it was shown that European parliamentary systems that had been beset by cabinet instability and an inability to govern had both fragmented party systems and a proportional type of electoral system. Logically, it was shown how that type of electoral system should encourage the proliferation and persistence of small parties and how the fragmentation of a party system should encourage dogmatic extremism, thus impeding the compromises necessary to form stable governing coalitions.

Despite the *prima facie* persuasiveness of the case made by the anti-P.R. crusaders, a growing number of anomalies began to be noticed in the decades immediately following World War II: nations that combined proportional representation with cabinet stability. (The converse putative relationship between the Anglo-American single-member district, plurality-electoral system, and a high degree of party aggregation approximating a two-party system, on the other hand, still appears to hold true universally.) Party systems did not necessarily fragment when P.R. was adopted. Moreover, systems consisting of more than two parties did not generate either political extremism or cabinet instability. The Scandinavian democracies and the Low Countries constitute the most obvious anomalies to the P.R. → instability theory.

The tendency of the leading scholars of the discipline, in the face of such contradictory evidence, was to reject outright the electoral-system—cabinet-stability theory as spurious. The existence of anomolous or deviant cases to social theory, however, does not entail the conclusion that the explicans is completely without causal impact on the explicandum. A more useful strategy in the face of anomolies to a theory that did appear to account for a range of other phenomena would be to ascertain those attributes common to the deviant cases and absent in those cases in which the theory held true, attributes that could logically account for the observed anomolies. Thus, in the case of Hermans' theory, it is one thing to say that the explanation that purported to account for differences in cabinet stability among Great Britain, Weimar Germany, Italy, and France does not hold true in Scandinavia, the Low Countries, and Israel. It would be theoretically more useful to delineate the attributes common to the disconfirming or anomolous group of systems in terms of generic variables.

In the example under discussion, the deviant cases are systems in which P.R. produced neither the party fragmentation nor the cabinet instability entailed by the electoral-system theory. These systems all seem to lack those cultural attributes that generate fissiparous tendencies in their stratification system. In those systems, the "interest aggregation" function, in the language of Gabriel Almond, has been inadequately performed. Thus, the theory must now hold that P.R. *permits* the fragmentation of party systems and the representation of extremist positions in those cultural contexts whose fissiparous tendencies discourage the formation of broad and stable political coalitions and otherwise promote extremist politics.

To give another illustration, observers of the American political scene have discerned a growing tendency in the 1980s for women to vote in a more liberal direction than do men (Holbert, 1982). This tendency appears to contradict the conventional wisdom among students of Western democracies, especially of Western Europe, that women act as a conservative political force. This author and others are involved in research to determine in which systems sex predicts voting choice at all and in which systems women tend to vote one way rather than another (Mayer and Smith, 1983). The task of the research is ultimately to specify how cultural or other contextual factors act as intervening variables between gender and voting behavior. Preliminary findings suggest that the salience of religiosity in a nation affects the impact of sex on voting behavior. Religious women tend to be more conservative than men; secularized women tend to be either more liberal or not significantly different in their voting behavior from males, depending on other individual level factors.

Thus, it is suggested that the contribution of comparative analysis to the building of explanatory theory is to distinguish the type of context in which a given explanation holds true and those types of contexts in which it does not. This identification of contextual qualifications as intervening variables to explanatory theory increases the complexity of such theory as well as its predictive accuracy and explanatory completeness.

COMPARISON AND THE PROBLEM OF MEASUREMENT

It follows from the foregoing that the goals of comparative analysis are best served when explanatory theory is applied to the widest possible variety of contexts. Hence, one of the reactions to the traditional noncomparative, single-nation emphasis of the old field of comparative government was to try to construct *general theories of politics*. This term meant theories that would hold true regardless of the various idiosyncratic contextual attributes of particular political or social systems.

This focus on building general theory borrowed heavily from the Parsonian school in sociology, the work of Talcott Parsons and his followers.[5] This orientation has been most notably represented in political science in the work of David Easton (1953, 1965, and 1971). Parsons began his intellectual career with the modest goal of a search for a general theory of human action or behavior; later Parsons was to reorient his efforts toward the prolegomena of a general theory of social systems. It is noteworthy that none of the general theorists ever claimed to have constructed such a general theory ready for testing against a body of empirical data. Rather their efforts have been focused upon the construction of concepts and logical systems that, in the effort to make them universally applicable, have been devoid of empirical content. The more formalized and creative examples of such logical systems (e.g., the work of systems theorists such as Parsons or Easton or of structural-functionalists such as Binder or Almond) contain the elements of explanatory theory except for rules of correspondence linking the concepts employed in these systems to sensory reality.

These general theorists were, of course, aware that their work fell short of explanatory theory in the accepted scientific sense of that term. They defended their efforts as steps *toward* the construction of explanatory theory. (Frequently, their efforts were, in fact, entitled "Toward a Theory of . . ." or, in the case of an article by Binder, 1957, "Prolegomena to a Theory of . . .") In eschewing the claim to be suggesting an explanatory theory as such, these general theorists thus insulate themselves from all of the criticisms that could be leveled at the epistemological shortcomings of their efforts. (The specifics of such criticisms have been thoroughly delineated elsewhere by this author, among others Mayer, 1972 and LaPalombara, 1970.) In leaving to others the task of deriving researchable propositions from their theoretic frameworks, these theorists have allocated to themselves the role of pointing out the difficult road we must travel without providing a hint of how to surmount the seemingly impregnable barriers that we will necessarily face en route.

It has been a central argument of this chapter that the epistemological imperatives of comparative analysis require the discovery of the logical relationships among the properties of phenomena, relationships that hold true across systems. This requirement entails the value of generality, that the relationships in question be applied to the widest possible variety of systemic contexts. Values must inevitably be compromised by and balanced against other values with which they conflict. Empirical testability and its concomitant imperative of precise rules of correspondence is no less a value than widespread, if not universal, applicability.

The conflict arises because indicators, those sensory phenomena that tell us whether, and the extent to which, the theoretic phenomenon is presumed to be present, are context-specific. While concepts may logically apply to a variety of political systems, the observations that denote their presumed presence or magnitude derive their meaning from the context in which they are found. A given frequency of reading a newspaper may indicate a high level of psychological involvement in politics in a context in which such newspapers are not easily obtained, but that same frequency may indicate apathy where such newspapers are easily accessible and such readership is a widespread cultural norm. Similarly, a group of Eastern European dissidents who huddle around a shortwave radio once a week at the risk of their lives to hear the latest news broadcast from the West, may indicate a higher level of political involvement than their American counterparts who casually watch the television news four or five times per week because the news happens to follow their favorite situation comedy. The same frequency of church attendance may not indicate the same level of religiosity in all religions and, hence, in all systems. Among Orthodox Jews, for example, attendance at synagogue service is largely a male duty; hence, many very observant Jewish women rarely attend such formal services. Observance of dietary laws may be a better indicator for them but not for people in religions in which such laws are less central. In one more example of the context-specific meaning of indicators, this author and his colleague, in their research on the impact of sexual consciousness on the voting behavior of women in Western democracies, had to measure the concept of a woman's vote, the extent to which women tend to vote for those concerns and values articulated by feminist leaders as central to their movement. The imperfect measure used was a vote for parties of the left on the assumption that such parties generally espouse those values of concern to feminist leaders (e.g., marketplace equity policies, access to abortion, a pacificist or accomodationist approach to foreign policy). However, the presumed validity of this common indicator is compromised by the fact that it is not self-evident that parties of the left will necessarily espouse such values and, conversely, that parties of the right will necessarily oppose them in all nations—with equal clarity. In some nations, the major electoral choices may not be perceived as clearly distinct with respect to feminist values and concerns; hence, the absence of a statistical relationship between gender and voting in such a setting may not have the same meaning for the extent of feminist consciousness as it would in a setting where parties of the left clearly differed from parties of the right on such values.

The goal is not commonality of indicators in each system under study but that the concepts retain a consistent meaning in each context in which they are applied. This goal may require the use of different indicators in different settings. Clearly, a measure of judgment and inference is involved in the selection of indicators to establish conceptual equivalence because of the absence of universally agreed upon, objective criteria to establish the validity of indicators.

Many concepts used in social research have theoretic meanings distinct from the measures that indicate the presence of such concepts and the strength of that presence. Such concepts are not *operationalized* in the commonly understood sense of that term. Dispositional attributes, such as alienation or frustration, can most easily be measured by behaviors that are inferred to indicate the extent to which such dispositions are presumed to be present. Concepts such as stability, modernization, or dependency are not defined merely in terms of the measures used to indicate their presence but rather are given essential meanings apart from their assigned indicators. Such creative utilization of indirect indicators expands the body of stochastic theory that can be rendered testable.

However, the use of such indirect indicators raises the question of *validity*—the extent to which the indicator actually measures the concept it purports to measure. The use of such indicators involves often unexplicated assumptions about the relationship between these indicators and their concepts. It is assumed in some of the literature on political violence, for example, that a growing gap between the formation and the satisfaction of wants will produce the psychological state of frustration. Such inferences about the properties of individuals from aggregate data constitute the oft-discussed ecological fallacy, the invalid presumption that what is true about the relationship among aggregates is not necessarily true for the relationship among individuals within such aggregates (Robinson, 1950). Clearly, scholars of the caliber of those who created the concept of systemic frustration were not unaware of this methodological vulnerability in their work. Critiques based upon this problem are pointing out the obvious. If social scientists are to measure the kinds of theoretic concepts with which they are necessarily concerned, imperfect inferences from the empirical data designated as indirect indicators of such concepts to the concepts themselves will be unavoidable. The extensive literature on the problem of validity leads to the conclusion that validity cannot be conclusively established. Problems of measurement can only be ameliorated; they cannot be eliminated without the concomitant elimination of theory itself.

The exacerbation of the problems of measurement posed by comparative analysis, the problem of "equivalence" or "the traveling problem," reflects the conflict between important methodological values: generality and empiricism. By using indirect aggregate-data indicators for dispositional attributes, researchers on the topic of violence such as Ivo and Rosalind Feierabend, Betty Nesvold, and Ted Gurr were able to apply these concepts to as many as 114 polities (Feierabend 1966, Gurr 1968). The advantage of taking into account as many distinct contexts as possible for the goal of specifying the impact of exogenous variables has been discussed above at length. The logistical and monetary barriers to the attempt to directly measure such dispositional attributes are well known. In the aforementioned studies, the imperfection of inferential measurement was the price of achieving that degree of universality in the data base. The price of questionable validity may exceed the benefit of added generality in a given case; that is a judgment to be made in individual cases. The aforementioned general theorists such as Easton and others of the Parsonian school pursued the value of generality at the expense of empirical content. It may be that some who object to inferential measurement err in the other direction. The point is that the precision and validity of measuring instruments or indicators on one hand and the cross-national applicability of concepts and the generality of analysis on the other constitute conflicting values to be balanced and compromised against one another. To pursue either one of these values to an absolute extent, in effect, denies the legitimacy of the other important values. Hence, the optimum solution for comparative political inquiry may entail indicators that are imperfectly valid and theory that is less than universal in scope.

CONCLUSIONS

The central theme of this chapter is that comparative analysis should be considered as a method that plays a central role in the explanatory mission of political science itself. It is assumed that political science is an enterprise with the goal of any other scientific enterprise: to develop theories that explain and predict the phenomena with which it is concerned. In pursuing this goal, all scientific enterprises employ certain criteria in the justification of truth claims. These criteria of justification constitute the essence of the distinction between science and what A. J. Ayer calls "metaphysics" (Ayer, 1952, p. 33) or, in Karl Popper's words, "the criterion of demarcation." (Popper, 1954, pp. 34–37, 42–4, Popper, 1963, chapt. 11) The application of these criteria in analysis is what we call the scientific method.

This chapter has argued that there is one such scientific method that can be applied, with appropriate modifications in the area of technique, to all forms of inquiry including the study of social and political phenomena. The claim made here, that the same epistemological criteria apply to the social and behavioral sciences as to the natural sciences, must be qualified by the almost inevitable presence of a large unexplained residual in the explanation of social and political phenomena. Such residuals are attributable to a repository of variables, variables that impact upon the phenomena with which we are concerned but are unanalyzed by and, hence, exogenous to all explanatory theory in political science.

Such exogenous variables frequently constitute attributes of the political or social system itself: the social, cultural, or historical context in which political behavior takes place. It was shown how cross-contextual analysis constitutes the best available method for ascertaining the impact of such contextual variables on the phenomena to be explained. Hence, the function of comparative analysis as a method is best fulfilled, *ceteris paribus*, when explanatory theory is applied to as wide a variety of contexts as possible.

Accordingly, analysis becomes comparative when explanatory theory is framed in such a way that it could be applied to data in two or more distinct contexts. These contexts may or may not involve more than one political system; however, the contexts must differ from one another with respect to at least one important attribute that may affect the magnitude or quality of the explicandum. This book recognizes that explanatory theory may be created based upon data from one context or one political system and that theory entails expectations about data from other systems or contexts. In this way, single-system or single-case analysis may serve as a *means* to comparative analysis. However, such single-system or single-case analysis as an *end* in itself, even if derived from a foreign government, is not *comparative politics* as that term is used in this book. The analysis of foreign governments as an end in itself does not serve the methodological function of comparative politics. Hence, data from foreign governments are useful only insofar as they have theoretic and comparative relevance.

The *ceteris paribus* qualifier referred to above implies a value conflict with cross-contextual generality. This conflicting value is that explanatory theory shall have empirical content. That is, the concepts that comprise such a theory should either be defined in terms of sensory data (operationalized) or assigned indicators that unambiguously determine the extent to which the concept is presumed to be present.

Since the meaning of actions or phenomena varies from context to context, it is rarely possible to operationalize many of the important concepts in political analysis. Moreover, the rules of inference from data to concept vary from one context to another. Hence, the maintenance of a consistent meaning for concepts becomes one of the difficult tasks of cross-contextual analysis.

The contextual relativity of the meaning or the measures of indicators constitutes the most serious impediment to the cross-contextual validity of empirically testable explanatory theory. Yet, this chapter argues that the building of such theory constitutes the *raison d'être* of comparative political analysis. Compromises must inevitably be made, it was argued, in the validity of measures used and in the geographical scope of theory in order to balance these important and conflicting imperatives. Subsequent chapters will examine the success and prospects of scholarship in comparative politics in filling this key theory-building role.

NOTES

1. See also Rapoport (1953).
2. This is the criterion of demarcation proposed by Karl Popper (1954) to distinguish scientific from nonscientific propositions.
3. This classification of methods is delineated in Lijphart (1971).
4. See also Milnor (1969) for the most recent and most naive example of a true believer in the single-factor (electoral system) explanation of cabinet stability.
5. For a sympathetic analysis of the whole of Parsons' contribution, see Mitchell (1967).

REFERENCES

Ayer, A. J. 1952. *Language, Truth and Logic*. New York: Dover Publications.
Binder, Leonard. 1957. Prolegomena to the Comparative Study of Middle East Governments. *American Political Science Review* LI (3, Sept.).
Blalock, Hubert M. 1964. *Causal Inferences in Non-Experimental Research*. Chapel Hill: University of North Carolina Press.
Brodbeck, May. 1968. "Explanation, Prediction, and Imperfect Knowledge." In *Readings in the Philosophy of Social Science*. New York: Macmillan.
Duverger, Maurice. 1963. *Political Parties*, translated by Barbara and Robert North. New York: John Wiley.
Easton, David. 1953 and 1971. *The Political System*. New York: Knopf.
Easton, David. 1965. *A Systems Analysis of Political Life*. New York: John Wiley.
Feierabend, Ivo and Rosalind Feierabend. 1966. "Systemic Conditions of Political Aggression: An Application of Frustration-Aggression Theory." *Journal of Conflict Resolution* X(3, Sept.):249–271.
Grofman, Bernard and Edward N. Muller. "The Strange Case of Relative Gratification and Potential for Political Violence: The V-Curve Hypothesis." *American Political Science Review* LXVII (2, June): 514–539.
Gurr, Ted. 1968. "A Causal Model of Civil Strife: A Comparative Analysis Using New Indices." *American Political Science Review* LXII(4, Dec.):1104–1124.
Hempel, Carl. 1968. "Explanatory Incompleteness." In *Readings in the Philosophy of Social Science*, edited by May Brodbeck. New York: Macmillan.
Hermans, F. A. 1951. *Europe Under Democracy or Anarchy*. South Bend, IN: University of Notre Dame Press.
Holbert, Ann. 1982. "What Gender Gap?" *New York Times* (Dec. 10):35.

Kaplan, Abraham. 1964. *The Conduct of Inquiry.* San Francisco: Chandler Publishing Company.
LaPalombara, Joseph. 1970. "Parsimony and Empiricism in Comparative Politics." In *The Methodology of Comparative Research,* edited by Robert T. Holt and John E. Turner. New York: The Free Press.
Lijphart, Arend. 1971. *American Political Science Review* LXV(3, Sept.):682–693.
Maslow, Abraham. 1970. *Motivation and Personality,* 2nd ed. New York: Harper and Row.
Mayer, Lawrence. 1972. *Comparative Political Inquiry.* Homewood, IL: The Dorsey Press.
Mayer, Lawrence and Roland Smith. 1983. "The Impact of Gender on Electoral Choice in Western Democracies." Paper delivered to the annual meeting of the American Political Science Association.
Milnor, A. J. 1969. *Elections and Political Stability.* Boston: Little, Brown.
Mitchell, William U. 1967. *Sociological Analysis and Politics.* Englewood Cliffs, NJ: Prentice Hall.
Nagel, Ernst. 1962. *The Structure of Science.* New York: Harcourt, Brace, and World.
Parsons, Talcott. 1949. *Essays in Sociological Theory.* New York: The Free Press.
Parsons, Talcott and Edward Shils. 1951. *Toward a General Theory of Action.* New York: Harper and Row.
Parsons, Talcott. 1957. *Social Theory and Social Structure.* New York: The Free Press.
Popper, Karl. 1954. *The Logic of Scientific Discovery.* New York: Harper and Row.
Popper, Karl. 1963. *Conjectures and Refutations.* New York: Harper and Row.
Przeworski, Adam and Henry Teune. 1970. *The Logic of Comparative Social Inquiry.* New York: John Wiley.
Rapoport, Anatol. 1968. "Explanatory Power and Explanatory Appeal of Theories." Unpublished paper prepared for a conference on explanatory theory in political science, University of Texas at Austin, February.
Rapoport, Anatol. 1967. *Operational Philosophies.* (pp. 53–64). New York: John Wiley. (Reprinted from New York: Harper and Row, 1953).
Robinson, W. S. 1950. "Ecological Correlations and the Behavior of Individuals." *American Sociological Review* XV(3, June):351–357.
Shively, W. Phillips. 1969. "Ecological Inference: The use of aggregate data to study individuals." *American Political Science Review* LXIII(3, Dec.), 1183–1196.
Sigelman, Lee and George Gadbois. 1983. "Contemporary Comparative Politics: An Inventory and Assessment." *Comparative Political Studies* 16(3, Oct.): 275–307.
Skinner, B. F. 1971. *Beyond Freedom and Dignity.* New York: Knopf.
Strauss, Leo. 1957. "What Is Political Philosophy?" *Journal of Politics* 19(3, Aug.): 352ff.

CHAPTER THREE

Development, Ethnocentrism, and Dependency: Theory and Polemic

It was not coincidental that the revolution in comparative politics discussed in the preceding chapters was accompanied by a concomitant "discovery" of the politics of what is generally understood to encompass those political systems among neither the Western industrialized democracies nor the relatively industrialized socialist autocracies of the Soviet bloc. Hence, the term "third world" is generally understood to refer to most of the political systems of Asia, Africa, and Latin America. However, the lines of demarcation in this tripartite classification of the world's political systems are imprecise, leaving a number of political systems about whose label in that classification reasonable observers may disagree. Are Greece and Spain, for example, to be grouped with the first or third world nations? Moreover, even when there is widespread consensus as to how to classify given systems, the range of diversity within each category is so great as to render the classificaiton useless for scientific purposes. India, for example, is probably third world to most scholars; yet, India may have more in common with some industrial democracies than it has with such relatively undeveloped nations as Upper Volta, Chad, or Lesotho. Clearly, problems of imprecise conceptualization abound in the study of "developing areas" or "third world nations," problems that we will presently consider in some detail.

The field of comparative politics in its prerevolutionary period, as is widely acknowledged and piously deplored, took on a parochial cast by confining itself to the major European powers. Technology, ideological changes, and the impact of World War II combined to make the salience of the rest of the world inescapable. Isolationism had been discredited by our World War II experiences; hence, it was no longer either politically respectable or physically feasible at the current state of technology, the imperatives of which made global interdependence and interaction inexorable. The collapse of the overseas empires of the Western powers led to a rapid growth in the number of sovereign, independent nations, nations that, in the nature of things, came into being with a disposition toward a suspicious if not adversarial relationship with the West. These systems were to constitute an inescapable political force that we in the West now had to confront and, hence, to understand. The need to understand this hitherto unexplored subject matter created a virgin frontier for new scholars seeking to make their names and build their careers. Scholars poured into this intellectual vacuum, and an avalanche of literature has continued to be discharged from it.

The conceptual tools of traditional political science were often ill-suited to the study of these non-Western nations. Constitutionally designated structures, the focus of the traditional approach, were frequently absent or poorly developed and bad, sometimes having taken on functions or meanings distinct from those that defined these structures in Western nations.

Hence, the pioneers in the study of non-Western or less-developed nations took the lead in introducing concepts from other social sciences to the study of politics. Concepts such as functionalism or those involving the attributes of social structures were introduced as tools for the study of such non-Western or less-developed systems (Almond, 1960).

Such conceptual tools from sister disciplines—especially sociology, anthropology, and social psychology—seemed to be highly useful for the explanatory focus of the new comparative analysis and of political science in general, whether dealing with the more- or the less-industrialized nations. Those constitutionally designated structures that have traditionally been identified as explicitly political do not exist in a vacuum; they are the product of the social, cultural, and economic contexts in which they are found. To explain such structures, one must analyze those less-explicitly political phenomena that determine their nature. In this way, the expansion of the geographic scope of comparative politics was accompanied by an expansion of its conceptual scope. Furthermore, this conceptual expansion of the province of political analysis was an inescapable concomitant of the newer explanatory focus of the field.

Hence, if, as was argued in the preceding chapter, comparative politics had an important role to play in the application of the scientific method to the study of political phenomena, the study of the less-developed nations within the field has had a unique contribution to make to that scientific enterprise. It is, therefore, fitting that the literature devoted to the non-Western or less-industrialized parts of the world be judged from the perspective of its contribution to that scientific enterprise.

This chapter will argue that the literature in this area fails to fulfill that scientific or explanatory mission for several reasons. First, much of the literature lacks the conceptual precision necessary for scientifically adequate explanatory theory, due in part to the conflicting imperatives between generality and empirical precision discussed in the preceding chapter. Concepts, when applied to a wide range of phenomena, tend to be imprecise in theoretic or essential meaning and to lack consistent and precise rules of correspondence to sensory indicators. Second, it will be argued that much of the literature has taken on a polemical or normative perspective.

Two frequently conflicting values that have explicitly or implicitly shaped so much of the literature in political science—order and justice—are values that have similarly been implicit in the literature on political development. The concern for order underlies a substantial literature that is concerned with the destabilizing effects of political change, a literature to be discussed in some detail below (Huntington, 1968; Olson, 1963). This concern for the value of order is frequently quite manifest in the literature. For example, the explicandum of the systems analysis and functionalist literature is explicitly the persistence or maintenance of the system. In fact, the functionalists define *function*, as opposed to *dysfunction*, as the consequences of phenomena or behavior that contribute to this system maintenance.

What is not always explicated in this literature is that order as a value can conflict with other values, such as some conceptions of social justice generally defined in terms of some measure of material egalitarianism. Conceptions of social justice imply some idealized state of affairs, a state that generally conflicts with the status quo. Hence, the goal of those who are concerned with some conception of social justice may not be system or pattern maintenance. The goal of such people may rather be the breakdown or at least change of the existing system.

The normative perspective that is becoming most apparent in the development literature is concerned with the fact of significant material inequality among nations. The explanations of such inequality are not clearly distinguished from the assignment of blame or moral condemnation for that state of affairs. The literature has, to a large extent, moved from the ethnocentric assumption that Western institutions and values constitute a normative standard by which the world should be judged to the contradictory assumption that Western values, institutions, and their influence have been dysfunctional for the well-being of the non-Western world.

Clearly, normative considerations are not incompatible with explanatory purposes; it is generally recognized that they should complement one another. However, this chapter assumes that explanatory and polemic purposes should and can be kept distinct from one another. It will be argued that much of the literature on dependency or other putative explanations of the inequality among nations that, to a greater or lesser extent, rely on a Marxian or Leninist perspective, fail to clearly distinguish explanatory from polemic purposes.

CONCEPTUALIZING POLITICAL DEVELOPMENT

The aforementioned problems of imprecise conceptualization and of a normative perspective both emerge in the effort to conceptualize political development. Much of this literature does not clearly distinguish underdevelopment as a state of being from development as a process of changing from one state to another. The term *developing areas* has sometimes been used virtually interchangeably with the concept of non-Western systems, even though development implies movement or change, and it is by no means self-evident that all non-Western systems are in fact developing.[1]

Another source of imprecision in much of the literature is the failure to distinguish political development from social and economic change. An interesting corollary question in this regard, a question to which inadequate attention has thus far been given, is whether the long-term maintenance of advanced industrial technology is feasible without aspects of cultural and political modernization. For example, Iran in the 1980s may be testing whether the modern military machine and industrial economy built under the reign of the Shah can be maintained on a cultural and political base of Islamic fundamentalism.

Initially, leading scholars concerned with the political analysis of the African, Asian, and Latin American systems attempted to make some order and sense of the bewildering diversity of the universe of political systems by developing classification schemes based essentially on their degree of what may be called *Westernization:* the extent to which they possessed the various attributes of liberal democracy. Gabriel Almond's pioneering effort to classify the universe of political systems resulted in the following four categories: Anglo-American systems, preindustrial systems, continental European systems, and totalitarian systems (Almond, 1956). Initial attempts to categorize an array of phenomena, generally in retrospect, are found to violate some of the rules for scientifically useful categorization; Almond's early effort, while heuristic and provocative, is vulnerable to such *post hoc* criticism. The precise epistemological grounds for such criticism have been expounded in detail elsewhere (Kalleberg, 1956; Mayer, 1972). The major point to be made here is that the categories are too broad and imprecisely defined to be empirically useful. Certainly the category of preindustrial systems encompasses an enormous variety of systems and an enormous range of degrees of industrialization. Within that category, one can identify some systems that aspire to, and even to a degree possess, some of the institutions or culture of liberal democracies, for example, India, Turkey, or Mexico. Other systems attempt to co-opt some of the rhetoric and imagery of Western democracy while explicitly rejecting its substance, for example, "tutelary democracy" under Sekou Toure in Guinea and "guided democracy" under Kwame Nkrumah in Ghana. Still others vehemently reject the values and substance of liberal democracy in every respect except for the technology that liberal democracy has produced, for example, Islamic fundamentalism as practiced in the Ayatollah Khomeini's Iran. The level of industrialization itself within the nations presumably included in the preindustrial category is enormous. For instance, if India is not in the preindustrial category, it is hard to know in what other category it could be placed; yet, it is at a very different level of industrialization than, say, Mauritania or Upper Volta. Similarly, other partially industrialized systems such as Argentina and Mexico present problems of being seemingly between categories in Almond's scheme.

Leaving aside the question of whether totalitarianism is a useful concept, a question to be considered in Chapter 7, that cell apparently also encompasses a great range of system types that share only the common attribute of not being democratic. (It is assumed here that the cell encompasses industrialized autocracies whether or not they are totalitarian in the strict sense, [such as Warsaw Pact nations] since such systems fit in no other cell).

Autocracies vary greatly with respect to the amount of control they are capable of effectively imposing. It will be argued in that chapter that much finer distinctions are called for in this regard by distinguishing the commitment to establish totalitarian control over all aspects of a social system (as in Iran or North Korea) from the greater or less actual establishment of such control (as in those states most frequently designated as totalitarian, such as Stalinist U.S.S.R. or Nazi Germany) and from those systems that have been autocratic in the sense of suppressing the legitimacy of opposition but that do not aspire to control all aspects of social life (as in South Korea or the Philippines) up to their apparent move toward more competitive political formats in the 1980s.

If four-cell classification schemes greatly oversimplify the universe of political systems, clearly two-cell schemes may be especially vulnerable to such criticism.

Several such schemes attempt to dichotomize the world into Western and non-Western types.[2] Lucien Pye's effort is somewhat more sophisticated than some of the earlier efforts to so bifurcate the political universe, in that he lists seventeen attributes—both social and explicitly political—that putatively distinguish Western and non-Western systems. The criticism raised here, however, is not with the complexity of the model. Rather, the question is whether the diversity of the world can usefully be forced into two categories. As noted above, the range of industrial modernization and the diversity of political formats within the category we tend to think of as non-Western is staggering. The same could easily be said of the alternative category. Italy may be more similar to some of the more industrialized non-Western states than to the Anglo-American or Scandinavian democracies. Clearly, some of the industrialized autocracies of the Communist bloc have at times had many of the social and political attributes that Pye lists as non-Western; yet, one would hardly group such systems with some of the very nonindustrialized systems of, say, sub-Sahara Africa in terms of system capabilities. Of course, scholars of this magnitude recognized that their non-Western categories constituted ideal types in the Weberian sense rather than descriptions of reality; actual social and political systems are explicitly recognized to contain a mixture of both traditional and modern attributes (Almond, 1960).

The essence of the criticism, then, is not with the number of attributes in each category or ideal type. Rather, it is that there are too few cells or ideal types in the classification scheme to impose any useful order on the political universe.

At a minimum, there is a failure to distinguish political development from industrial or technological development. Leaving aside for the time being the question raised at the outset of this chapter—whether the technological state of a mature industrial order can be developed and sustained in a context of non-Western cultural and political institutions—it is surely possible to conceive of such a combination of advanced technology and industrialization existing in such a non-Western cultural and political milieu for a period of time. The Soviet Union, at least in its Stalinist period, may have been a case in point, as was, perhaps, Nazi Germany.[3]

Furthermore, the Western versus non-Western dichotomy does not distinguish between a "developed" or "modern" political system and liberal democracy, as that format has been known in Western Europe or the Anglo-American systems. Despite lip-service agreement given to Macridis' early injection against the parochial and normative ethnocentrism of traditional comparative politics, there was a tendency in the early grapplings with the concept of political development to consider systems modern (and, implicitly, better) to the extent that they became more like us. For instance, the functional categories that Gabriel Almond developed to analyze (and, implicitly, to evaluate the modernity of) non-Western systems were explicitly drawn from the analysis of Western systems.

However, the Warsaw Pact nations, clearly not liberal democracies, possess many attributes of modernity. Hence, the initial task seems to be to distinguish political modernization from industrialization and technological modernization, and these phenomena from democratization. It should be theoretically possible for technological modernization to take place without political development, and it should be equally possible for these two phenomena to occur without democratization. These possibilities, in turn, raise the question of the relationship between these three variables: industrialization, political development, and democratization.

Samuel Huntington has made a major contribution in this regard. His writings on the concept of institutionalization offer a conceptualization of a more explicitly *political* development that is clearly distinguishable from the literature that conceptualizes and measures political development as social mobilization (Huntington, 1965a). One may distinguish a third school of thought with regard to conceptualizing political development, the conceptualization of development as an increase in the capabilities of political systems (Diamant, 1966; Almond 1956; Eisenstadt, 1963). Scholars in this third school are essentially concerned with the capability of a system's institutions to adapt to stress generated by changes in the quantity and quality of demands; hence, this school is related to the institutionalist school. Scholars in the institutionalist school and those concerned with system capabilities implicitly share the value of stability and order; their concern is with the persistence of the system and its adaptation to a changing environment.

Daniel Lerner's model of development is one of the early classic statements of the mobilizationist perspective. Lerner hypothesized that the process of urbanization begins the breakdown of traditional perspectives and ties as it broadens the horizons of traditional man, thus allowing new patterns of relationships to form. A crucial aspect of this reorientation is the spread of literacy, which allows people to assume the roles of a more modern order. Literacy first causes and then is reciprocally stimulated by the development of a mass media. Finally, these developments encourage the development of a participant society (Lerner, 1958). The causal sequence of his model might be represented thusly: U→ L→ M→ P, where U = urbanization, L = literacy, M = media growth and P = participant society. The approach of Lerner and his mobilizationist followers entails an unexplicated presumption that development would lead to democratization in an essentially linear process—that is, once the process of mobilization was underway, although the rate of change may vary, the movement toward modernization and an increasingly responsive, participant system is both inexorable and unidirectional.

Yet, as Guillermo O'Donnell has persuasively demonstrated with respect to Brazil and Argentina, bureaucratic authoritarian regimes may appear in the modernization process of some nations, regimes that halt or reverse any tendency toward participatory democracy. Moreover, the inherent nonadaptive, routinized attributes of bureaucracy may cause such regimes to halt or stagnate the development process itself, contradicting any assumptions of linearity in the development process.

Karl Deutsch's seminal article also has been cited as an epitome of the mobilizationist perspective. Deutsch offers seven indicators of the overall process of mobilization (Deutsch, 1961). Deutsch assumes that these indicators, correlated with one another as they are, constitute aspects of a single underlying process and that they will promote major modernizing changes in the political process itself. The underlying assumption is that the pressures, generated by a significant expansion of the politically relevant portion of the population and, consequently, of the demands and stress they place on the political system, will force that system to make the requisite structural changes to adapt to that pressure.

This assumption has, in various forms, provided the basis for a number of well-known theories or hypotheses in the social sciences. For example, Arnold Toynbee's "challenge and response" thesis in his classic *A Study of History* held that the greatest civilizations were faced with a measure of adversity, the challenge of which led to their greatness (Toynbee, 1946). Similarly, Harold Lasswell has hypothesized that power seekers may be explained as individuals seeking to overcome some ego deprivation in their past (Lasswell, 1948). Each of these theorists hides behind the hypotheses-saving corollary that the challenge or adversity must be great enough to provoke the adaptive response but not so great as to cause the civilization, system, or individual to give up, withdraw, or be destroyed. How does one know if the challenge was great enough but not too great? One knows by the nature of the response the theory purports to "explain." This is, of course, a *post hoc* explanation that, in affording no predictive power, violates the criteria of scientific explanation established in the preceding chapter.

The institutionalist and, implicitly, the system-capacity schools of development, as we will see below, do not take it as a given that systems will respond to challenges by adapting to higher levels of stress. Rather, for them, that is the potentially empirical question to be answered by research. Whether or not *mobilization*, defined as an expansion of the politically relevant sectors of the population, constitutes the essence of the modernization process is a semantic question. Whether the political structures of a society will adapt to such modernization is a potentially researchable one. Huntington also defines the essence of modernization as mobilization in the sense in which that term is used here but, as we have noted, distinguishes the concept of political development as institutionalization.

McCrone and Cnudde have attempted to distinguish the causal from the spurious relationships among the four variables that underlie the mobilizationist model: urbanization, education or literacy rates, media exposure, and participation (McCrone and Cnudde, 1971). Their principal contribution was to empirically confirm the causal path suggested by Lerner. Using prediction equations and path coefficients more sensitive to causal impact than correlation coefficients, they have empirically tested and confirmed the previously speculative conclusion that urbanization indirectly supports the spread of participation by directly promoting the spread of education, which, in turn, promotes literacy and media exposure, which then promotes participation or, as McCrone and Cnudde phrase it, "democratic development." The paper thus demonstrates how the technique of causal modeling can subject multivariate speculation to empirical scrutiny.

The dependent variable or explicandum of the preceding analysis—democratic development—is measured by a series of indicators that were suggested in an earlier piece by Cutwright

(Cutwright, 1963), indicators that render the concept a continuous variable rather than the dichotomous typology suggested by Lipset's oft-cited attempt to delineate those social and economic attributes regularly associated with either stable democracy or the lack thereof (Lipset, 1959). A major advantage of Cutwright's measurement is that a continuous variable is subject to correlational or regression analysis. Another advantage is that it avoids the inherent liabilities in the process of dichotomous classification, some of which were considered above with respect to the Western versus non-Western dichotomy. The range of differences among the states within a category such as democracy places doubt on the scientific utility of the concept. If democracy implies certain values, such as accountability of elites, mass participation in the decision-making process, or political competition, such values could be possessed to a greater or lesser extent. Hence, finer distinctions could be made by rendering democracy a continuous variable rather than a discrete, dichtomized type.

Cutwright's conception of democracy is clearly a function of the indicators by which he chooses to operationalize it. He refers to it as an index of political development; however, he clearly is measuring the extent to which a system has a democratic format. The index includes such things as the presence of opposition parties in a parliament or of competively elected executives. Clearly, the Soviet bloc nations would score poorly on such an index; yet, with their massive administrative sector, they are a very different type of political system than would be found in sub-Sahara Africa or Micronesia.

The goal of rendering the concept of democracy a continuous variable is certainly admirable for the reasons stated above. Yet, it is difficult to avoid conceptualizing democracy as an attribute. Generally, the concept is indicated or operationalized by the presence of competition for political office. While values such as accountability, in theory, could be possessed to a greater or lesser extent, in practice, such values have not been measured independently from some concrete procedures to realize them, procedures such as regularly scheduled competitive elections that are not matters of degree. While party fragmentation is certainly a matter of degree, this is not the same thing as competition. Competition is either there or it is not. The inescapably qualitative nature of the concept is revealed in Cutwright's attempt to render it otherwise. He measures the number of years the system has possessed the attributes of democracy; hence, the concept becomes something that systems have or lack for greater or lesser periods of time rather than something that they have to a greater or lesser extent.

Beyond the tendency of the mobilization literature to fail to distinguish democracy from political development, there is a widespread lack of consensus in the literature in general on the conceptualization and measurement of both democracy and political development. Obviously, the correlates of such concepts will be a function of the way the concepts are defined and measured. The lack of anything resembling a consensus on the conceptualization and measurement of political development constitutes an enormous barrier to cumulative research on the causes and consequences of such development.

The conceptualization of development as some variant of the mobilizationist school implies unstated values. The authors of that literature seem to regard a democratic political format as desirable both from an instrumental perspective and as an end in itself. The instrumentalist perspective constitutes a rather direct challenge to such institutionalists as Huntington by suggesting that democracy is actually a more efficient means of allocating resources to promote economic growth, and maintaining order by adjusting to the changing needs and demands of society.[4] Theoretically, there is a potential empirical question here. Does that class of nations that have adopted the political format of a bureaucratized autocracy—roughly what Apter calls a "mobilization system"—have a better record with regard to the indices of political instability and violence than those systems that have adopted a more or less democratic format—roughly, what Apter calls a "reconciliation system" (Apter, 1965)? However, for several reasons, no empirical research has been undertaken that resolves that question. In the first place, so few nations have even adopted, let alone maintained, such a democratic format that there are not enough cases to reasonably test a hypothesis. More importantly, the problem of measurement for such key concepts as the level of institutionalization or of democratization has not yet been consensually resolved.

Lipset's seminal article, "Some Social Requisites of Democracy," did find an empirical relationship between economic development and democracy. Lipset suggested that the former attribute facilitates the establishment and maintenance of the latter (although, in a classic hypothesis-saving retreat, he eschews any explicit inference of causation) (Lipset, 1959). Pye suggests the reverse direction of causation, that democracy facilitates economic development. The question of the direction of causation can be resolved only with diachronic analysis, and the longitudinal data for such an analysis is only now becoming available. Since studies such as the aforementioned ones by Lipset and Cutwright are derived from data taken at one point in time, the direction of causation must be inferred without help from the data themselves.

There is a different implicit value in the institutionalist perspective on development, that of order and stability. The title of Huntington's book, *Political Order in Changing Societies*, reveals the underlying concern of that analysis: how to maintain a degree of order, stability, or pattern maintenance in a political system in the face of a rapidly changing socioeconomic context. It would be inaccurate to assert that institutionalists like Huntington manifest no concern at all with competing values such as a more egalitarian political structure or broadening the base of political participation. Indeed, Huntington has collaborated with Joan Nelson in an analysis of the causes and consequences of participation in developing nations. They argue that participation becomes valued for its own sake at higher levels of development, although it is unclear whether the authors so value it themselves, despite the extensive analysis they undertake of its determinants. It should be noted that even in a book devoted to the phenomenon of participation, Huntington emphasizes that values such as participation and equality can conflict and compete with such other values as political stability and socioeconomic development.

Quoting from his earlier work, *Political Order in Changing Societies*, Huntington (1976, p. 162) claims that "the political essence of revolution is the rapid expansion of political consciousness . . . Revolution is the extreme case of the explosion of political participation" (Huntington, 1968). Thus, far from positing a causal or symbiotic relationship between expanded participation and the modernization of political institutions, Huntington suggests that the two may be inversely related (Huntington, 1963). Modernization, for Huntington, involves the capacity of man to act to control his environment, which in turn, entails centralizing effective authority and freeing it from the debilitating fetters of medieval institutions and conceptions of law. The Anglo-American conception of the rule of law reflected the persistence of medieval constraints on the discretion of political leadership, on their ability to act and to shape their environment. Huntington's insight that the Anglo-American (and especially the American) passion for constraining political power resulted in a loss of political efficiency is hardly revolutionary; students of American politics have recognized this reality for quite some time.[5] It is interesting, however, that the mobilizationists chose to assume the opposite, that somehow the pressures of expanded participation will somehow result in political institutions successfully adapting by becoming more efficient.

The point is that the difference between the institutionalist and mobilizationist perspectives on development is only partially based on disagreement over how the process operates; it is also based upon a disagreement over value priorities. The adherents of these positions disagree on whether a system facing the increased stress of expanded mobilization will more probably adapt, thus becoming more efficient, or more probably break down. They also implicitly disagree on whether the benefits of the changes generated by the expanded mobilization will outweigh the costs of the increased probability of some instability, on whether the value of change is more important or desirable than the value of order.

With regard to the former potentially empirical question, whether rapid change still, in fact, generates system breakdown, empirical research has not produced a definitive answer, nor is such an answer in the offing. The concepts involved in this question have not been defined with sufficient precision to permit systematic empirical testing. No indicators logically suggest themselves for unambiguously distinguishing between adaptive system change and system breakdown. After all, revolution itself might be posited as a type of adaptation in the face of the increased stress of rising mobilization. Professor Huntington has perceptively suggested that revolution generally results in strengthened political institutions (Huntington, 1968). Furthermore, no suggestion has been forthcoming as to how one could distinguish between moderate and rapid rates of mobilization change. Although the logical argument that rapid mobilization will increase the probability of system breakdown has been eloquently and persuasively spelled out, the theory remains conjectural and beyond empirical analysis.

EXPLAINING UNDERDEVELOPMENT

While normative perspectives, with varying degrees of explicitness, underlie efforts to conceptualize political development and modernization, such perspectives assume even greater importance in the various attempts to explain the enormous gap in levels of material well-being between the relatively industrialized nations of Europe, the Anglo-American democracies, and presumably Japan, on the one hand, and the less industrialized nations of Asia, Africa (presumably excluding South Africa), and Latin America on the other. Such normative perspectives extend to the point of blurring the distinction between positing causes and assessing blame in the sense of imputing nefarious motivation on the part of putatively exploitive nations and institutions.

Clearly, the commericial, industrial, and scientific revolutions were manifested in the Western world centuries before they substantially affected the nations of Africa, Asia, and Latin America. These revolutions ushered in an enormous growth in the gross national products (G.N.P.) of the affected nations and, ultimately, in their levels of material well-being. Despite the undeniable fact that industrialization and social modernization (in Lerner's mobilizationist sense of the term) were of uneven benefit at best and clearly dysfunctional for material well-being to many segments of formerly agrarian societies in the short run, it is equally undeniable that individuals across the social spectrum are ultimately better off in a material sense in relatively mature industrial societies than in agrarian ones. The per capita income of many of those citizens in Western democracies that are classified as in a state of poverty would make them relatively well-off in most nations of the third world. (See Figure 3.1)

The unequal distribution of the world's resources has contributed to a disproportionate share of human misery in many third world nations as reflected in such aggregate data as the differing rates among nations with respect to life expectancy, infant mortality, malnutrition, and so forth. Data such as per capita income are imperfect indicators of human well-being. Life in a subsistence agrarian economy where individuals consume what they produce and produce only what they consume may be better in most respects than life in an industrializing economy with all of the social dislocations of the early stages of industrialization, despite the larger per-capita income and G.N.P. in the latter type of system. However, most third world systems are not primitive agrarian systems but, rather, industrializing systems. Moreover, on most measures of human well-being, mature industrial systems fare better than either agrarian or partially industrialized systems. Figure 3.2 shows a correlation between an index of material well-being (per-capita G.N.P.) and a measure of level of industrialization (percent of work force in agriculture). The point of the clearly expected strength of association is that with all of the putatively dislocating and dysfunctional effects of the industrializing process, not only are people of the industrial societies demonstrably better off by Western standards of material well-being than those of the pre-industrial world, but also a given increase in the level of industrialization tends to be associated with proportionate gains in the indicators of material well-being.

Development, Ethnocentrism, and Dependency 77

national well being

[Bar chart showing number of nations above poverty (~50) and below poverty (~165), with y-axis "number of nations" from 0 to 180 and x-axis "poverty line"]

national well being

[Pie chart: 23% of the nations of the world have per-capita incomes above the American poverty line figure; 77% of the nations of the world with per-capita incomes below the American poverty line]

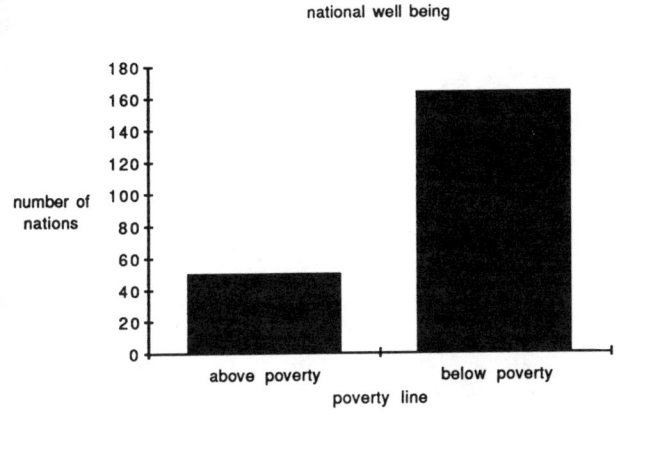

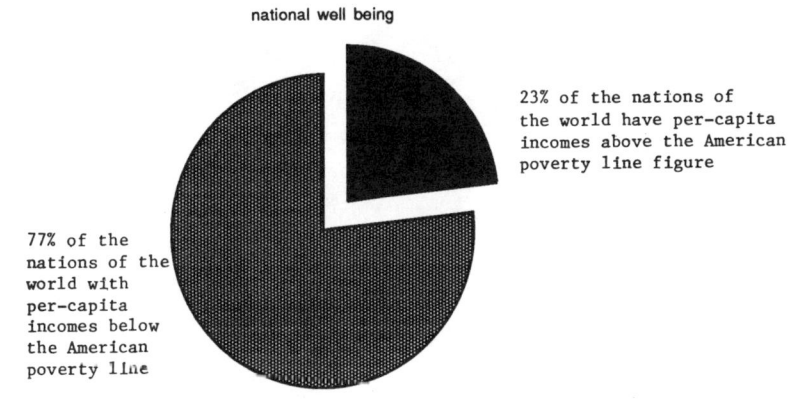

Figure 3.1. Figure 3.1 shows that of 211 listed nations, the 1985 per-capita income of 162 or 77% of them is below the American single poverty line figure for that year of $5469 while only 49 or 23% of them exceed that threshold with respect to per-capita income. Thus a person at poverty line in the United States would be at average or well above average income in over three quarters of the nations of the world. While such an American is impoverished *relative* to other Americans, an American at the poverty line would be very well off relative to average residents of most less developed nations.

$r = -.79$ $r_2 = -.62$

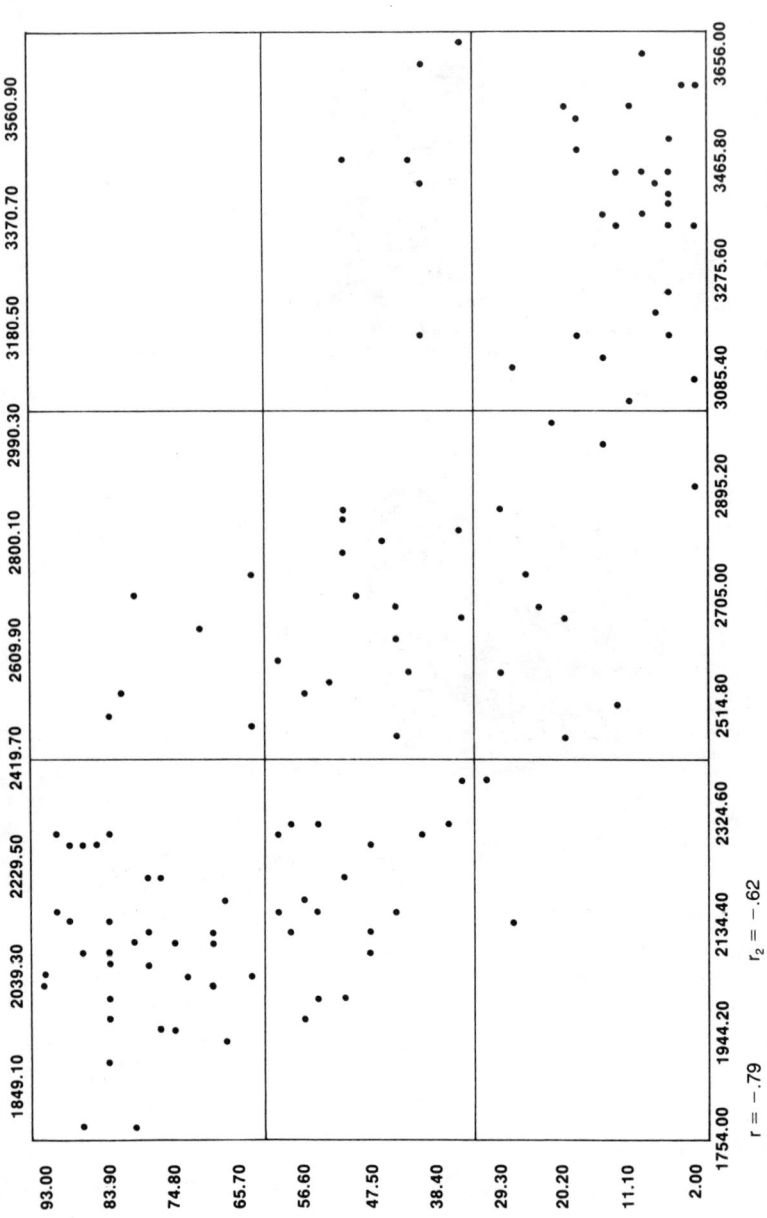

Figure 3.2. The relationship between percent of the work force in agriculture and available per diem calories per capita

Data Source: Charles Taylor and Davic Jodice, Eds. *The World Handbook of Social and Political Indicators*, Vol. 1, 3rd ed. (New Haven, CT: Yale University Press, 1983).

MARXISM, LENINISM AND, UNDERDEVELOPMENT

Despite the foregoing caveats that these measures of material well-being reflect a certain Western parochialism and imperfectly reflect the quality of life in agrarian societies, the fact remains that the vastly unequal distribution of such indicators among nations is widely perceived as a moral problem of such significance that a growing and widely discussed body of literature has developed that purports to explain this inequality (while, with varying degrees of explicitness, condemning it), to assess blame for it, and to recommend the remedy for it. This literature, generally known as *dependency theory*, constructs an explanation of third world underdevelopment that closely resembles the theory of imperialism that V. I. Lenin adopted from such writers as J. A. Hobson.

Hobson (1905, pp. 71–89) blames international finance capital in general and Jews in particular for both the colonial exploitation of the third world and for the wars of Europe that he imagines are engineered by the Jewish banking families. "Does anyone seriously suppose," he writes, "that a great war could be undertaken by any European state or a great state loan subscribed if the House of Rothschild and its connections set their face against it?" Hobson was formulating a conspiratorial explanation for underdevelopment, and for centuries the Jews have been the classic scapegoats for various conspiracy theories. In seeing (and selling) the idea of the Jew as the quintessential paragon of capitalist exploiter, Hobson was setting the foundation for the widespread view among many third world elites today that Zionism is an instrument for capitalist exploitation of third world peoples.

Some dependency theorists claim that their theory should be distinguished from Leninism on the question of whether capitalism caused dependency and, in fact, preceded it or whether the same factors and process that produced the capitalist world system also produced underdevelopment and dependency. Nevertheless, leading proponents of dependency theory such as

Bodenheimer, Frank, and Dos Santos argue in a Leninist vein that the imperatives of modern capitalism require it to seek to exploit other systems in order to serve its own needs.[6] A Marxian analysis of capitalism and its requirements underlies both the dependency and Leninist theories of imperialism and renders them alike in their analyses of the causes of the perpetuation of underdevelopment and inequality and in the remedy that logically follows from those analyses.

Marx predicted that mature capitalism would collapse, virtually of its own weight, from recurrent crises generated by perpetual overproduction. This conclusion flows from the assumed labor standard of value that Marx lifted uncritically from economist David Ricardo, that the value of a product equals the labor that went into producing it. The entrepreneur who puts up the capital at a risk to reap profits extracts those profits from laborers to whom legitimately belong the fruits of their labor. Since laborers, due to a "reserve army of unemployed" and an interchangeability of workers, have no bargaining position, entrepreneurs can and will force workers to work longer and produce more without additional compensation. The laborer becomes increasingly alienated from the fruits of his labor and is increasingly unable to purchase that which he has produced. Hence the inevitable problem of overproduction, a lack of secure outlets for a growing supply of capital, and economic crises. These crises drive more and more failing entrepreneurs (or bourgeoisie) into the swelling ranks of the working class or proletariat. Capital becomes thus concentrated in fewer and fewer hands; hence, a diminishing handful of bourgeoisie try to maintain an exploitive relationship over a swelling army of oppressed proletarians.

Lenin's adaptation of J. A. Hobson's economic interpretation of imperialism served the initial function of salvaging the foregoing Marxian analysis from disconfirmation by the nonoccurrence of facts logically entailed by Marxian economic theory: an increasingly shrinking and isolated entrepreneurial class, recurring economic crises, and the eventual collapse of the system. Secondly, Lenin's writings purport to account for their establishment of Marxian socialism in essentially agrarian or peasant societies.

This development contradicts Marx's theory of history that held socialism to be a dialectical product of the contradictions of maturing industrial capitalism. Thirdly, Lenin's writings offer an explanation of third world underdevelopment that assigns the blame for that state of affairs on the imperatives of the capitalist system, not on the attributes of the less-developed nations themselves. Lenin's explanation thus goes far in maintaining the dignity and self respect of those materially less well-off systems by removing from them the stigma of their plight. Each of these points will be elaborated in greater detail below.

Lenin performed a classic "saving the hypothesis" function for Marxian theory in explaining away the apparently disconfirmatory fact of the continued existence and even growing economic prosperity and political health of the world's capitalist systems. He argued that the collapse of such systems was averted (or at least delayed) by siphoning off the overproduction or "surplus value" of capitalist exploitation into the captive markets of the nonindustrialized world. This process preserves an artificial prosperity for capitalist systems and prolongs their otherwise doomed existence. The industrial proletariat, sharing in the ill-gotten fruits of this exploitive relationship between capitalist and less-developed nations, do not develop the class consciousness—the sense of a sharing among fellow workers of a realization that they were being exploited by the bourgeoisie—necessary to alienate the working class from the system and cause them to bring about that system's collapse. This failure to develop class consciousness among the proletariat, the lack of crises causing the bourgeoisie to fall into the ranks of the proletariat, and the overall prosperity of the system all have the effect of preventing the predicted collapse of capitalist systems.

This Leninist exigesis of Marxism makes Marxism especially relevant and appealing to third world nations. His use of the theory of imperialism to explain underdevelopment shifts the cause (and, implicitly, the blame) for this underdevelopment from the attributes of third world nations themselves to the putatively exploitive activities of Western capitalists. This explanation, in part, accounts for the fact that the Marxist-Leninist model has far and away been the more popular model of nation building among those nations that have come into being since World War II, despite the fact that it is virtually self-evident to most citizens of the liberal democracies of Europe, North America, and Britain with her Older Dominions that some variant of the liberal democratic model is the best available type of political system in which one could live. Israel is the only post-World War II nation that has, without interruption, maintained what most regard as a democratic state. Some further explanation of the appeal of the Leninist model in the third world seems to be in order, given that the model does not protect such civil libertarian values as individualism and tolerance of diversity.

Marxism itself constitutes a theoretical system that is compatible with the structure of many non-Western philosophical systems in that they each tend to be closed and comprehensive attempts to subsume most of human history and most aspects of life in one system of thought that is insensitive to outside information. Secondly, Marxism, purporting to be materialistic, addresses itself to the dominant concern of the third world—material well-being. Values such as tolerance of diversity are mere abstractions and not of primary concern to those who are living at or near the subsistence level and who have not been socialized into placing a value on such things. Moreover, some Western values are in direct conflict with important values of the non-Western world. For example, the Western value of secularism and the separation of church and state is not a value to the peoples of Islam, where the state is viewed as an instrument of the faith. Thirdly, Marxism claims a "scientific" status that purports to give the triumph of the oppressed an inevitability. Such a "the meek shall inherit the earth" claim, buttressed by a plausible claim of scientific inexorability, has an obvious appeal to those who otherwise perceive themselves to be in a state of hopeless subordination and material misery.

As suggested above, it is the Leninist exigesis of the theory of imperialism that makes Marxism especially appealing to the third world. This putative explanation is a simplified, conspiratorial view of the situation that lends itself well to the consumatory ideological base that, as Apter points out, modernizing systems frequently adopt because they are compatible with their own cultures (Apter, 1965).

DEPENDENCY THEORY AS AN EXPLANATION OF UNDERDEVELOPMENT

Dependency theory asserts, in the Leninist vein, that capitalism survives and prospers by exploiting the resources of the less-developed nations. Some dependency theorists, in fact, go farther than classical Leninists in holding that capitalism developed and grew out of this exploitation of less-developed nations, that the development of capitalism and of underdevelopment was part of the same historical process, while Marxist-Leninists accept the independent development of capitalism and characterize the putative exploitation of the non-Western world as a futile attempt to forestall the inevitable collapse of the capitalist system. Dependency theorists characterize the relationship of the non-Western world to the West as one of unmitigated exploitation of the former by the latter. Julius Nyerere, President of Tanzania, put it bluntly when he charged an implicitly monolithic West, "You are rich because we are poor; we are poor because you are rich." In other words, the material well-being of the industrial world, by this view, was created by expropriating and exploiting the resources of the non-Western world, thereby preventing the development of that part of the world, a development that presumably would have otherwise occurred in due course. Hence, underdevelopment, in dependency theory arguments, suggests that the image of precolonial Africa as underdeveloped is a myth created by "imperialism's image makers." Thus, in the early 1400s, Michael Parenti claims, Niger, Mali, and the Guinea coast produced fine fabrics and leathers, Katanga Zambia and Sierra Leone produced copper and iron, and Benin produced brass. These enterprises, however, are hardly indicators of "development" even on the economic dimension. They seem to constitute either cottage-industry types of pursuits or the extractive enterprises that frequently define the preindustrial stages. They certainly do not demonstrate the level of technology and productive efficiency associated with economic modernity.

This view that the well-being of the West is built upon the imperialistic exploitation of the non-Western world seems to imply that those nations that colonized the most and exploited the most would be among the richest nations, while those nations without substantial colonial holdings and without substantial trade with the third world would be behind the other industrial powers in development and material well-being. Yet, as one passionate critic of the dependency explanation of underdevelopment, P. T. Bauer, points out, some of the most prosperous and developed industrial nations have had until recently few contacts with the third world and certainly have not been noted as colonia powers: Canada, Australia, Japan, and the Scandinavian democracies (Bauer 1976). On the other hand, Spain and Portugal were among the most notoriously exploitive colonial powers; yet, they have remained among the least developed and least prosperous of the European nations. The dependency perspective seems to suggest that Western influence is the major impediment to development and prosperity in the third world; yet, nations that have been subjected to a minimum of such influence, e.g., Ethiopia and Liberia, are among the poorest nations on their continent. Hence, one of the major logical entailments of dependency theory does not conform to empirical reality.

An additional logical entailment of dependency theory is that one should expect a negative relationship between the degree of economic dependence and the responsiveness (or, in Almond's terms, "responsive capacity") of third world elites to the demands and interests of their respective systems. After all, these elites are installed and maintained by Western capitalist powers to serve the needs of the Western capitalist "core" at the expense of the third world "periphery." Indeed, Kenneth Bollen has presented a regression analysis to empirically demonstrate the negative relationship between economic dependence and democracy (Bollan, 1983). However, as Mark Gasiorowski points out in a devastating critique of Bollen's analysis and the dependency theory that underlies it, Bollen's findings depend on the *nonsystematic* elimination of a number of deviant cases or "outliers" based upon a questionable reclassification of several nations in a tripartite scheme labelling them as core, periphery, and semi-periphery (Gasiorowski, 1988). Aside from the simplistic nature of Snyder and Kirk's original scheme and their lack of unambiguous criteria for so classifying nations, Bollen lacked any consistent or principled justification for his reclassification, a reclassification that rendered possible his finding of a statistically significant negative relationship. Bollen's work demonstrates an apparent ignorance of the principles of taxonomy all too common among political scientists. Gasiorowski's analysis empirically rejects the principle entailed by dependency theory that economic dependency is negatively related to democracy. *More importantly, his analysis demonstrates how even empirical data can be statistically manipulated to produce results that conform to polemical purposes and predetermined conclusions.*

Susan Bodenheimer, one of the leading proponents of modern dependency theory, claims that the imperatives of capitalism as a world system have created an economic "infrastructure" in the non-Western nations that serves the needs of the capitalist world system and restricts the alternatives available to the dependent nation (Bodenheimer, 1971). Elites are created in the dependent states whose position rests on serving the needs of the international system. Their policies are directed toward the extraction of raw materials that serve the needs of industrial states rather than the nurturing of native industry. Dependent states serve as semi-captive markets for the oversupply of finished goods emanating from Western industry; hence, dependent states have little option but to buy back goods processed from their own raw materials or resources at a cost that gives great profit to the capitalists. Industrial states keep the technology needed to process such raw materials esoteric to themselves through the system of patents. Bodenheimer denies any genuine autonomy of satellite nations. Despite the formal sovereignty of non-Western nations, such nations are subjected to an economic (or "neo") imperialism, a conceptualization that expands the traditional meaning of imperialism (Bodenheimer, 1971). Neo-imperialism seems to mean that the legal autonomy of non-Western nations is undermined by the coercion of economic resources. Thus, the basis of neo-imperialism is economic; in classic Marxian fashion, the relations among nations is solely and completely understood in terms of economic factors (Bodenheimer, 1971).

The proponents of dependency theory offer little, if any, supporting hard data, let alone anything resembling a suggestion of precisely what it would take to wholly or partially falsify the theory. Such data as are offered usually take the form of documenting the material inequality that the theory purports to explain, a classic case of "the fallacy of affirming the consequent" (Blalock, 1960). A few exceptions do exist, such as Richard Vengroff's empirical test of the implications of dependency theory in African nations. Vengroff's data disconfirm the expectations generated by the theory (Vengroff, 1977). Dependency proponents offer data documenting that more money is taken out of less-developed nations as evidence of exploitation; yet, the fact that profits are acquired from risky capital investments is neither surprising nor consistent with any traditionally understood conception of exploitation. Such profits do not preclude benefits accruing to the less-developed nations from these capital investments. This generalized indictment of the profit motive as coterminous with exploitation of the consumer of processed goods is consistent with Bodenheimer's remedy for the perceived ills that she addresses. Bodenheimer concludes that the only way to break the cycle of dependency is by replacing capitalism with socialism, despite the fact that socialist states have not modernized more rapidly or successfully than capitalist states and socialist industrial powers have not been notably less exploitive of agrarian or less-developed nations than the more or less capitalist counterparts. In fact, that the nations that have, to a greater or lesser extent, followed the capitalist model of modernization, such as Japan and Hong Kong, have stood out in most measures of material well-being.

It is being suggested here that simple, single-factor explanations of complex social, political, and/or economic phenomena should be inherently suspect. Dependency theorists argue that the internal socioeconomic structure (or, in their terminology, "infrastructure") of third world nations is primarily determined by the pressure of Western capital investment. Frank and Bodenheimer were primarily writing about underdevelopment in Latin America. The total U.S. investment in Latin American in 1965 averages out to about $44 per capita from a total of $11 billions. This is not a high proportion of the G.N.P. of those nations and is hardly sufficient in and of itself to determine the socioeconomic structure of those societies.

Clearly, the socioeconomic structure of societies is affected by a variety of system-level attributes, including cultural patterns, historical experiences, physical and demographic patterns, and so forth. Monte Palmer lists seven system-level structural, cultural, or demographic factors that he claims *tend* to characterize third world systems (Palmer, 1980): (1) a shortage of entrepreneurs and innovators, (2) the family orientation of firms leading to ascriptive recruitment and avoidance of expansion, (3) antipathy of the masses to savings and capital accumulation, (4) a propensity of the masses to "squander their meager resources on feasts and celebrations," (5) the increasing fragmentation of wealth and land due to traditional inheritance practices, (6) the propensity of the masses to seek immediate gratification (to be "present oriented" in the terminology of Edward Banfield's pejorative characterization of America's poor) (Banfield, 1968) and (7) a tendency for most individuals to think small and safe.

Palmer presents no systematic empirical evidence to support his characterization of third world systems; indeed, such vaguely defined tendency statements may be inherently incapable of being empirically falsified. How could one measure, for instance, the degree to which people seek immediate gratification or are present oriented? Furthermore, any attempt to generically characterize "traditional societies" is rendered suspect by the enormous variety of social and cultural patterns among those societies commonly included in the concept of non-Western or third world systems.

However, the foregoing caveats aside, a number of specialists on such systems either impressionistically or empirically have found some of Palmer's attributes frequently appearing in some third world systems, while other attributes on the list appear in other third world systems. While the infusion of Western capital may offer inducements for forms of enterprise that are dysfunctional for domestic industrial development, the attributes of some systems may also be dysfunctional for such development. Values that are pervasive enough to characterize some cultures may encourage saving, economic risk taking, innovation, acquisition, or other entrepreneurial activity, while alternative values that characterize other cultures may discourage such activity. Some scholars, such as McClelland (1961), have qualified or modified the famous Tawney-Weber thesis that the values associated with Protestant theology were conducive to the development of capitalism while the values associated with Catholic theology were dysfunctional to such development. However, such scholars do not refute the basic premise that cultural attributes (such as child-rearing patterns) associated with Protestant societies have been conducive to such entrepreneurial behavior. Value systems that stress the afterlife or divine grace as opposed to worldly well-being are not conducive to the effort needed to generate such well-being, an effort at the foundation of the commercial revolution. This movement from a feudal, peasant-based economic order to a commercial order is part of what is held to define the modernization process.

Modernization also entails the development of modern science, and modern technology is based upon modern science. Value systems that are based on closed, comprehensive thought systems are not conducive to the open inquiry on which modern science is based. Scientific epistemology regards conclusions as tentative, contingent upon the relevant evidence insofar as it is known (as discussed in Chapter 2). When societies are dominated by a dogma, inquiry into the validity of ideas is discouraged. When the truth is known with certainty, further inquiry is useless. Since scientific epistemology seems to require a relatively open society, some scholars have noted it was no accident that the zenith of power of the then-dogmatic church in Europe in the Middle Ages coincided with what we call "the Dark Ages," the nadir of intellectual, scientific, and material development—in other words, the modernization process—in the Western world (Meehan, 1965, p. 39). A concern with rooting out and punishing heresy may not be compatible with the scientific enterprise of adjusting the corpus of knowledge to fit a constantly growing body of data. It remains to be seen whether relatively closed societies such as Iran or the Soviet Union can, in the long run, maintain the technology needed for modern armies and an expanding economy while at the same time rejecting the values underlying the scientific epistemology on which such technology is based. If the answer turns out to be *no*, will the pattern be to generate an "opening" of such closed societies or to cause a stagnation or decline in the state of technology in such an inhospitable cultural climate?

Another internal factor that can affect the level of a system's ability to modernize and its overall level of material well-being is that nation's rate of population growth. Modernization requires a growth in capital accumulation, the allocation of resources to the process of expanding and transforming the means of production. In the face of an increasingly finite supply of resources, the result is fewer resources allocated to consumption. Yet, a rapidly rising population places enormous pressure to increase the resources available for consumption. This pressure is especially critical in the presence of significant increases in the rate at which the population is being mobilized, as discussed above.

Not only does population growth mean more individuals among whom to allocate increasingly finite resources, but it means that a greater proportion of the population will be youths who are only consumers but not yet producers. Hence, rapid population growth is a double-barreled impediment to economic growth and development. The percentage of the population that is of working age has increased in all Western nations during the period from 1970 to 1975 but has decreased in most third world nations during that period. Some advocates of dependency theory, such as Parenti, explicitly reject the demographic explanation by arguing that population density in some third world nations does not exceed that of many Western industrialized nations. The problem, however, as the foregoing analysis has made clear, is not density per se but the rate of population growth. It is the number of children per family that determines what percent are purely consumers. Moreover, a rapid increase in population size consumes resources over and above the level the system was structured to provide. Clearly, the Western systems are structured and possess the technology to provide for a higher population density than less-developed nations.

The populations of many third world systems have been growing at extremely rapid rates compared to the populations of Western nations. For instance, between 1940 and 1982 and operating from an approximately equal base, the population of the United States increased by around ninety million people while that of Latin America increased by around two hundred ten million. This exponential population growth in third world nations is a result of two factors: cultural proclivities toward high birth rates in third world nations combined with dramatic reductions in the death rates. The birth rate per thousand people per year in developed nations in 1975 was 17.0 while the corresponding rate for less-developed nations was 37.4, or 220% higher. The high birth rate in less-developed nations is not a recent phenomenon; however, it was previously balanced by a correspondingly high death rate, especially with regard to infant mortality, thereby keeping third world populations within manageable bounds. With the rapid infusion of Western technology—especially medical technology, sanitation, and hygiene—on a traditional cultural base, the death rate declined markedly while the birth rate remained high. In the past twenty-five years, the average life expectancy in less-developed nations has increased from 35 to 50 years. The traditional proclivities toward high birth rates were appropriate for societies from two standpoints: first, the agrarian nature of traditional society made it economically desirable for a man to have many children to help with the manual work in the fields and, second, a smaller proportion of the children survived into adulthood.

Western nations have adapted to the new demographic imperatives of industrial and post-industrial systems with significantly lower birth rates than even a generation ago. However, institutions in non-Western nations have been a force against a similar adaptation of birth rates. The cultural value of large families in much of the third world has already been identified as such an institution. The Catholic Church with its papal injunctions against most effective forms of contraception, against abortion and generally in favor of fecundity, has also been identified as having this impact in many of those third world areas in which it has substantial following. Clearly, the Church's impact on fecundity has not been uniform in all nations in which it has a substantial following. For instance, between 1970 and 1975, the population of Catholic Italy grew by 8.7% while that of Mexico grew by 38.5%. One may be tempted to point to the oft-cited "macho" element in the Latin culture as a factor that inhibits family planning, and something like this concept impressionistically seems to be operating in a number of Latin American nations; however, the population of Argentina grew by only 18% in that period.

Beyond Catholic nations, large families remain a well-established cultural value in other third world nations, such as India. Family planning there is less a matter of technology than of cultural acceptance.

In no way is it being suggested that the values that promote high birth rates or that inhibit entrepreneurial behavior are intrinsically undesirable. Rather, it is being suggested that these values entail choices, choices that have consequences for the level and pace of development and industrialization. It is not being asserted here that such demographic factors constitute the definitive explanation of differing levels of development. Rather, the point is that the foregoing consequences of the values in question constitute at least one plausible alternative explanation of the unequal distribution among nations of the attributes of modernization and material well-being.

The existence of such an alternative explanation places the simplistic single facts or explanations of such dependency theorists as Bodenheimer in the category of polemics rather than analysis. When she singles out the alleged exploitive impact of Western capitalism as the single or dominant cause of third world "under-development," she ignores equally plausible alternative explanations in order to support a policy goal or set of values that were previously determined. At the close of her article, she concludes that socialism is the panacea to break the self-perpetuating structure of dependency (Bodenheimer, 1971, p. 176). Yet, this inference is clearly not supported by the data.

This simplistic identification of world capitalism as the cause of unequal development is brought into question in an article by Dirk Berg-Schlosser, who typologizes African political systems and then rates their performance in terms of per capita growth in G.N.P. and a physical quality-of-life index developed by the Overseas Development Council, both rough indices of development in the sense in which that term is used here (Berg-Schlosser, 1984). Berg-Schlosser found that *polyarchies* (a term roughly coterminous with *liberal democracy*) perform significantly better on the aforementioned indices of development than do "socialist" systems. Berg-Schlosser's criteria for typologizing African systems lack rigorous precision; however, he clearly does not allow for the possibility of democratic socialism. His attributes for the category of socialist systems include a single party system, one of the essential attributes of political autocracy. However, socialist states in the African context tend to be political autocracies. Despite the methodological critiques of imprecise conceptualization that may be leveled at Berg-Schlosser's work, it may fairly be said that the work does not support the conclusion that poor performance on indices of economic growth is mainly attributable to the outside force of dependency or may be remedied by the adoption of a socialist economic system. Indeed, Berg-Schlosser incorporates a measure of dependency in his model and fails to find that it explains any significant part of the variation in economic performance.

The dependency theorists have clearly pointed out a dimension of the development process that had heretofore been overlooked: How Western investment in third world nations may act to discourage the kind of entrepreneurial activity that leads to industrialization and modernization. In this sense of balancing the naive "white man's burden" outlook of viewing Western influence in the African, Asian, and Latin American worlds as an unmixed blessing, the dependency theorists have contributed to our understanding of reality.

Yet, if contact with the West was not an unmixed blessing, neither was it an unmixed curse. Western influence facilitated a fair amount of technology transfer (despite third world complaints about patent monopolies). There are a number of goods manufactured in third world nations that were developed in the West. Moreover, Western technology gave value to many of the resources of third world nations, such as Malaysian rubber or Arab oil. The development of such technologies involves risk and the expenditure of resources (not to mention creativity). If the implicit demand of the dependency theorists were granted and new technology became, in fact, common property, it is doubtful that risks would be taken and resources expended for such technological development.

For dependency theory to be taken seriously as the major explanation of underdevelopment, it would have to do four things. First, it would have to show that it is superior to and, in a sense, would have to refute, the various aforementioned alternative explanations of underdevelopment. This it has not done. Second, it would have to answer the question (posed by Thomas Sowell, among others) (Sowell, 1983, pp. 34–43) as to why third world underdevelopment preceded by centuries the capitalism that is supposed to have caused and perpetuated it. The dependency theorist explains how the industrialized capitalist nations exploit their advantage in technology and resources; however, those theorists do not explain how that advantage was obtained in the first place. They ignore the question of why the commercial and industrial revolutions came to pass first in England and thereafter in Western and North-Central Europe, not in the Latin, Asian, Near Eastern, and African civilizations, because that question would interfere with their goal of assigning blame for third world underdevelopment on the capitalist world and promoting socialism as the hope of third world well-being.

Third, dependency theory would have to yield some propositions that are, in fact, falsifiable by contemporary social science criteria and that withstand such empirical scrutiny by being in conformity with the preponderance of relevant data. Robert Packenham has argued that some of the basic propositions entailed by dependency theory are inherently not testable. He points out that the theory rests upon a convergence of interests, not behavior, and interests must be subjectively inferred. Packenham, therefore, claims that these propositions are "true by definition" and that social science is conceived by dependency theorists to be a "tool in a political struggle" (Packenham, 1983) rather than a set of criteria for inquiry. Specifically, one of the propositions of dependency theory is that the native elites of periphery nations serve the needs of transnational corporations rather than the needs of the native masses. However, as Peter Evans points out, "needs of native masses" is not a social science concept but a normative judgment (Evans, 1979).

Fourth, the theory would not only have to be testable but actually in conformity with the preponderance of data. However, a number of anomalies exist between the entailments of the theory and some undisputable data. For instance, rather than acting in a dependent fashion, the native elites often act in ways clearly inimical to the manifest interest of multinational corporations as evidenced by the more than 500 expropriations of the facilities of such corporations between 1960 and 1975 (Duran, 1983). Such elites clearly can and do behave independently of the pressures of Western and corporate capital. Another logical entailment of the theory is that the gap between the rich nations and poor nations should continue to increase since the dependency relationship in theory is self perpetuating. Yet, in the history of modern nations, no nation seems to remain permanently at the top in terms of wealth and power. What Duran has called "dependency reversal," the effective termination of any reasonable conception of a dependency relationship, does in fact occur.

These considerations, plus the existence of alternative explanations of the same disparities in levels of development putatively "explained" by dependency theory, lead to the conclusion that dependency theory, however useful it may be in modifying or qualifying alternative theories of underdevelopment, is not a scientifically adequate explanation of underdevelopment or of the economic and power disparities among nations, nor is it likely to produce such an explanation. It is probably best understood in the words of Packenham as a "tool" in a "political struggle" that is a rationale or instrument for attacking the economic systems of Western industrial democracies and trying to bring about the displacement of such systems with socialism as that system is understood by such dependency advocates as Bodenheimer and Frank.

CONCLUSIONS

The *raison d'être* of the new comparative politics, it was argued in the preceding chapter, has been to adopt a method that is useful for constructing scientifically acceptable explanations of the phenomena in which we, as political scientists, are interested. This and subsequent chapters, therefore, examine the leading books and articles in the various areas or dimensions of the comparative field to determine the extent to which that literature does or is likely to contribute to this putative explanatory purpose.

The sub-field of comparative politics that specializes in the less developed or third world nations of Asia, Africa, and Latin America has attracted a preponderance of the most prestigious scholars in the comparative field and has produced much of the field's most discussed literature. For reasons that have been considered above, there had been until recently a definite relationship between an interest in either one of the less-developed areas or the subject of political development and change, on the one hand, and an apparent commitment to the goals and values of the revolution in comparative politics on the other. Among the most visible and prolific of the prophets exhorting us to the promised land of the new comparative politics, many of the names are associated to a significant extent with the developing-areas dimension of the field. Scholars such as Gabriel Almond, David Apter, Samuel Huntington, and Lucien Pye have achieved much of their well-deserved reputations through their work on the less-developed systems.

Yet, despite the concerted efforts of some of the outstanding scholars in the field of comparative politics, it must be concluded from the analysis in this chapter that very little in the way of explanatory theory, in the sense of that term as discussed in Chapter 2, has emanated from all of this effort. Nor is it likely that the kind of work considered in this chapter will lead to such explanatory theory in the foreseeable future. Two reasons have been discussed for the failure of the new comparative politics to live up to its "promise" in this area.

The first reason is the generality or level of abstraction of much of the conceptualization and the consequent lack of the precise empirical content necessary to generate testable propositions. This state of affairs may be an unavoidable consequence of the effort to generalize over such a diverse array of systems as those deceptively grouped under such labels as *underdeveloped, developing, non-Western,* or *third world systems* as if they were a monolithic array. What Giovanni Sartori has called "the travelling problem" (Sartori, 1970)—the lack of conceptual equivalence as concepts are translated into specific behaviors and events in given systems—is particularly acute among third world systems. Specific behaviors or events take on different conceptual implications in different contexts. Because of the imprecise empirical content of much of the most respected theorizing about the nature of underdevelopment and of the process of development, it is possible to read much of the frequently cited and prestigious literature in this area without encountering a single testable proposition.

Stochastic theory may be justified for its hueristic function when a field of inquiry is in its infancy. At that point, insightful scholars serve a useful function in suggesting what propositions may be worth testing. However, at some point, a serious scientific enterprise needs to produce explanatory theory with predictive power; hence, theorists need to assume the responsibility for the testability (or empirical content) of the fruits of their mental efforts, rather than leaving it for lesser souls to wallow about in the more mundane tasks of data collection or what Thomas Kuhn has called "paradigm articulation" or "normal science." The experience of several decades of theorizing about political development in the era of the new comparative politics seems to teach that unless the theory-creation function is performed with a concern for its empirical content or testability, much of the theory that is created will be inherently non-testable.

The second reason for the failure of the new comparative politics to develop explanatory theory in the sub-discipline of political development or third world studies is that many of the scholars in this area view political analysis as a tool for polemic purposes, an instrument to persuade their audience that the displacement of what they view as a world capitalist system by some form of socialism is necessary, moral, and inevitable. The polemic purpose of the leading advocates of dependency theory is undisguised. Bodenheimer explicitly argues that displacement of the world capitalist system by socialism is the only effective strategy of undoing the system of dependency relations that she so clearly deplores. Fernando E. Cardozo (in Packenham 1983, pp. 30–31) clearly links the entire idea of dependency to a Marxist perspective. "The idea of dependency," he says,

> is defined in the theoretical field of the Marxist theory of capitalism. Once this is established, there is no need to deny the existence of a theoretical field for dependency itself, but this latter theoretical field is limited by and subordinated to the Marxist theory into which dependency analyses are inserted.[7]

The teleological orientation of a Marxian perspective is well known; that perspective seeks not to explain in the scientific sense of that term but to persuade that an idealized state of affairs is both inevitable and desirable.

It has been shown how dependency theory and related putative explanations of either underdevelopment or the inequality of material well-being among and within nations are scientifically inadequate. The increasing preoccupation of scholars who deal with third world systems with the dependency perspective impedes the explanatory promise of this subdiscipline of the comparative politics field.

NOTES

1. For some of the better known and most fully developed arguments that such non-Western societies may tend toward stagnation rather than change, see Riggs (1964).
2. The most sophisticated of these is Pye (1958). For earlier examples of this genre, see Kahan, Pauker, and Pye (1955) and Riggs (1959).
3. The Third Reich has been interpreted as a revolt against modernization and Western values. This point will be elaborated in chapter 7. For example, see Turner (1972).
4. One of the most explicit and articulately argued examples of this perspective may be found in Pye (1966).
5. This argument is made most concisely in Wade and Bennet (1969). Huntington (1965b) himself explicated the implications of his argument for American politics some time ago (1965).
6. Bodenheimer (1971) says ". . . a Marxist theory of imperialism addresses itself directly to the economic basis of American politics and the causes of dependency and underdevelopment in Latin America" (p. 172).
7. Quoted from Packenham (1983).

REFERENCES

Almond, Gabriel. 1956. "Comparative political systems." *Journal of Politics* 18(3 Aug.):391–409
Almond, Gabriel. 1960a. "A functional approach to comparative politics." In *Politics of the Developing Areas*, edited by Gabriel Almond and James Coleman. Princeton, NJ: Princeton University Press.
Almond, Gabriel. 1960b. "A Developmental Approach to Political Systems." In *Politics of the Developing Areas*, edited by Gabriel Almond and James Coleman. Princeton, NJ: Princeton University Press.
Apter, David. 1965. *The Politics of Modernization*. Chicago: University of Chicago Press.
Banfield, Edward. 1968. *The Unheavenly City*. Boston: Little, Brown.

Bauer, P. T. 1976. *Dissent on Development*. Cambridge, MA: Harvard University Press.

Berg-Schlosser, Dirk. 1984. "African Political Systems: Typology and Performance." *Comparative Political Studies* 17(1, April):121–144.

Blalock, Hubert M. 1960. *Social Statistics*. New York: McGraw Hill.

Bodenheimer, Susan. 1971. "Dependency and Imperialism: The Roots of Underdevelopment." In *Readings in U.S. Imperialism*, edited by K. T. Fann and Donald Hodges. Boston: Porter Sargent.

Bollen, Kenneth. 1983. "World System Position, Dependency and Democracy." *American Sociological Review* 48(4):468 & 479.

Cutwright, Phillips. 1963. "National Political Development: Its Measurement Correlates." In *Politics and Social Life*, edited by Nelson Polsby, Robert Dentler, and Paul Smith. Boston: Houghton Mifflin.

Deutsch, Karl. 1961. "Social Mobilization and Political Development." *American Political Science Review* LV(3, Sept.):493–514.

Diamant, Alfred. 1966. "Political Development: Approaches to Theory and Strategy." In *Approaches to Development, Politics, Administration, and Change*, edited by John D. Montgomery and William Siffin. New York: McGraw Hill.

Duran, Charles. 1983. "Structuring the Concept of Dependency Reversal." In *Studies of Dependency Reversal*, edited by Charles Duran, George Modelski, and Colin Clarke. New York: Praeger.

Eisenstadt, S. N. 1963. "Bureaucracy and Political Development." In *Bureaucracy and Political Development*, edited by Joseph La Palombara. Princeton, NJ: Princeton University Press.

Evans, Peter. 1979. *Dependent Development: The Alliance of Multi-national State and Local Capital in Brazil*. Princeton, NJ: Princeton University Press.

Gasiorowski, Mark. 1988. "Economic Dependence and Political Democracy: A Cross National Study." *Comparative Political Studies* 20(4, Jan.):489–515.

Hobson, J. A. 1905. *Imperialism: A Theory*. London: George Allen and Unwin, Ltd.

Huntington, Samuel. 1965a. "Political Development and Political Decay." *World Politics* XVII (S, April):386–430.

Huntington, Samuel. 1965b. "Congressional Responses to the Twentieth Century." In *Congress and America's Future*, edited by David Truman. Englewood Cliffs, NJ: Prentice-Hall.

Huntington, Samuel. 1968. *Political Order in Changing Societies*. New Haven, CT: Yale University Press.

Huntington, Samuel and Joan Nelson. 1976. *No Easy Choice: Political Participation in Developing Societies*. Cambridge, MA: Harvard University Press.

Kahan, George M., Guy Pauker, and Lucien Pye. 1955. "The Comparative Politics of Non-Western Countries." *American Political Science Review* 49(4, Dec.):1022–1041.

Kalleberg, Arthur. 1956. "The Logic of Comparison: A Methodological Note on the Study of Political Systems." *World Politics* 19(Jan.):69–82.

Lassell, Harold. 1948. *Power and Personality*. New York: The Viking Press.

Lerner, Daniel. 1958. *The Passing of Traditional Society*. Glencoe, IL: The Free Press.

Lipset, Seymour. 1959. "Some Social Requisites of Democracy." *American Political Science Review* 53(1, Mar.):69–105.

Mayer, Lawrence. 1972. *Comparative Political Inquiry*. Homewood, IL: The Dorsey Press.

McClelland, David. 1961. *The Achieving Society*. New York: The Free Press.

McCrone, Donald and Charles Cnudde. 1971. "Toward a Communication Theory of Democratic Development: A Causal Model." In *Macro Quantitative Analyses*, edited by John Gillespie and Betty Nesvold. Beverly Hills, CA: Sage Publications.

Meehan, Eugene. 1965. *The Theory and Model of Political Analysis*. Homewood, IL: The Dorsey Press.

Novack, Michael. 1982. "Why Latin America is Poor." *The Atlantic* 29(3, Marc.):66–73.

Olson, Mancur. 1963. "Rapid Growth as a Destabilizing Force." *Journal of Economic History* 16(4, Dec.):529–552.

Packenham, Robert. 1983. "The Dependency Perspective and Analytic Dependency." In *North-South Relations: Studies of Dependency Reversal*, edited by Charles Duran, George Modelski, and Colin Clarke. New York: Praeger.

Palmer, Monte. 1980. *Dilemmas of Political Development*, 2nd ed. Itasca, IL: Peacock Publishing.

Parenti, Michael. 1989. *The Sword and the Dollar: Imperialism and the Arms Race* New York: St. Martin's Press.

Pye, Lucien. 1958. "The Non-Western Political Process." *Journal of Politics* XX(3, Aug.):468–486.

Pye, Lucien. 1966. *Aspects of Political Development*. Boston: Little, Brown.

Riggs, Fred. 1959. "Agraria and Industria." In *Toward the Comparative Study of Administration*, edited by William Siffin. Bloomington, IN: University of Indiana Press.

Riggs, Fred. 1964. *Administration in Developing Countries: The Theory of the Prismatic Society*. Boston: Houghton Mifflin.

Sartori, Giovanni. 1970. "Concept Misinformation in Comparative Politics." *American Political Science Review* LXIV(4, Dec.):1033–1053.

Sowell, Thomas. 1983. "Second Thoughts About the Third World." *Harpers* 267(1602, Nov.):34–43.

Toynbee, Arnold. 1946. *A Study of History*, abridged by D. C. Somervell, Volume 1. New York: Oxford University Press.

Turner, Henry Ashby. 1972. "Fascism and Modernization." *World Politics* 24(4, July):547–564.

Vengroff, Richard. 1977. "Dependence, Development, and Inequality in Black Africa." *African Studies Review* 20(2, Sept.):17–26.

Wade, Quentin and Thomas Bennet. 1969. *American Politics: Effective, Responsible?* New York: American Book Company.

CHAPTER FOUR

Industrial Democracies

The body of literature dealing in one way or another with industrial democracy is too vast to be analyzed adequately in one book, let alone in one chapter. Accordingly, some narrower focus is needed to render this chapter manageable. An analysis of the success of the literature in conceptualizing the subject matter with sufficient precision for the development of explanatory theory, in identifying major trends or deviations from classical, or conventionally understood, patterns in the operations of such systems, and in determining the impact of such trends on the essential values that constitute the very nature of industrial democracy will constitute the focus of this chapter. Important determinants of the nature and operation of industrial democracies, specifically their party systems, their sociopolitical cleavages, and the cultural context in which they operate, will be treated in separate chapters for reasons pertaining to the extent of these topics and of the literature dealing with them, although it is realized that industrial democracies cannot be analyzed or explained with any reasonable degree of completeness in the absence of considering such factors.

Specifically, it will be argued that the essence of industrial democracies lies in the procedures, institutions, and patterns of interaction by which decision makers are chosen and decisions made, procedures and institutions intended to render authoritative decisions accountable to a significant portion of the society that such political systems ostensibly govern. Further, it will be argued that the literature has clearly identified trends in the nature of these procedures, institutions, and patterns, trends that are a product of the evolving state of technology and that impact upon the structure of accountability. Such analysis of the impact of advancing technology and the structure of accountability constitutes a significant advance over the pre-1950s literature and even over some more recent writings from that same perspective.

The aforementioned literature has not, however, coalesced into a coherent theory of the impact of such trends, a theory based upon the essential values that define the *raison d'être* of industrial democracy itself. A persisting ambiguity on the essence of industrial democracy prevents the building of such a body of coherent theory. Hence, it seems appropriate to discuss the phenomenon of industrial democracy, especially with respect to the failure to build a consensus on its essence.

CONCEPTUALIZING INDUSTRIAL DEMOCRACY

The literature dealing with Western democracies has failed to unambiguously conceptualize the essence of that phenomenon. Frequently, scholars discussing the phenomenon do not even try to do so. Rather, they proceed to discuss types and attributes of democracy without delineating its essence. Even when attention is given to the problem of conceptualizing democracy, there is no consensus on the precise criteria for assigning given nations either to the class of systems we call democracies or to that residual class of non-democracies conveniently called autocracies (discussed at length in Chapter 7). Arend Lijphart (1984, p. 1), for example, refers to democracy as "government by the freely elected representatives of the people," and further holds that a country is democratic to the extent that it acts "in accord with the people's preferences." Lijphart does not trouble himself with such questions as how the preferences of the people are determined and measured. It is unclear, for instance, as to the degree of specificity with which such preferences will be measured. Given that, presumably, there is some degree of autonomy of any governmental decision-making process from the impact of public opinion, how much convergence or correspondence between governmental and societal preferences is required to classify a state as democratic? Can the degree of such correspondence conceivably be measured and, if so, how can cut-off levels of such correspondence distinguishing democracies from autocracies be justified? Furthermore, since Lijphart identifies both a majoritarian model of democracy in which a government must maintain some correspondence with or responsiveness to a majority of voting citizens and a consensus model in which minority veto groups can negate and thus impose policy choices, it is unclear as to precisely who the "people" are with whose preferences government must be in some degree of "accord."

Lijphart's conception of democracy contains two kinds of criteria: procedural and substantive. The procedural criterion involves the question of how decision makers are chosen and how decisions are reached among them. This question is logically distinct from the substantive question of the content of these decisions. One may argue that the question of whether a regime is or is not democratic is solely a function of whether elites are chosen and decisions made by democratic procedures, irrespective of the policies adopted. Joseph Schumpeter's conceptualization of democracy as merely a system in which "individuals acquire power to make authoritative political decisions by means of a competitive struggle for the people's vote" is one of the best known of this procedural genre of conceptualizing democracy (Schumpeter, 1950). Another procedural approach is to define democracy in terms of the scope of the politically relevant state of the population, specifically in terms of providing the mechanism and/or opportunity for the widest proportion of the population to participate in and influence the political decision-making process (Dahl, 1970). Seymour Lipset combines both criteria in his definition (Lipset, 1963).

Some scholars have either expressly or implicitly attached substantive criteria to their conceptualization of democracy, either in addition to the aforementioned concept or as the essence of the concept. The various conceptualizations of equality constitute the most frequently adduced substantive criteria for inclusion among that class of systems we call democracies. Equality is frequently conceptualized to refer to what may be called political equality, a condition in which

> all full citizens must have unimpaired opportunities: (1) to formulate their preferences . . . (2) to signify their preferences . . . (3) to have their preferences weighted equally.

Dahl (1971, pp. 1–2), who offers the foregoing criteria, holds that a democracy must be continually responsive to the preferences of its citizens "considered as political equals."

Lewis Lipsitz also typifies those political scientists who incorporate the criterion of equality in their conceptualization of democracy. Arguing from the indisputable premise that disparities in the distribution of material well-being inevitably are translated into corresponding disparities in political influence, he concludes that under such disparities of wealth and power, "democracy will probably be drained of its meaning" (Lipsitz, 1986). Lipsitz goes on to dismiss the Schumpeterian definition as a "minimalist position" as opposed to a "maximalist position" that conceptualizes democracy not only in terms of political procedures but in terms of the egalitarian values Lipsitz would like to see achieved. Yet, his maximalist view would mean that, to a greater or lesser extent, all of those nations he lists as established democracies fall short of his ideal type. Hence, such a type may provide normative ends in view but it lacks explanatory utility in the sense that term was used in the preceding chapter.

Political equality, thus conceptualized, constitutes a standard to which all the industrial nations we normally consider democracies will, to a greater or lesser extent, fall short.[1] In no modern system do all citizens even have what might reasonably be called autonomous political preferences formed independently of opinion leaders.[2] Political activity is not only, in fact, confined to a narrow elite; large sections of the citizenry clearly lack the essential resources to articulate their preferences, even when they have preferences coherent enough to justify such articulation.[3] Moreover, the opportunities for citizens' preferences to have an impact on public policy are clearly a function of unequally distributed socioeconomic circumstances, among other factors.

Moreover, the enormous problems of measurement entailed by the criterion of the responsiveness of public policy to its people have never been seriously addressed. Given the inevitability of the conflict of interests in any reasonably complex society, the responsiveness criterion raises questions about the people to whom policy should respond. Moreover, the varying degrees of intensity with which preferences are held place varying degrees of pressure on the system to respond in a certain way; hence, the research task is complicated not only by the familiar case of a passionate minority overcoming a passive majority, but also by the question of how passionate a minority of a given size must be in order to overcome a given sized majority, as well as how to measure degrees of passion and commitment.

Since the rational, activist citizen has been clearly shown to be largely mythical, and since public opinion is largely formulated and disseminated by opinion leaders, government does not respond to autonomously formed and held social preferences in any meaningful sense. The criterion of responsiveness is clearly related to the idea of citizen involvement, since a capacity to respond to the preferences of the citizenry in general requires that those preferences be somehow articulated. Gabriel Almond and Bingham Powell (1984) have even suggested that democracy be thought of as a matter of degree—"The more citizens are involved and the more meaningful their choices, the more democratic the system" (p. 47).

The scope of citizen participation as a criterion for how democratic a system is presumed to be, taken by itself, would seem to impute a democratic value to those autocracies whose legitimacy rests on the claim to represent, in a Rousseauian sense, the true will of a mobilized populace, systems that more or less embody what Talmon meant by "totalitarian democracy," or Neumann by the term "Caesaristic dictatorship" (Talmon, 1952; Neumann, 1957). Such a criterion would seem to detract from the democratic character of systems in which a large percentage of the populace is politically passive or inert, whether out of basic satisfaction with system performance, a widespread deference to political authority, or even a lack of widespread socialization and recruitment into their political roles. Despite such popular passivity, these systems may, in fact, choose their leaders by genuinely competitive (and hence "fair") elections and respect the basic individual liberties that define an open society. One would not want to characterize the Philippine political system of 1986, for example, as more democratic than the United States on the basis of a Philippine election characterized by a large turnout but also by numerous instances of voter intimidation, violence, bribery, and outright dishonesty in the tabulation of results, while American presidential elections are routinely ignored by a third or more of the eligible voters.

The criterion of meaningfulness of choice lacks the necessary precision to form the basis of an unambiguous distinction between democracies and autocracies or an intersubjective rating on the degree of democracy. Does a meaningful choice imply a clear principled or ideological distinction between parties or candidates? The extent to which such a choice is actually present in competitive party systems is a subject of growing concern in the literature, as will be discussed at some length in the next chapter. For now, it can be noted that the ideological distance between parties is measureable (Sigelman and Yough, 1978) and negatively related to the success and stability of democratic government. Democracy, after all, requires that losers in the political competition accept the outcome, which, in turn, presumes that the rules of the game are more important than the outcome; such an attitude can be found only when there is not much at stake in the democratic election. The meaningful-choice criterion thus raises a serious question about whether those nations in which programmatic or philosophical positions of political competitors are either too amorphous to generate such a choice or tend to converge will be considered less democratic than nations whose electoral process is wracked by polarized competition on the most fundamental issues. Many scholars consider such centripetal convergence on issues and lack of passion, or lower level of political activism, to constitute a sign of political health.

Hence, while it has been shown that the ideological distance between parties is measurable, the level of principled distinctiveness in electoral choice as a criterion of democracy presents serious difficulties. The lack of agreement among scholars as to whether the distinctiveness or polarization of electoral choice is positively or negatively related to the essential values of democracy prevents that criterion from forming the basis of a cumulative body of explanatory theory. This lack of agreement on the impact of that criterion emanates from an absence of consensus on the essential normative value(s) entailed by the concept of democracy. This problem is discussed below at some length.

For the goal of building a cumulative body of explanatory theory, the simple criterion of regular competitive elections offers a number of advantages as a definition. First, it is useful to keep the definition analytically distinct from the values entailed by that definition. In that way, the question of the utility and effectiveness of democracy, as descriptively defined, in promoting the normatively posited essential values becomes a potential subject for inquiry rather than true by definition. To include a value such as equality as part of the definition of democracy obviates the question of whether or to what extent democracy promotes that value.

A second advantage of the simple Schumpeterian definition is that it has face validity; it does not offend widespread, commonsense understanding of the nature of the democratic phenomenon. Democracy may entail more than this to many people, but to nearly everyone in the Western world, it entails at least this much. Such common understanding would do much to promote the goal of building explanatory theory cumulatively.

A third advantage of this definition is that it is relatively precise because it minimizes ambiguity over which nations will be included by this criterion in the democratic category. The ambiguity that does exist in this criterion is in the concept of genuinely competitive. The concept entails the legitimacy of active opposition and an electoral process that is free from intimidation and fraud significant enough to determine the outcome of the election. Hence, the apparent combination of intimidation, vote buying, intentional miscounting of votes, and other techniques of vote fraud by which Ferdinand Marcos engineered his election "victory" over Corazon Aquino in February 1986, would remove the Phillipines from our democratic category. Marcos apparently felt almost no constraint on his discretion to enrich his personal situation at public expense and with good reason: he could assume that his power would be protected by his control of the process. The absence-of-fraud-and-intimidation corollary to the genuinely-competitive-election criterion of democracy, if consensually adopted, would expose the untenable nature of numerous attempts to stretch the category of democratic nations to include nations like the Philippines under Marcos in order to justify a continued or expanded American financial and military commitment to them. Voting fraud does occur, of course, in those nations whose democratic nature is virtually unquestioned in the West. For example, it is apparent that voting irregularities occurred in Chicago in the 1960 presidential elections, and some reasonable men are unsure as to whether the outcome might have been altered in a scrupulously "honest" election. However, the magnitude of such fraud does not approach the magnitude of the Philippine situation and, aside from the question about the 1960 American election, national election results in the West have not been reversed by such manipulation of the electoral process.

A fourth advantage of the Schumpeterian definition is that it allows the inclusion of states consensually recognized as democratic but which would not meet some of the other criteria offered. For example, the meaningfulness of the competition criterion is held by some to imply something about the opposition's chances of actually winning control of the central government—to elect a prime minister, president, or their equivalent. Implicitly, then, hegemonic regimes such as Sweden, Japan, or India are either less democratic or non-democratic.

Yet, there are three possible types of explanation for one party or set of elites maintaining a hegemony of power over a long period of time with each of these explanations entailing a different impact on the accountability of elites. One is that the incumbent elites suppress and deny the legitimacy of opposition candidates and of their political activity. A second is that the incumbents perpetrate a sufficient amount of vote fraud, bribery, or harassment of opposition activity to ensure that the incumbents win. The situation in the Philippines to which we referred above fits this type. Mexico may also fit this category as the Party of Institutionalized Revolution has been accused of a significant amount of vote stealing, although it probably would win a "fair" election. The third scenario is where one party or set of leaders maintains its hegemony by creating a widespread perception of satisfactory performance. The security and well being of the Swedes under their welfare state has been said to render that nation's politics "boring", meaning that the opposition lacks issues around which they might mobilize support for their challenge. When elites maintain their hegemony because voters are at least passively satisfied, surely those elites are more accountable than when elites maintain their power by suppressing opposition. Mexico may lay some claim to this third category as well; hence, even the legitimacy of competition as a criterion of democracy may leave ambiguity in classifying particular cases. However, such ambiguity is minimal compared to such aforementioned criteria as the meaningfulness of electoral choice and the scope of citizen participation.

It is being suggested that Schumpeter's conception of democracy offers the least ambiguity for classifying particular states without sacrificing face validity in the sense of making a principled distinction between democracies and autocracies that is congruent with widely accepted impressionistic judgments about which nations ought to belong to which category. Democracy, thus defined, may require certain attributes from its sociocultural and economic context to thrive, persist, or even come into being. However, the relationship between such attributes and "healthy" democracy constitutes a potentially researchable question. Such attributes may or may not contribute to the well-being of democracy, but they do not constitute part of its defining essence. The inclusion of such sociocultural attributes (for example, a tolerance of pluralism and of different normative or political judgments or respect for civil liberties broadly defined) in the definition of democracy resolves the real question of the relation between these sociocultural attributes and our defining political procedures tautologically. The preservation of a distinction between the essence of a phenomenon and that which may (or may not) support the existence or well-being of that phenomenon is important in allowing for inquiry into what does or does not actually support the phenomenon itself. Thus, the inclusion of a civil libertarian culture in the concept of democracy precludes inquiry into the question of the extent to which such cultural attributes are necessary or supportive of democratic procedures.

ACCOUNTABILITY AS THE BASIC DEMOCRATIC VALUE

The conceptualization of democracy as competition for political office, in addition to its justification in terms of face validity, entails a normative component. After all, democracy is not merely something that distinguishes one group of nations from other nations but something that makes that group of nations preferred in the Western world. The procedures that define the essence of political democracy may be instrumentally justified in terms of some substantive ends that establish the priority of one conceptualization of this normatively positive term over competing conceptualizations.

Democracy is a term to which claim has been laid by a number of very distinct sociopolitical formats. Sekou Toure of Guinea claimed to be practicing "tutelary democracy." Kwame

Nkrumah of Ghana claimed to be practicing "guided democracy." The Soviets have characterized their system as "democratic centralism." The term has such a normatively positive connotation that very different systems based upon very different values have applied it to themselves. It is the position of this chapter that those Western nations based on political competition have a unique claim to this term because of their contribution to an outcome or value more essentially tied to the idea of democracy than the outcomes of alternative formats that have co-opted the term.

Originally, in its Greek roots, democracy entailed the idea that the populace controlled its rulers. Whatever good this concept may constitute in itself, it seems primarily directed toward the idea that rulers are accountable to those that they rule. The actuality of popular control of government seems today to be an increasingly unrealistic standard.

In one of the notable examples of a growing body of literature perceptively reassessing the actual nature of modern democracy, Eric Nordlinger argues that democratic governments choose among policy alternatives much more autonomously from the preferences of the societies they rule than one would conclude from classical democratic theory, a theory that stresses a society-centered explanation for government actions (Nordlinger, 1981). Nordlinger argues that even when governmental and dominant societal preferences appear to diverge, government may utilize one of several strategies to either change the latter to a position of convergence or to neutralize or render ineffective the will and resources of those who hold divergent preferences. The significance of work such as Nordlinger's is that it devastates the justification of democracy as a government meaningfully controlled by "the people" (meaning a majority of nongovernmental actors).

One may question whether the state, in the sense of legally or constitutionally designated officials, effectively uses its "autonomy-enhancing" resources and strategies so effectively as to render state action as autonomous from all nongovernment actors as is implied by Nordlinger. It will be shown that other assessments of modern industrial democracy render the formal state less autonomous of certain powerful social and economic forces than Nordlinger's theoretical analysis seems to imply.

It is clear, however, from Nordlinger and others, that a justification of democratic government based upon a claim that such governments substantially reflect the "will of the people" will not withstand realistic analysis. Thus, it is not only accepted as true to the point of being trite that actual decision-making power in any society is in the hands of a few—an elite[4]— or even that such an elite is not the product of some correctable pathology in the society, such as an uninformed electorate, but that in any reasonably complex large organization, let alone sociopolitical system, in which there is a high degree of functional specialization of roles, elitism or oligarchy is inevitable.[5] Thus, government by the few, and even government that is not responsive in a policy-specific sense, is a necessary product of the process of modernization that makes leadership or government itself a specialized function based upon esoteric skills and information. This observation may be little more than noting that in a modern society the job of the government is to govern—not merely to sense the pulse of public opinion and follow its dictates in a clerical fashion.

Modern political scientists have, in their critiques of classical democratic theory, persuasively made a case for what democracy is not. However, it is the position of this chapter that they have not replaced classical democratic theory with a conceptualization of democracy that is both empirically and normatively justifiable.

As implied above, an empirically useful definition must distinguish with as little ambiguity as possible between those nations we consensually and impressionistically identify as democracies and those we do not. This criterion is, for the most part, met by the Schumpeterian conception of democracy: regular competition for public office. However, if Nordlinger's argument is granted that modern democracies act autonomously from societal preferences and that actual impact on the policy-making process is confined to a small elite, the question arises as to what advantages are gained from the process of competitive elections. If the people do not govern themselves either directly or through their representatives or do not even closely control and determine policy outcomes, why is democracy a preferred system?

It is suggested that, to the degree that elections are competitive, the elites who do govern are accountable to their society for the impact of the policy choices they make. *Accountability* is defined here as a perception by the elites that their political fortunes will be better off to the extent that they can justify the impact of their governance in terms of some conception of the public interest. This perception limits the range of policy choices and actions available to the occupant of the elite role to those choices or actions he or she believes can be so justified.

Accountability, thus conceptualized, is a matter of degree rather than a discrete dichotomous variable. Elites are more or less accountable, depending on the breadth or narrowness of the discretion available to them without jeopardizing their political well-being or, otherwise put, depending on the amount of popular dissatisfaction the elites can afford to generate without jeopardizing their political fortunes. Clearly, it would take far less dissatisfaction with a regime to prompt citizens to vote for a legitimate opposition in a regularly scheduled election than to risk life and limb in armed revolt against an entrenched autocracy. To take a less extreme example, it would take less dissatisfaction to vote for an opposition party or candidate that had a realistic chance of winning than it would to support an opposition that, while legitimate, had only a remote chance of unseating a dominant or hegemonic regime. The more dissatisfaction with system output it would require to generate opposition, the broader the discretion of elites without concern for the justifiability of their behavior and policy choice in terms of the public interest.

The mere fact of competitive elections—elections in which opposition is legitimate—generates a degree of accountability that is not approached by autocracies in which opposition is suppressed. Where opposition is legitimate, a hegemonic elite maintains its dominance because society is at least passively satisfied. The long dominance of the Swedish Social Democrats, for example, was clearly related to the absence of a viable issue around which to mobilize the passions of a coherent opposition while Sweden enjoyed a long period of economic prosperity, economic security, the absence of great levels of inequality in the distribution of material well-being, and the national security that comes from the absence of external threats.

In nations in which opposition is legitimate but in which elections and election results are so managed and readjusted by the incumbents that the results are predetermined, incumbents have a freer hand to largely ignore the justification of their frequently self-serving policies. The cases of the Marcos regime in the Philippines, of the Party of Institutionalized Revolution in Mexico, and of the Chun Doo Hwan regimes in South Korea illustrate this type of absence of accountability. Such nations should, therefore, be excluded from the category of political democracies, although such nations may possess a number of the attributes commonly associated with that political format. It may be argued, however, that such nations constitute a particular variant of autocracy because of the relative openness with which opposition is permitted to flourish. While Marcos apparently stole the Philippine election of 1986 with massive vote fraud, it is impossible to imagine a Soviet counterpart of Ms. Aquino similarly mobilizing opposition to the Kremlin. A mobilized opposition of a given level of intensity becomes more probable in such relatively open autocracies than in relatively closed ones, and perceptive leaders in the relatively open type may well concern themselves with some attempt to justify their rule to avoid the fate of a Marcos. Yet, such leaders, freed from institutionalized mechanisms to replace them, apparently do not perceive that they are under significant restraints on their policies and official acts, as attested by the rampant corruption and economic chaos generated without apology by the Marcos and recent Mexican regimes.

The degree of accountability thus varies, both within the category of democratic nations and within the category of autocracies, but it varies significantly less within those categories than between them. It is argued here that the value of accountability as an outcome of competitive elections justifies the adoption of that procedural standard for distinguishing democracies from autocracies. Such an operational definition avoids the problem of setting criteria for the category that no nation fully meets.

The explanatory purpose of a concept entails a descriptive, rather than a normative, orientation—to provide precise criteria for grouping and making distinctions between sensory phenomena, rather than to set standards for the way phenomena ought to be. However, definitions, once stipulated, cannot avoid a normative component in social research. Political scientists define democracy and attempt to stipulate the factors that support or threaten it because it entails certain values. Yet, the literature has not produced a consensus on precisely why democracy should be promoted or preserved. Some critics of American democracy imply material equality as the criterion of a just society (Rawls, 1971), a position that would render the United States one of the less "truly" just nations in that category.

Accountability constitutes an alternative criterion for the evaluation of protean variation in formal and informal structures and in trends among democracies, a criterion that is more political and that has more face validity than such criteria as economic equality and social justice. Although fragmentary evidence raises questions about the success of such efforts thus far, it is theoretically possible for a regime to successfully implement a high degree of redistribution of material values while eschewing the legitimacy of political competition. The classification of political systems along a political dimension (democracy, autocracy) may be related to classification along an economic dimension (free enterprise capitalism, welfare state capitalism, state socialism), but these two dimensions should remain conceptually distinct, thus permitting conjecture about the relationship between political format and economic outcome to remain questions for inquiry rather than impressionistic givens. The criterion of accountability permits the analysis of variations in political structures or institutions with respect to their impact on an essentially political value.

THE STRUCTURE OF ACCOUNTABILITY AND THE PROBLEM OF POWER

The best of the large body of literature that focuses on the variation in constitutionally designated structures, that which goes beyond a largely descriptive purpose, frequently addresses the impact of such structures and the pattern of interaction among them (referred to in this book as the political format) on the goal of rendering political elites more accountable. Such structures become part of what the present author calls the structure of accountability. This accountability is a product of the procedures entailed by the political format and depends on the extent to which the actual political decision-making procedures are congruent with those delineated by the political format.

Thus, the efforts of scholars such as Lijphart (1984) and Livingston (1976) to ascertain how the variation in political format among major democracies impacts on democratic values presumes that the real power to make those decisions that actually allocate values lies within the constitutionally designated political format. These works, among others, suggest that a critical difference exists between the type of solution offered by the British model and that offered by the American model to the eternal problem of power.

The essence of the problem is that the power to govern cannot be separated from the power to abuse. The power to act in the interest of society necessarily entails the power to act for or against the public interest, since power includes the choice of how to act.

The solution of the British majoritarian or Westminster model, to use Lijphart's terminology, is to concentrate power so as to clarify the lines of responsibility and then to hold those power wielders accountable for its use. The solution of the American model, or the consensus model, again in Lijphart's terminology, is to divide power among a number of autonomous power wielders so that no actor has enough power to abuse without the spontaneous concurrence of other autonomous actors. Given the improbability that a widespread consensus would spontaneously occur with respect to any controversial issue of public policy, the American or consensus model is really a blueprint for political stalemate. Hence, over the years, a chorus of voices from among scholarly observers of the British system have urged varying degrees of reform of the American system along British lines.[6] Such analyses are of value in overcoming a widespread ethnocentrism regarding the political format of one's own nation as the only conceivable or effective solution to the problem of power, as well as in explicating the logic of how each system is designed to resolve the problem. However, as actual proposals for reform, such analyses ignore the extent to which institutional choices are reflections of deep-seated cultural attributes, a relationship discussed at greater length in Chapter 6.

The same presumption that actual political power resides in those structures constitutionally designated for that purpose implicitly underlies a body of literature concerned with the reform of such institutions. While much of the classic literature in this area focuses on the overanalyzed British constitution, other industrial democracies have not been neglected (Crick, 1965; Amery, 1964; Williams, 1968). Such works recommend techniques for streamlining institutions to make them more efficient at coping with the growing imperatives of modernity as, for instance, making greater use of the principle of functional specialization in the structure of legislative committees and making the member of parliament a full-time, well-paid official with adequate staff and logistical support. Many of the best of these works, such as that of Crick, recognize that the political institutions they seek to reform, because of the inefficiencies being discussed, no longer play the central role assigned to them in constitutional theory. The implicit presumption of such proposals of reform, however, is that the constitutionally designated structures can, with the implementation of these proposals, reassert their classic theoretical role in the policy-making process.

Yet, the thrust of the growing corpus of literature on "postindustrial societies" is that an important ineluctable trend in such societies is a transfer of actual political power from the constitutionally designated political institutions to a technocracy, the locus of which is outside the political sector. Such a trend would render the question of the nature and reform of the political sector largely moot.

SPECIALIZATION AND THE PROBLEM OF POWER

One of the revelations of hitherto ignored or even repressed reality that accompanied the revolution in comparative politics was the growing awareness of the political role of the administrative sector. The field of comparative administration became one of the real growth industries of the 1960s as an increasingly large corpus of literature appeared not only to inform us that, lo and behold, Woodrow Wilson's 1887 idealistic dictum about the separation of politics and administration increasingly did not describe reality, but further to logically analyze the implications of this newly discovered political role of actors operating within the constraints of administrative structure and norms.

Students of the phenomenon of political development perhaps took an early lead in producing a substantial literature on what Fred Riggs called "the heavy weight of bureaucratic power" in the political process (Riggs, 1964). Hence, the study of "development administration" took on many of the attributes of a distinct field with its own literature and courses and the implicit *raison d'être* that the role of administration in such third world systems was somehow *sui generis*.[7] Riggs and other scholars of this genre reasoned that Western imperial powers, understandably more interested in enhancing their effectiveness in the implementation of policies designed to control and exploit their third world dependents than in fostering the instruments of political autonomy, built and fostered strong administrative structures while neglecting those representative structures most capable of mobilizing and responding to native demands. Logically, it has been pointed out, administrative structures are not designed to maximize the values of adaptability and responsiveness; hence, societies dominated by such structures are ill-suited for the challenge of sociopolitical modernization. The heavy weight of bureaucratic power may foster stagnation rather than development in such less-developed systems. This argument has largely been confined to the level of logical analysis; only a few attempts have been made to subject this widely postulated conventional wisdom to empirical analysis.

Conventional wisdom is taken here to mean that which is widely or consensually accepted as impressionistically true but which has never been empirically verified. Because we must, of necessity, treat so many concepts that inherently pose difficult problems of measurement and even greater problems of equivalence in conceptualization across cultural contexts, a distressingly large portion of our most widely cited explanatory theory remains in the form of conventional wisdom. One of the most satisfying and important tasks in the theory-building enterprise is the role of the discipline's "gadfly" who creatively devises a way to subject such conventional wisdom to empirical tests and who occasionally finds that the data do not support the assumed truths.

Lee Sigelman has ably assumed the gadfly role on more than one occasion. In that capacity, he has provided one of the few attempts to subject this conventional wisdom about the predominant role of the bureaucracy in less-developed systems to empirical test. Sigelman found that, contrary to the expectation entailed by the imbalance thesis, bureaucratic dominance of the political sector is negatively related to bureaucratic modernity or development. The imbalance thesis holds that as the administrative sector becomes more modern and hence stronger, it tends to overpower the weaker political sector. While Sigelman found the diametric opposite, these findings are based, by his own admission, on judgmental data (Sigelman, 1972). Sigelman replicates these findings with other data that, while more explicitly ordinal and based on more precise criteria for classification, remain essentially judgmental (Sigelman, 1974). Although judgmental and clearly inconclusive, these data draw the "heavy weight of bureaucratic power" thesis of Riggs and others into serious question. Such empirical pinpricks in our overinflated balloons of conventional wisdom constitute a useful caveat against our frequently heavy reliance on such assumptions.

The impressions of bureaucratic instrusions in the political process that Riggs and others have formed with respect to third world systems have occurred to students of Western democracies as well. The inevitable political role of administrative officials in the political processes of first world nations has been noted by scholars for decades. In one group of first world systems, the attributed cause of the excessive role of the public bureaucracy in the political process is the same as in the third world—an ineffective and poorly legitimized political process. The Third and Fourth Republics of France constitute two of the best examples of this situation (Diamant, 1957; Ehrman, 1961). This scenario is of limited significance in the first world, since most Western democracies possess reasonably effective and legitimate political institutions. However, there is a growing concern about declining legitimacy and effectiveness in many of these democracies, a concern that is addressed at some length below.

A growing chorus of scholars has been arguing that in the most developed politics, the so-called postindustrial societies, a strong political role for the administrative sector is an inevitable concomitant of the very process of modernization. A literature has developed identifying and discussing the implications of the phenomenon called the postindustrial society, a phenomenon generally identified as those societies in which a majority of people are employed in the tertiary or service sector of the economy.[8]

The present author, among others, has raised the question of whether postindustrial society ought to be regarded as a distinct phenomenon from a *relatively* mature industrial society (Mayer and Burnett, 1977). There are advantages to regarding the maturity of industrial societies, as measured by the percentage of workers in the tertiary sector or by other appropriate indicators, as a continuous rather than a discrete variable. Clearly, there are or have been societies that fall just short of Bell's rigid threshold criterion but exhibit most of the attributes of such postindustrial systems and, in fact, resemble such systems far more than systems that barely exceed the threshold for the industrial category. Since the indicators are amounts or values rather than attributes, the mathematical and conceptual advantages of a continuous variable ought to be utilized. However, the discipline seems to have a penchant for catchwords, slogans, or "talismans" that have become *de rigueur* among the *cognoscenti* of the field, catchwords that often become a substitute for analysis and that obscure more than they reveal. However, the concept of postindustrial society is definitely "in", and the literature on it is burgeoning.

The essential attribute of the concept of postindustrial society for the purposes of formulating and implementating public policy is its advanced state of technology. The body of human knowledge has expanded to the point of being beyond the grasp of individuals or small, coherent institutions; hence, a heavy reliance on the principle of functional specialization and expertise in the policy process is inexorable. As Bell repeatedly tells us, we live in a "technocracy" in which effective control of the policy process, the actual discretion in determining who gets how much of what, has fallen into the hands of those who are technologically competent to comprehend the issues, the policy alternatives, and their respective probable impacts. These "technocrats", or experts, tend to be found either in the higher levels of the civil service or administrative sector of government or outside government in organized interest groups.

Classic bureaucratic rules optimize the values of predictability and efficiency—desirable attributes for the implementation of policy—while working against the values of adaptability and responsiveness—imperatives for the formulation of policy in a successful democracy (March and Simon, 1967).[9] Crozier perceptively analyzes how this bureaucratic mind-set tends to create policy that is noncreative, nonadaptive and nonresponsive. Such a highly bureaucratized political system becomes what he calls "the stalled society" (Crozier, 1973). A system based upon rigidity and routinization will resist change for as long as possible, and, in such a system, change can be initiated only by remote centralized authority, says Crozier. Yet, without the capacity to change, the system cannot adapt and respond to a nonstatic environment (Crozier, 1964).

That there is such a phenomenon as a bureaucratic mind-set and that this is dysfunctional for the political role of senior civil servants has been documented by Robert Putnam and others (Putnam, 1973). Based upon interviews with senior civil servants in Great Britain and Italy, Putnam identified what he termed the "classical bureaucrat," one who believes that he should be insulated from sociopolitical pressures with which he has little patience or understanding, in order to make the right decisions based upon what he considers his superior technical expertise. He tends to "go by the book" in applying rules without regard to any unique or extenuating circumstances in a particular case. Putnam's finding that such "classical bureaucrats" are more prevalent in Italy than in Great Britain is not surprising from what is known about the cultural patterns of these two nations and further supports Crozier's suggestion that the character of a nation's civil service will reflect its political culture. Putnam's work is an early example of a now growing but sparse body of data on the political role of the higher civil service.

REPRESENTATIVE BUREAUCRACY

The problem of the political role of the civil service has been addressed by an appeal to make the admittedly politically active administrative sector more representative of the social and ethnic cleavages in the society. The concept of representative in this literature is usually used in the sense of a proportional correspondence of the social, political, and ethnic attributes of the bureaucratic elites to the distribution of such attributes in the general population (Kingsley, 1964),[10] a concept that the present author calls sociological representation. This literature tends to take on the purpose of exhortations for reform rather than of explanation and is based upon several assumptions. One is that the real function of the higher civil service is primarily political and hence ought to be constituted in a way consistent with a political rather than an administrative role. However, to deny the administrative role of the civil service is not only to distort reality in the other direction but to ignore the source of the expertise that gave the civil service its political role in the first place.

This presents what the author of this book has elsewhere called the paradox of modern bureaucracy (Mayer and Burnett, 1977). The imperatives of mature industrial societies demand increasing reliance on technical competence and expertise for decision making; hence, these bureaucratic attributes of specialization and recruitment on the basis of expertise render the civil service a politically salient institution. However, these very same attributes render the civil service less suitable for fulfilling its political function with responsive and adaptive capabilities. Representative bureaucracy implies recruitment on the basis of ascriptive criteria, which must necessarily compromise the traditional recruitment on the basis of merit or skill, criteria that lead to the bureaucratic attributes of expertise and functional specialization that render civil servants politically relevant in technologically advanced societies.

Another assumption is that psychological representation—an understanding of and sympathy for the values, interests, and demands of the various segments of society—is a function of the concept of sociological representation as defined above. Thus, it is assumed that only individuals who belong to certain groups or who have matured as members of these groups can be trusted to guard and promote the interests of such groups. The assumption is manifested in the effort to achieve cultural proportionality in the civil service of such culturally segmented systems as Belgium, Canada, the Netherlands, and Austria (with its *proporz* system). Yet, it is well known that there is no necessary correspondence between the ethnic, gender, racial, or other sociological attributes of a person and that person's attitudes about the putative interests of that group. For example, with respect to attitudes about the feminist movement or the issues with which it is concerned, gender is a poor predictor (Mayer and Smith, 1985). There are as many female "male chauvinists" as there are males. Many whites are among the strongest and most passionate advocates of the goals of the Black community and its civil rights movement.

The entire concept of representative bureaucracy seems to ignore the fact that it is part of the very essence of bureaucracy to be nonresponsive to the momentary passions of the multitude and, in the sociological sense, nonrepresentative. It is not only hard to imagine a bureaucracy that is a sociological microcosm of the larger society; its nonrepresentative character is greatest at the higher and more politically salient levels of the civil service.

NEO-CORPORATISM

Accountability as a value is being weakened in Western democracies by the general devolution of actual decision-making power from the prime ministers, presidents, or equivalent heads of government and legislators whose accountability is structured by the political format to what Daniel Bell has called the technocracy whose authority lies outside this structure of accountability. The growing political role of the higher civil service just discussed is one manifestation of the growing political salience of the technocracy.

Another manifestation of the political salience of the technocracy is the extent to which actual policy formulation is in the hands of the organized interests whose leadership possesses the specialized knowledge about their particular sector of society or the economy. These organized interests are, of course, not part of the constitutionally designated decision-making process; hence, their role in the political process lies outside the formal structure of accountability. The actual effect of the policy-formulation role of organized interests on the democratic value of accountability varies with what Schmitter calls "the mode of interest mediation" (Schmitter, 1979). These modes or types include pluralism, syndicalism, and corporatism—the latter term being usually accompanied by a prefix such as *neo-*, *societal*, *state*, or *liberal*, permitting varied applications of the term *corporatism* to widely differing contexts, reflecting the conceptual anarchy in the burgeoning literature on it.

The literature on corporatism has been characterized as one of the real "growth industries" in the discipline (Panitch, 1980). The concept of corporatism refers to a category of several forms of interest group participation in the national decision-making process, forms that putatively characterize the actual rather than constitutionally designated political format of postindustrial societies (another of the *au courant* concepts in the literature). The question of whether the concept of neo-corporatism (or its related variants) has any explanatory value in the discipline depends on the extent to which the concept identifies and interprets a precisely defined set of trends in the political processes of these postindustrial democracies and, further, on the extent to which the concept of corporatism (with or without the *neo* prefix) is clearly and precisely distinguished from other modes of interest mediation, such as pluralism.

The term has traditionally been associated with its application in fascist Italy. Its image has thereby been generally associated with autocracies of the right; hence, a modification and/or expansion of the concept is required for its application to Western industrial democracies. In its fascist manifestation, corporatism referred to a mode of managing the inevitable interests that arise out of a functionally differentiated society, a society in which these interests are managed from above by nonvoluntary units or agencies created by the state and granted a representational monopoly within their respective categories. Phillipe Schmitter, probably one of the two or three leading authorities on present applications of the concept, modifies the above definition in the following way: the representational units are recognized or licensed by the state but not necessarily created by it, and these units accept certain controls in the selection of leaders and the articulation of demands, rather than the Italian style of using these representational units to manage these interests by and in the interest of the state (Schmitter, 1979). Corporatism, as thus conceptualized by Schmitter, is theoretically compatible with a variety of regime types, yet distinguishable from the Anglo-American concept of pluralism, a system in which the representational units are voluntary and competitive, as opposed to those in a corporatist system, which are compulsory and noncompetitive.

Within the general concept of corporatism, Schmitter distinguishes between two subtypes: societal and state. The latter is a categorical name assigned to those manifestations of corporatism associated with autocracies, essentially as it was manifested in its fascist roots. The former term, essentially equivalent to what Gerhard Lembruch means by liberal corporatism, constitutes the adaptation of the concept to the pattern of interest-group mediation increasingly found in Western democracies. In expanding the conceptualization of corporatism to such parliamentary democracies, scholars such as Schmitter and Lembruch have detracted from its precision and coherence. The dimension of interest mediation that runs from full co-optation to complete autonomy admits an infinite number of degrees of autonomy in between. Thus, the dividing line between corporatism or neo-corporatism and the lack thereof is imprecise at best. The United States is widely accepted as one of the noncorporatist states (Salisbury, 1979); yet, there may have been a significant measure of co-optation of some of that nation's peak interest associations, such as the American Farm Bureau Federation by the Department of Agriculture. Some United States organizations seem to many to have acquired peak status (e.g., professional organizations such as the American Bar Association or the American Medical Association, or the AFL-CIO) while other scholars, such as Salisbury, characterize these organizations as relatively weak and ineffectual (Salisbury, 1979). Clearly, this is a judgment call of assigning a discrete, qualitative label to a manifestation of an essentially continuous variable. Similarly, judgment is equally involved in the process of declaring when it is that competition—putatively a characteristic of interest-group interrelationships under pluralism—blends into cooperation, based as they both are on a process of bargaining. It appears that there is a greater and clearer distinction to be made between state corporatism, based as it is on state command of interest associations, and so-called liberal or societal corporatism than between societal corporatism and pluralism.

The corporatist literature contributes a focusing of attention on an important attribute of postindustrial democracies, namely that constitutionally designated decision-making processes are no longer at the core of those decisions that actually allocate the values of those societies. The implications of this idea give new life to a suggestion that has been advanced and then rejected on numerous occasions, namely that actual political processes may be more a function of the imperatives of the state of technology than of variations in the constitutionally designated structures. It has been argued here and in the corporatist (and other) literature that, in mature industrial societies, the advanced state of technology renders heavy reliance on impersonal market forces highly impractical if not totally atavistic. Hence, planning becomes inexorable. Planning presumes predictability and, therefore, control. In that context, consensus building replaces the unrestrained competition of the conventional pluralist model.

It is, therefore, being suggested that, in advanced pluralist democracies, a decision-making process of cooperative bargaining among key elements in the higher civil service and of peak organizations representing major elements in the economic and industrial order (i.e., the technology) will replace either the formal, rationalized process that is constitutionally designated or the outcome of party competition. The process by which decisions are made will tend to be similar in advanced industrial democracies, regardless of constitutional or ideological differences among them.

In its extreme versions, such as its Marxist manifestations, technological determinism explains not only process but policy as well. That contention is not being advanced here, however. Policy choices are affected not only by process and technology but by normative considerations as well, the values that define the essence of a political system. Technological imperatives may constrain policy choices, but they don't make them. Despite the suggestions that have emanated from the anticapitalist left with varying degrees of explicitness that the choice between American and Soviet influence is morally neutral, it is assumed here that normative constraints will prevent the one superpower from pursuing policy options and goals adopted by the other.

The argument here is, therefore, one of a qualified convergence theme for advanced industrial societies—a growing pattern identified by the neo-corporatist literature as well by the literature on the administrative state that defines the decision-making processes of such systems, while significant distinctions remain among systems with respect to patterns of policy substance, distinctions immutably rooted in the normative essence of sociopolitical systems.

If the neo-corporatist literature is merely saying that the imperatives of technology have required new patterns of extra-constitutional decision making in domestic policy among the technocracy and in increased levels of state control, the argument is unassailable. Explicit recognition of this process antedates the revival of the concept of corporatism (with or without its *neo* prefix). It is not clear, however, that stretching the concept of corporatism from its widely understood authoritarian moorings to a broad pattern of decision-making processes adds to one's understanding of the pattern or to one's ability to explain the variations in such processes.

Corporatism is posited as the co-optation of interests by the state to make policy impacts more predictable and thus to facilitate the displacement of a disposition to rely on market forces with an emphasis on economic planning, an imperative tied to the needs of technologically advanced capitalist systems (Causon, 1978; Pahl and Winkler, 1974). The extent to which the distinct interests have been co-opted by the state and to which cooperation has replaced competition is never carefully measured or supported by actual data. The process is merely asserted. Yet, some scholars offer data that bring such assertions into question (Cox, 1981). It is clear from examining these data that competition between divergent interests may have been reduced in some cases but definitely has not been eliminated in the various institutionalized patterns of interest mediation grouped under the concept of corporatism.

Moreover, the very diversity of economic relationships subsumed under the concept of corporatism renders the theoretical utility of the concept questionable (Cox, 1981). The very *au courant* popularity of the term has led to its indiscriminate use and misuse, a confusion emanating also from the imprecise empirical content of the term (Metcalf and McQuillan, 1979).

The central problem is to develop modes of public policy formulation and implementation for advanced industrial democracies that afford the capacities of coordinating the diverse competing interests of such systems into efficient problem-solving capabilities, while, at the same time, providing for the structuring of accountability consistent with political democracy. The substitution of an empirically imprecise term for a serious analysis of this problem contributes nothing to the explanation of the processes and outputs of such industrial democracies.

DEMOCRACY AND THE CRISIS OF LEGITIMACY

The term "crisis of democracy" is another term that has become *au courant* among the *cognoscenti* of the discipline. As with other aforementioned concepts that have become the focus of a burgeoning literature, this concept is as empirically vague as it is academically popular. In its dominant usage, it seems to relate to a growing inability of governments of advanced industrial democracies to satisfy the skyrocketing expectations of a mobilized, consumption-oriented population in an increasingly complex, interdependent world.

Governments, by this interpretation, are "overloaded" with more demands than their institutions can process. Moreover, the problems that governments are increasingly expected to resolve have their roots and causes in domains beyond the effective control of such governments. This is especially true in the face of the high degree of interdependence in the modern world.

The problem of inflation is frequently cited as exemplifying an unsolvable crisis. A widespread scourge among Western industrial societies, inflation has roots in such factors as the more or less effectively administered price of energy and, thus, in the internal politics and external conflicts of nations beyond the control of the West. Hence, the problem lies in large part beyond the traditional remedies of monetary and fiscal policies prescribed by the economic establishment and among the alternatives available to Western governments. The reduction of the rate of inflation in the 1980s came about with the internal disarray of O.P.E.C., not as a result of any national policies.

The unsolvability of many of the problems and issues of industrial democracies is a function of two attributes of such societies, as suggested in a perceptive analysis by Michael Crozier (Crozier, Huntington, and Watanuki, 1975; Dahrendorf, 1980). In this concept of "demand overload," Crozier is alluding to the fact that postindustrial societies generate maximum want formation. Not only are the communication grids highly developed (in Karl Deutsch's conception of a cybernetic approach to development) (Deutsch, 1961 and 1966) and literacy rates expanded in such systems but, in addition, liberal democracies carry an ideological baggage that values citizen politicization and activity as well as a responsive capacity of government to needs and demands as perceived by its citizens. Clearly, in autocracies, based upon the theory that the public interests, general will, or spirit of the folk—whatever the concept is called—is embodied and defined by the elite, the political system will be under considerably less stress to respond to societally generated demands. Thus, to the extent that industrial societies in general may be rendered ungovernable by demand overload, industrial democracies may be particularly so rendered.

The second aspect of industrial societies that, according to Crozier, contributes to the crisis of ungovernability is the heavy weight of bureaucratic power. In an analysis that forms the core of his writings, Crozier focuses on the structural unsuitability of the bureaucratic form of organization, especially as manifested in such "classical" bureaucratic settings as in France, Germany, and Italy, for the formulation as opposed to the mere implementation of public policy (Crozier, Huntington, and Watanuki, 1975; Crozier, 1964). The classical model, as it has evolved from its initial formulation in the writings of Max Weber, emphasizes the attributes of routinization and predictability, autonomy from external or societal pressures such as public opinion and voting, and a high degree of functional specialization. In contrast, the formulation of policy should entail the political values of adaptability, responsiveness and accountability to public needs and pressures, and responsibility to leadership (i.e., hierarchy which is, in fact, undermined by functional specialization).

Many of the expectations of the mobilized population of the advanced industrial world inherently conflict with one another. For example, there are the traditional materialist expectations of economic growth that still concern some parts of the population conflicting with the imperfect triumph of such postmaterialist values as environmentalism.

Governments, it has been argued, must be able to convert the expectations of the government into a level of output satisfactory to maintain their political health. In autocracies, this ability can translate more into control of the input, but, in democracies, the literature suggests a greater "responsive capacity" is required to maintain the equilibrium of the system. Citizens, this reasoning goes, must believe the regime or the political system will make reasonable progress in solving the problems of greatest concern to them, or they will begin over time to withhold or withdraw their diffuse support of the system. This withdrawal leads to what has been called a "crisis of legitimacy."

Legitimacy is one of those soft concepts with widely agreed upon and theoretically significant meaning with which political scientists must freqeuntly deal but which present seemingly insurmountable difficulties for the goal of measurement. The legitimacy of a system is widely accepted irrespective of the policy outputs or any independent measure of the success of that system. It is clearly related to the idea of diffuse support for the system as developed by David Easton. Legitimacy has been indirectly or approximately measured in sample survey work by questions on perceptions about the system (e.g., the amount of pride in the system, expectations that it will treat the respondent fairly; Almond and Verba, 1965); however, lacking a norm or a base against which to evaluate and interpret this data, statements about the relative degree of legitimacy of political systems are not rigorously empirical.

Yet, it is clear from a large and diverse body of literature that legitimacy is widely presumed to be a fundamental prerequisite to stable government in general and stable democracy in particular. The loss of legitimacy in some form, moreover, seems to be one of the first indications of an increased probability of antisystem violence (Gurr, 1968; Brinton, 1938). Without legitimacy, system support depends upon specific performance; yet, no system has the resources or control of outcomes to satisfy most expectations. Moreover, since demands compete with one another in a zero-sum situation, the satisfaction of the demands of some interests requires the rejection and consequent alienation of others.

Several decades ago when modern comparative politics was in its infancy, Herbert Spiro, in a textbook on Western democracies that few textbooks have since approached with respect to the creative and insightful formulation of explanatory theory from a consistent, clearly articulated conceptual framework, suggested that consensus on fundamental procedures was a requisite of stable democracy (Spiro, 1959). Since the concept of fundamental procedures refers to those means of choosing elites that define the very essence of the system, Spiro's procedural consensus is close to what we mean by legitimacy. Spiro further suggested that such fundamental procedural consensus is acquired by time; procedures become accepted when they have been around for many years. These fundamental procedures last, in turn, when they become accepted or acquire legitimacy before they are called upon to resolve elusive and complex issues, when the question of regime is resolved first, and when other issues are resolved sequentially.

Mayer and Burnett took this analysis a step further in suggesting that the key to constitutional stability is to resolve the question of regime prior to the technological modernization that necessarily mobilizes the masses and generates the range of substantive issues (Mayer and Burnett, 1977). In Europe, the Napoleonic Wars seem to constitute the watershed that would forevermore leave the continent with a mobilized mass population imbued with the idea that they possessed rights. Nations that legitimized their constitutional format before that period have enjoyed constitutional stability since. Those nations that, for a variety of reasons, failed to resolve their question of regime before the eighteenth century have ever since been arguing the extremely divisive and complex issues of the nineteenth and twentieth centuries in constitutional terms. In other words, in such imperfectly legitimized systems, solutions to substantive problems were posited as alternative changes in the constitution or nature of the regime.

As Chapter 3 has suggested, this analysis leads to a pessimistic prognosis for the constitutional health of those third world systems seeking to establish regime legitimacy while governing an already mobilized and politicized population. Huntington's concern for order in modernizing systems is another statement of this theoretical perspective (Huntington, 1968 and 1965). His concept of institutionalization is very close to what is meant here by regime legitimacy, and, indeed, Huntington discusses the concept of legitimacy itself at some length. The present author has expressed doubts whether Huntington's prescription for order, the suppression or delay of mass mobilization, is possible at this stage of technology. Not only is technology here to stay with all of its inexorably mobilizing imperatives (e.g., urbanization, literacy, media growth), but ideas that promote such mobilization (e.g., the ideals of the French Revolution, Marxism, liberal democracy) are already out of the bag and can never be completely forgotten or suppressed. Hence, continued constitutional instability among third world nations seems to be a likely attribute of the foreseeable future.

However, the question that concerns us here is legitimacy and constitutional stability among industrial democracies. The so-called crisis of legitimacy clearly implies that a loss of regime legitimacy is becoming as endemic to the industrial world as the failure to attain it has been in the third world.

There is growing evidence of a widespread perception that governments in Western democracies are no longer effective in processing issues and solving problems. Long-term economic growth to absorb population growth and, more importantly, to alleviate issues over the distribution of material well-being by expanding the G.N.P. and raising everyone's standard of material well-being absolutely, if not relatively, can no longer routinely be assured. The inevitable scarcity of resources and limits on the ecological capacity of the planet to absorb the by-products of infinitely increasing productivity must at some point put an upper limit on economic growth.[11] Thus, the old aphorism about a rising tide floating all boats no longer applies; a zero-sum economic world pertains, and there will now be winners and resentful losers in the increasingly intense conflict among interests.

It is possible to show empirically that heads of government have become significantly more vulnerable in democratic systems in recent years compared to the rest of this century. Votes of no confidence occur where they were previously thought to be an empty threat, hegemonic parties suddenly find themselves voted out of office, and major shifts in party systems have occurred in which traditionally dominant parties find themselves voted of office and excluded from governing coalitions, while passionate and principled new parties appear in legislatures for the first time.[12] All of these changes may be taken to indicate a growing lack of satisfaction with the performance of governments.

This perception of the failure of governments to respond to vaguely articulated needs and demands of society and to satisfactorily solve the major problems facing society is perhaps less a statement about the competency of elites than a statement of what may be called the ungovernability thesis. One finds a few scholars who go so far as to suggest that advanced industrial democracies may be ungovernable in the sense that the problems they face may be beyond the reach of any policy alternatives available to them (Dahrendorf, 1980; Deutsch, 1981). One example of such a problem was the worldwide inflation and economic crisis generated by the geometric increase in the price of energy, a phenomenon emanating from international events beyond the control of the governments in question. This is merely one instance of the high degree of interdependence of political systems that reduces the theoretically sovereign control such systems have over the well-being of their citizens and subjects. Governments are no longer able to come before their subjects and convincingly declare that during their administration they have effectively resolved most of their society's problems. In other words, there is a small but growing body of yet inconclusive data that indicate people no longer perceive that their governments are effective and that further indicate people in increasing numbers have lowered their expectations that government, by formulating and implementing the correct policy options, can improve their status or well-being (Kavanaugh, 1980).

Legitimacy does not refer to dissatisfaction with specific performance, however. Rather, it connotes a feeling of being part of and perceiving that one has a stake in the well-being of the system itself, irrespective of one's satisfaction or lack thereof with specific output or performance. The idea is that legitimacy enables a system to withstand the inevitable performance failures and citizen dissatisfactions faced sooner or later by all systems without losing the level of support necessary for the maintenance of public order. The literature has carefully preserved the distinction between specific and diffuse support. However, scholars are increasingly raising a question about the impact of long-term dissatisfaction with specific performance on diffuse support or legitimacy. The question is especially pertinent for a system such as the United Kingdom, whose legitimacy has been so taken for granted as to have virtually become conventional wisdom. This legitimacy was acquired and strengthened over a very long period of system success; however, the United Kingdom has been experiencing a clear, long-term decline in international strength and prestige and in economic prosperity. Early data indicate some decline in the legitimacy of the regime. While the legitimacy of the regime remains strong in comparison with some other nations, it apparently is not as strong as it once was, as indicated by such summarizing epithets as "the collapse of deference" or "the civic culture is declared to have collapsed" (Beer, 1982). This body of data suggests that the theoretical distinction between diffuse and specific support of a system may be less useful than assumed by such general theorists as Easton, since the loss of the latter seems to result in the loss of the former.

The broader question raised in this chapter is one of the real source of the decline in legitimacy that may be perceived as a trend in advanced industrial democracies. The foregoing literature postulates the cause as the intractable nature of the problems and issues confronting such systems, rendering them "ungovernable." This decline in the effectiveness of such systems to resolve specific issues is held to ultimately diminish their legitimacy or diffuse support. The loss of legitimacy, however, may be more than a matter of the inability of government to formulate problem-solving policy choices; it may be structural.

The theme of a structural failure of democracy runs throughout this chapter. Democratic theory, it has been argued here, is based on the substantive value of rendering elites accountable to the citizens they govern or to those who are significantly affected by the decisions of these elites. Yet, because of the imperatives of an advanced state of technology and the attributes of a postindustrial society, policy is increasingly being made outside of the structures and processes designed to render elites accountable. The rise of the administrative state—a concept that refers to the growing political role of the public bureaucracy—and the rise of neo-corporatism are both manifestations of the broader phenomenon of the increasing dominance of technocrats in the policy process. Technocrats, individuals who, by definition, act upon knowledge and skills esoteric to their roles, cannot, in any meaningful sense, be held accountable to citizens who do not share in that knowledge or those skills. Democratic theory has not fully adjusted in a coherent fashion to this reality of the postindustrial world.

It may be further suggested that citizens perceive this loss of control over decision makers and decisions that affect their lives. What is happening is not as much a perception of long-term ineffectiveness of government as a perception that citizens have lost their capacity to hold elites accountable, an unarticulated realization that decisions about matters that vitally affect their lives are beyond their control and, for that reason, unresponsive to their needs. Democratic government is not so much ineffective as irrelevant to the perceived needs of citizens.

NOTES

1. See Verba, Nie, and Kim (1978). Even when writing a book that documents the great actual variation in political influence that is exercised by individuals, the authors begin by asserting an egalitarian criterion from which they show reality deviating.

2. There is a vast corpus of research documenting the extent to which the typical citizen in industrial democracies is marginally aware of existing issues, unable to articulate alternatives of public policy to address such issues, and even lacking in any significant amount of knowledge and information about public affairs. Perhaps the most famous is the cross-national survey reported in Almond and Verba (1965), especially Chapter 2.

3. For example, see Nie and Verba (1975), pp. 1–53.

4. Among the classic advocates of this elite perspective are Pareto (1935), Mosca (1939), and, with respect to the American case, Mills (1946).

5. The "iron law of oligarchy" was formulated by Italian sociologist Roberto Michels (1915 and 1959).

6. This literature is summarized in Livingston (1976).

7. Among the early examples of this literature are LaPalombara (1963), Swerdlow (1963), and Montgomery and Siffin (1966). The LaPalombara volume, while focusing on "developing nations," does not confine its analyses to these parts of the world.

8. The leading or seminal work in this group is Bell (1973). See also Lindberg (1976).

9. For a summary of this literature, see March and Simon (1967).

10. See, for example, Kingsley (1964). For a review and critique of the literature, see Meler (1975), Mosher (1968), and Krislov (1974).

11. See, for example, Meadows (1972) and Renshaw (1976). Note Robert Lineberry's succinct phrase "the management of scarcity" in Chapter 8 of Lineberry (1977).

12. Mayer's unpublished manuscript "A Note on the Vulnerability of Democratic Elites" presents data that show that destabilizing events (for example, votes of no-confidence and changes in the identity of the prime minister) were more frequent in the 1970s than in the 1950s to a statistically significant extent.

REFERENCES

Almond, Gabriel and G. Bingham Powell. 1984. *Comparative Politics Today*, 3rd ed. Boston: Little Brown.
Almond, Gabriel and Sidney Verba. 1965. *The Civic Culture*. Boston: Little Brown.
Amery, L. S. 1964. *Thoughts on the Constitution*. London: Oxford University Press.
Beer, Samuel. 1982. *Britain Against Itself: The Political Contradictions of Collectivism* III:184ff.
Bell, Daniel. 1973. *The Coming of Post-Industrial Society*. New York: Basic Books.
Brinton, Crane. 1938. *The Anatomy of a Revolution*. New York: W. W. Norton.
Causon, Allen. 1978. "Pluralism, Corporatism, and the Role of the State." *Government and Opposition* 13(2, Spring):178–198.
Cox, Andrew. 1981. "Corporatism as Reductionism: The Analytic Limits of the Corporatist Thesis." *Government and Opposition* 16(1, Winter):78–95.
Crick, Bernard. 1965. *The Reform of Parliament*. Garden City, NY: Doubleday Anchor.
Crozier, Michael. 1964. *The Bureaucratic Phenomenon*. Chicago: University of Chicago Press.
Crozier, Michael. 1973. *The Stalled Society*. New York: Viking Press.
Crozier, Michael. 1975. "Western Europe." In *The Bureaucratic Phenomenon*. Chicago: University of Chicago Press.
Crozier, Michael, Samuel Huntington, and Joji Watanuki. 1975. *The Crisis of Democracy*. New York: New York University Press.
Dahl, Robert. 1970. *Modern Political Analysis*, 2nd ed. Englewood Cliffs, NJ: Prentice-Hall.
Dahl, Robert. 1971. *Polyarchy*. New Haven, CT: Yale University Press.
Dahrendorf, Ralf. 1980. "Effectiveness and Legitimacy: On the Governability of Democracies." *The Political Quarterly* 51(4, Oct.–Dec.):393–410.
Deutsch, Karl. 1961. "Social Mobilization and Political Development." *American Political Science Review* LV(3, Sept.):493–514.
Deutsch, Karl. 1966. *The Nerves of Government*. New York: The Free Press.
Deutsch, Karl. 1981. "The Crisis of the State." *Government and Opposition* 16(3, Summer):331–343.
Diamant, Alfred. 1957. "The French Administrative System: The Republic Passes but the Administration Remains." In *Toward the Comparative Study of Public Administration*, edited by William Siffin. Bloomington, IN: University of Indiana Department of Government.
Ehrman, Henry. 1961. "French Bureaucracy and Organized Interests." *Administrative Science Quarterly* 5(1, March):535.
Gurr, Ted. 1968. "A Causal Model of Civil Strife: A Comparative Analysis Using New Indices." *American Political Science Review* LXII(4, Dec.): 1104–1124.
Huntington, Samuel. 1965. "Political Development and Political Decay." *World Politics* 17(2, April):386–430.
Huntington, Samuel. 1968. *Political Order in Changing Societies*. New Haven, CT: Yale University Press.
Kavanaugh, Dennis. 1980. "Political Culture in Great Britain: The Decline of the Civic Culture." In *The Civic Culture Revisited*, edited by Gabriel Almond and Sidney Verba. Boston: Little, Brown.

Kingsley, J. Donald. 1964. *Representative Bureaucracy: An Interpretation of British Civil Service*. Yellow Springs, OH: Antioch Press.
Krislov, Samuel. 1974. *Representative Bureaucracy*. Englewood Cliffs, NJ: Prentice Hall.
LaPalombara, Joseph. 1963. *Bureaucracy and Political Development*. Princeton, NJ: Princeton University Press.
Lijphart, Arend. 1984. *Democracies: Patterns of Majoritarian and Consensus Government in Twenty-One Countries*. New Haven, CT: Yale University Press.
Lindberg, Leon. 1976. *Politics and the Future of Post-Industrial Society*. New York: David McKay.
Lineberry, Robert. 1977. *American Public Policy*. New York: Harper and Row.
Lipset, Seymour. 1963. *Political Man*. New York: Doubleday Anchor.
Lipsitz, Lewis. 1986. *American Democracy*. New York: St. Martin's Press.
Livingston, William S. 1976. "Britain and America: The Institutionalization of Accountability." *The Journal of Politics* 38(4, Nov.):879–894.
March, James and Herbert Simon. 1967. *Organizations*. New York: John Wiley.
Mayer, Lawrence. Unpublished manuscript. "A Note on the Vulnerability of Democratic Elites."
Mayer, Lawrence and John Burnett. 1977. *Politics in Industrial Societies: A Comparative Perspective*. New York: John Wiley and Sons.
Mayer, Lawrence and Roland Smith. 1985. "Feminism and Religiosity: Female Electoral Behaviour in Western Europe." *West European Politics* 8(4, Oct.):38–49.
Meadows, Donella. 1972. *The Limits to Growth*. New York: Universe Books.
Meier, Kenneth J. 1975. "Representative Bureaucracy: An Empirical Analysis." *American Political Science Review* LXIX(3, June):526–542.
Metcalf, Les and Will McQuillan. 1979. "Corporatism or Industrial Democracy." *Political Studies* XXVII(2, June):266–282.
Michels, Roberto. 1915 and 1959. *Political Parties*. New York: Dover Publications.
Mills, C. Wright. 1946. *The Power Elite*. New York: Oxford University Press.
Montgomery, John D. and William Siffin. 1966. *Approaches to Policy Administration and Change*. New York: McGraw Hill.
Mosca, Gaetano. 1939. *The Ruling Class*. New York: McGraw Hill.
Mosher, C. 1968. *Democracy and the Public Service*. New York: Oxford University Press.
Neumann, Franz. 1957. *The Democratic and Authoritarian State*. New York: The Free Press.
Nie, Norman and Sidney Verba. 1975. "Political Participation." In *Handbook of Social Science*, edited by Fred Greenstein and Nelson Polsby. Reading, MA: Addison-Wesley.
Nordlinger, Eric. 1981. *On the Autonomy of the Democratic State*. Cambridge, MA: Harvard University Press.
Pahl, R. E. and J. T. Winkler. 1974. "The Coming Corporatism." *The New Society* 30(627, Oct.):72–76.
Panitch, Leo. 1980. "Recent Theorizations of Corporatism: Reflections on a Growth Industry." *British Journal of Sociology* 31(2, June):159–187.
Pareto, Vilfredo. 1935. *Mind and Society*. New York: Harcourt Brace Jovanovich.
Putnam, Robert. 1973. "The Political Attitudes of Senior Civil Servants in Western Europe." *British Journal of Political Science* 3(3, July):257–290.

Rawls, John. 1971. *A Theory of Justice*. Cambridge, UK: Cambridge University Press.

Renshaw, Edward. 1976. *Adjusting to a No-Growth Economy*. North Situate, MA: Duxbury Press.

Riggs, Fred. 1964. *Administration in Developing Countries: The Theory of the Prismatic Society*. Boston: Houghton Mifflin.

Salisbury, Robert. 1979. "Why No Corporatism in America." In *Trends Toward Corporatists Intermediation*, edited by Phillipe Schmitter and Gerhard Lembruch. Beverly Hills, CA: Sage Publications.

Schmitter, Phillipe. 1979. "Modes of Interest Mediation and Models of Social Change in Western Europe." In *Trends Toward Corporatists Intermediation*, edited by Phillipe Schmitter and Gerhard Lembruch. Beverly Hills: Sage Publications.

Schmitter, Phillipe. 1979. "Still the Century of Corporatism?" In *Trends Toward Corporatists Intermediation*, edited by Phillipe Schmitter and Gerhard Lembruch, pp. 6-52. Beverly Hills, CA: Sage Publications.

Schumpeter, Joseph. 1950. *Capitalism, Socialism, and Democracy*, 3rd ed. New York: Harper & Row.

Sigelman, Lee. 1972. "Do Modern Bureaucrats Dominate Underdeveloped Politics? A Test of the Imbalance Thesis." *American Political Science Review* LXVI(2, June):525-528.

Sigelman, Lee. 1974. "Bureaucratic Development and Dominance: A New Test of the Imbalance Thesis." *Americn Political Science Review* XXVI(2, June):308-314.

Sigelman, Lee and Syung Nan Yough. 1978. "Left-Right Polarization in National Party Systems: A Cross-National Analysis." *Comparative Political Studies* 11(3, Oct.):355-381.

Spiro, Herbert. 1959. *Government by Constitution*. New York: Random House.

Swerdlow, Irving. 1963. *Development Administration: Concepts and Problems*. Syracuse, NY: Syracuse University Press.

Talmon, J. L. 1952. *The Origins of Totalitarian Democracy*. London: Martin Secker and Warburg, Ltd.

Verba, Sidney, Norman Nie, and Jae On Kim. 1978. *Participation and Political Equality: A Seven Nation Comparison*. New York: Cambridge University Press.

Williams, Philip. 1968. *The French Parliament: Politics in the Fifth Republic*. New York: Praeger.

Wilson, Woodrow. 1887. "The Study of Public Administration." *Political Science Quarterly* 11(2, June):197-222.

CHAPTER FIVE

Parties and Political Behavior

Research on political parties, focusing as it has on such measurable phenomena as voting behavior and the bases of electoral support, exemplifies more than most other areas of concern the kind of empirical rigor implied by the idea of a science of politics. It is, therefore, not surprising that work in this area has been one of the dominant interests in modern comparative politics, both quantitatively and qualitatively. Unlike other areas of research in the field, in which most of the key concepts lack empirical referents and raise difficult problems in cross-cultural equivalence, research on voting behavior and electoral cleavages lends itself to the rigorous quantification that allows the use of sophisticated mathematical techniques and electronic data processing. The data from such research present relatively fewer questions of interpretation and equivalence.[1]

Yet, vote counting alone will not advance the explanatory aims of a science of politics unless such data are integrated into and interpreted by a body of theory. One may reasonably inquire into the theoretic significance of any apparently rigorous and mathematically sophisticated piece of research. Not only must patterns and trends in electoral behavior be discerned and delineated but the causes and impacts of such patterns and trends ought to be offered in the form of testable propositions.

Moreover, voting and electoral behavior do not exhaust the attributes of parties in which political scientists are legitimately interested. For example, trends in program and ideology should logically have a reciprocal relationship to electoral behavior and cleavages; yet, data on program and ideology are neither as rigorous nor as accessible as those aforementioned electoral data. The importance of work in this area, an area in which the literature is just now being developed, cannot be overestimated, since the pattern of interaction among parties and electoral behavior is presumably, in part at least, a response to the ideologies and programs on which parties base their appeals.

The literature of parties, vast as it is, encompasses a number of distinguishable dimensions, each of which manifests a number of distinguishable characteristics. These dimensions include the literature on party systems (encompassing not only the causes and impacts of the number of parties but their electoral strength and the pattern of interaction among them), the causes and impacts of variations in the party-systems dimension, the programs and ideologies on which parties, to a greater or lesser extent, base their electoral appeal, social cleavages and voter alignments, the congruence between party cleavages and social or electoral cleavages, party organization and cohesion, and, ultimately, how all of the foregoing factors come together to determine the role that parties actually play in their nation's political process.

The prospects for integrating research on political parties into anything resembling coherent explanatory theory using parties as either explicans of other political phenomena or as explicanda in and of themselves suffers from the diverse and only loosely related nature of the questions asked, of the subject matter on which one focuses, and of the methodology and techniques being used. While the literature on voting behavior is often rigorously quantitative, research in areas such as program and ideology or internal party organization is often impressionistic and narrative in style. Thus, research in any one aspect of parties tends to appear in isolation from other aspects of the topic without justification for the theoretical importance of the questions being asked.

Yet, it may be suggested that a variable exists that could serve as a potential integrating focus of this diverse corpus of research, a variable on which each of these aforementioned research topics has a significant impact. The roles that parties actually play in the processing of issues in relatively industrialized democracies, roles that correspond, to a greater or lesser extent, to the functions that parties fulfill in ideal-type models of the democratic process, constitute the variable that can be used to integrate these diverse dimensions of the comparative political parties literature.[2] The extent to which given parties or party systems fulfill these putative functions depends upon how these respective parties or party systems manifest themselves on such variables as the type of party system; the nature of the party organization or structure; whether the party adopts an ideological, programmatic, or catchall basis of electoral appeal; the content of such programs or ideologies; and the congruence of these bases of appeal with the sociological basis of each party's electoral support.

THE RELEVANCE OF PARTIES

Much of the early literature assumed that parties filled their putative roles or performed their idealized functions. Such literature focused on these aforementioned attributes of parties or party systems based on an unstated assumption that these attributes made a difference in how the idealized functions were performed. Thus, one could find books and articles on the organization of parties and on internal party democracy.[3] Other works may discuss party program or ideology. Still others focus, to a greater or lesser extent, on the social bases of electoral support. Topics such as these may conveniently be thought of as the input side of any prospective theory on the role of parties in Western democracies.

However, as will be shown below in greater detail, a growing number of scholars are suggesting that the output side of this "model," the actual processing of issues in modern democracies, operates more or less independently of these input variables.

It is being suggested that the ideological or programmatic bases of appeal of political parties reflect issues that are no longer salient to postindustrial societies. The process in question was originally perceived as "the end of ideology" in mature industrial societies by some scholars interested in delineating the implications of the newly popular concept of postindustrial society (Lipset, 1963), a process disputed by other scholars (La Palombara, 1956). The dispute may be viewed as one that is essentially semantic; the conclusion about whether ideology has declined as a salient force in the Western world turns out to be a function of how ideology is conceptualized. Lipset and Bell regard ideology as the great thought systems generated by the idiosyncratic nature of the modernization process in the West, a process that created controversies surrounding the social dislocations of early industrialization, over the role of organized religion in an increasingly secular and pluralistic society, and over the structure of accountability in the constitutionally designated format. The parties to these controversies tended to promote and defend their goals in terms of ideologies in the traditional sense of that term: closed, comprehensive systems of thought.

Dissenters from the decline-of-ideology position, in contrast, use the term *ideology* in the sense of any principles that guide actions or determine choices. Robert Putnam, for example, defines an ideological political style as a tendency to generalize rather than to particularize, to utilize deductive thinking, and to refer to future utopias. In short, he uses the concept of ideology to refer to a tendency to utilize principle as a guide to political choice and action. Based on this conceptualization, Putnam finds from interview data drawn from members of the British and Italian political elite that, contrary to conventional wisdom, there is no relationship between an ideological political style and political intolerance (Putnam, 1971). Much of the apparent surprise at this finding is eliminated when one reflects upon the fact that it is the closed or dogmatic aspect of the traditional conceptualization of ideology that, by definition, generates the intolerance associated with that term. As the term *ideology* is used by Putnam and LaPalombara, it is indistinguishable from the term *principle* and thereby loses whatever independent theoretical utility it may have had.

Beyond the semantic expansion and obfuscation of the concept, the decline-of-ideology thesis runs into the objection that ideology—however defined—has not become less salient to postindustrial politics but, rather, has changed in content. One of the most important bodies of research concerned with Western democracies is the finding of Ronald Inglehart that the salient values in these societies have undergone a generational metamorphosis (Inglehart, 1947). Specifically, Inglehart finds that the generation that experienced a milieu of scarcity—i.e., the Great Depression—during its formative years is primarily concerned with material values while those whose formative years occurred in a milieu of relative prosperity take material well-being for granted and tend to focus on life-style values—what Inglehart calls "postbourgeois values," values concerned with morality, patriotism, family structure and behavior, and the like. While there are some differences among scholars with regard to how these value changes should be conceptualized, there is general agreement that the values of Western publics are in a state of flux. As documented in Russell Dalton's recent impressive synthesis of cross-national research on the attitudes and behaviors of Western publics (Dalton, 1988), some researchers describe the process as a transition from "old politics values" such as economic growth, public order, and national security to "new politics values" such as individual freedoms, social equality, and the quality of life (Miller and Levitin, 1979). Others conceptualize this process of change in terms of a transition from strict adherence to a moral code to greater personal autonomy (Harding, 1986). The best available data from the early 1980s confirms the consensus that, regardless of how the change is conceptualized, the basic values of Western publics are in a state of flux (Dalton, 1988).

The implications of these findings for the role of political parties are profound. The cleavages on which many of the political parties and party systems are based presume the dominant salience of the traditional materialist values and the dominance of class as the primary basis of political conflict. This presumption is especially true for parties of the left, whose fortunes depend on their ability to mobilize the support of a working class clientele, parties whose names include terms like *Labor* or *Social Democrat*, but it is also increasingly true for the center right, whose appeal is decreasingly based on the declining salience of religiosity and increasingly based on those middle class and professional strata who are opposed to a significant expansion of the egalitarian redistribution of material well-being associated with the modern welfare state.

Yet, to the extent that materialist or class-based issues do not structure the political conflict, the potential clientele of these parties will not be available for mobilization. Those who would be liberal on materialist issues tend to be conservative on lifestyle issues. People with less education tend to be among the economic "have nots" and to favor the egalitarian redistribution of materialist values. However, those same people tend to be less tolerant of challenges to dominant life-styles, culture, or morality; hence, they are conservative on postbourgeois issues. Similarly, the younger upper middle to upper classes, usually well educated, do not identify with many of the values that now constitute the social agenda of the political right. These values include such things as the traditional monogomous family structure and the suppression of sexual expression that occurs outside that structure. Support for the criminalization of abortion and opposition to sex education and birth control by leaders of the right have the effect of imposing adverse consequences on the sexual license they seek to suppress. The well-educated upper-middle classes are less likely to be traditional on such issues and, in any event, more likely to be tolerant of unconventional behavior.

Hence, to the extent that the Inglehart "silent revolution" describes reality, a serious question is raised about the adaptability of parties and party systems to the new structure of social cleavages.[4] Research into this important area is just now emerging, and the early data indicate an adaptation crisis, the failure of political parties to base their appeals on the issues that are most salient to the emerging generation of voters. Parties of the left, in particular, have found themselves vulnerable to a decline in the commitment of their traditional base of support, the less-educated working class, who, when cohesively mobilized on a haves versus have nots perception of the political universe, constitute a natural majority. Parties of the left that, in essence, must take an antiestablishment or pro-change position find that their traditional working class clientele frequently take the opposite stance (Sankiaho, 1984).

On many of the emerging postbourgeois issues, such as support for environmentalism, feminist concerns, or nuclear disarmament, the existing party system has not presented reasonably clear and meaningful choices to the voters. Voters who feel passionately about one or more of the postbourgeois issues frequently have been unable to find a champion of their cause among the more traditional parties. Consequently, research has been finding that emerging attitudes on postbourgeois issues are not reflected in voting behavior.[5] The growing masses of Europeans who passionately favor bold, unilateral moves toward nuclear disarmament generally find none of the traditional major parties taking a clear stance for that position. Similarly, the existing party structures, based as they are on the traditional bourgeoisie-working class cleavages, provide no clear outlet for such concerns as environmentalism.

Two possible consequences have been suggested from this growing incongruence between salient issue concerns of society and the bases of appeal in the party system. One is a realignment of the social bases of electoral support, including adaptation of existing parties to the new societal cleavages or the emergence of new parties. The other is a dealignment of voters who may no longer tend to express a party identification to the extent that they did some years ago.

Inglehart himself predicted the emergence of new left parties throughout Europe to provide an outlet for the demands of the postbourgeois liberals (Inglehart, 1947). Parties of what may be called cultural defense, such as Belgium's *Volksunie* or *Rassemblement Wallon*, Canada's Free Quebec, and Britain's Scottish National Party have gained strength, reflecting the growing salience in some settings of the preservation of the cultural distinctiveness and often the creation of the political autonomy of subcultures. Parties have also emerged representing the growing salience of other postbourgeois issues and orientations. The Green Party of the Federal Republic of Germany constitutes one of the noteworthy examples of this phenomenon in its attempt to mobilize the environmentalist and pacifist forces not championed by any of the existing parties. A third type of new party that has appeared to some extent in apparent response to the Inglehart revolution is parties designed to appeal, in a general rather than in an issue-specific way, to an educated, urban clientele—a kind of "yuppies" party, to borrow a new American colloquialism—exemplified by *Democraten 66* of the Netherlands.

Most of these newer parties, however they may represent postbourgeois or postmaterialist concerns, remain electorally insignificant. The Belgian parties of linguistic and cultural defense have come to constitute important exceptions to that rule, a situation that will be explained in another context below.[6] Other postmaterialist parties, such as the Greens of West Germany, despite some recent gains, remain distinctly minor. Although the concerns of the Green Party may be shared by a significant portion of the German electorate, such concerns are not represented by any of the viable choices in the West German Party system (Dalton, Flanagan, and Beck, 1984). Similarly, to the extent that postmaterialist values in Great Britain are most closely approximated by the relatively recent rise of the Social-Democratic-Liberal Alliance, these values will likely not be represented in the electoral struggle for control of the government in the foreseeable future. Due to the peculiarities of the Anglo-American plurality electoral system and the geographical distribution of Alliance support, the Alliance remains a rather distant and insignificant third in parliamentary strength.

Moreover, some of the critical issues of the postmaterialist age are simply not clearly represented by any party, major or minor. There are no feminist parties (or their antithesis), for example. Issues emanating from the increasingly abrasive clash between traditional moral values and the rising demand for individual choice on such matters as sexual behavior, abortion, divorce, and the like are avoided by the traditional major parties like a plague, a phenomenon that largely explains the phenomenal rise of single-issue interest groups.

Even with regard to materialist concerns about the distribution of material well-being, new realities are emerging that existing parties cannot absorb in their ideological baggage. For example, the postindustrial world is moving toward an age of scarcity, an age in which economic growth will be limited by a finite supply and rising costs of resources such as energy. Yet, the economic policies presented by traditional parties presume the possibility of indefinite economic growth. Limits on such growth obviously make the issue of the distribution of an increasingly fixed, if not declining, G.N.P. much more intense. Clearly, solutions to such economic realities will have to come from outside the existing party system.

The point is that the political cleavages and issues represented by the interparty electoral struggle for control of the government in Western democracies have not adapted to and are, therefore, not congruent with the social cleavages and issues that structure Inglehart's postindustrial segment of society. To the extent that the postmaterialist segment is increasingly coming to dominate Western society as a whole, the party system will be increasingly irrelevant to the processing of issues. This fundamental conclusion that appears in a number of sources (Rose, 1984; King, 1969) raises a question about the utility or futility of research on parties and electoral behavior as a vehicle for explaining the political process.

PARTY SYSTEMS, POLITICAL STABILITY, AND ELECTORAL SYSTEMS

A putative relationship between the nature of the party system and cabinet stability in parliamentary democracies and a relationship between the nature of the party system and the type

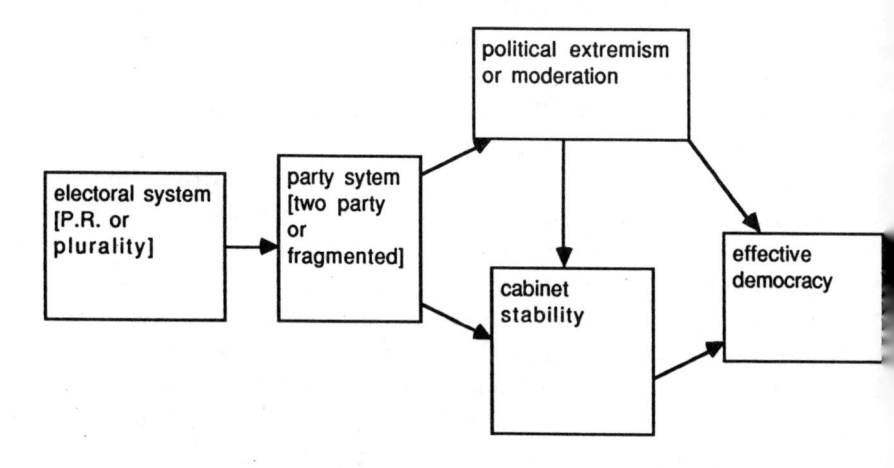

```
┌─────────────┐      ┌──────────┐         ┌──────────────┐
│ electoral   │      │party sytem│  ───▶  │political extremism│
│ system      │ ───▶ │[two party │         │or moderation  │
│ [P.R. or    │      │ or        │         └──────┬────────┘
│ plurality]  │      │fragmented]│                │
└─────────────┘      └─────┬─────┘                ▼
                           │           ┌──────────────┐    ┌──────────────┐
                           └─────────▶ │cabinet       │───▶│ effective    │
                                       │stability     │    │ democracy    │
                                       └──────────────┘    └──────────────┘
```

Figure 5.1. Hermans' Implicit Causal Model

of electoral system constitute some of the earliest attempts at causal analysis in the comparative politics literature on parties. The causal model that dominated the literature went as follows: the type of electoral system determines the type of party system and the nature of some parties, which, in turn, determine the stability of the system (see Figure 5.1). This causal model, whose chief advocates were Ferdinand A. Hermans and Andrew Milnor (Hermans, 1941; Milnor, 1969) became almost an object of ridicule among serious scholars for reasons that are analyzed below, and interest in the impact of electoral systems faded from the mainstream of political research.

In recent years, however, there has been a renewed interest in the study of the impact of electoral laws on political outcomes. Bernard Grofman and Arend Lijphart have come forth with two volumes of essays on the subject in the past couple of years (Lijphart and Grofman, 1984; Grofman and Lijphart, 1986). Interest in electoral system reform would logically be stimulated by pressures for change in the party system. It will be argued below that electoral systems tend to be selected to support the existing party system; hence, the perpetuation of any given electoral system tends to work against any fundamental change in the party system itself. The Inglehart revolution discussed above generated pressure for adaptation of the existing party systems to new social cleavages. Parties are appearing in response to such pressure for adaptation, parties such as the Greens in West Germany and the Social Democrats in Great Britain that, to a greater or lesser extent, are more reflective of postmaterialist than bourgeois values. These parties articulate the demands of a genuine constituency; yet, such articulation has been suppressed to some extent by the existing electoral system. The Greens have only recently overcome the five percent rule in West Germany to receive any representation despite growing public support, and the Social Democratic-Liberal Alliance, by virtue of its relatively even geographical distribution of support and the plurality electoral system, has been drastically underrepresented in Parliament. Although the popular vote received by the Alliance in 1983 was close to that of Labour (26% as opposed to 28%), Labour won nine times as many seats (Lakeman, 1984).

Such underrepresentation or suppressed articulation of growing and often passionately held interests and political perspectives generates a sense of injustice. The perception of injustice is perhaps the key ingredient in fostering pressure for fundamental change, especially when the source of the perceived injustice has been identified. Hence, we have the renewed interest in electoral system reform.

The concept of political stability, the principle dependent variable in the Hermans, et al. model, covers two distinct variables: constitutional stability and cabinet stability. The former refers to the frequency of fundamental changes in the regime format, which, in turn, reflects the disposition in a system to argue substantive political issues in terms of alternative regime formats, what Herbert Spiro calls "fundamental legalism" (Spiro, 1959).

The latter term is applicable only to parliamentary systems in which the government may theoretically be removed by the will of the legislature. It refers to the frequency with which the government (the prime minister or his equivalent and the cabinet) is compelled to resign in the face of a motion of "no confidence" or censure by the legislature. These two conceptualizations of political stability frequently are not clearly distinguished in the literature; yet, there is a more or less explicit suggestion in the literature that a breakdown in the latter will ultimately cause a breakdown in the former. This idea is never put in quantified terms with specified threshold levels and, hence, is not rigorously falsifiable in the form of more than x amount of cabinet instability will result in y amount of constitutional instability in z circumstances. One cannot even say at what point cabinet instability will result in any unspecified but significant increase in the level of constitutional instability. The variable of constitutional instability inherently involves such a small N that statistical techniques are inappropriate for manipulating such data. Hence, the variable of constitutional stability may well be indirectly indicated by some measure of system alienation among the politically relevant public, a measure based on survey data.

Cabinet instability offers a larger but still small N. By regarding the events that comprise a measure of cabinet stability in a finite number of parliamentary democracies and in a given time frame as a "sample" of a diachronically expandable universe, statistical techniques may legitimately be applied to such data. Cabinet stability is a more complex concept than is generally recognized in the literature that deals with it in that it is manifested in a variety of events that must be tallied and weighted in an overall index of cabinet instability: governments falling into the hands of another party as a result of a vote of censure or no confidence, governments falling on a confidence motion but being reconstituted by the same personnel or leadership, governments falling on a confidence motion and being reconstituted by the same party but with different leadership, governments winning a confidence vote, governments calling an early election and losing, and governments calling an early election and winning. Moreover, instability may be indicated not only by the nature and number of events but by their duration. The fragmented party system of the Netherlands produces relatively few "events" or cabinet crises, largely because each given crisis takes so long to resolve. It has taken up to a year to work out the necessary bargains and compromises to reconstitute a government in that system. Hence, the duration of destabilizing events must be weighted into any composite index of cabinet instability.

The choice among electoral systems had been dichotomized in the early literature into a choice between the Anglo-American system of single-member districts with plurality vote (usually and hereafter called the *plurality system*) and *proportional representation*. The latter term refers in practice to a number of distinct electoral systems that, to a greater or lesser but always imperfect extent, approximate the ideal of pure proportionality.

Pure proportionality implies that the percentage of seats that a party gets in the legislature from a given election approximately equals the percentage of total votes that the party received in that election. Such a system would seat in the legislature individuals who represent parties receiving any measurable amount of electoral support, however small. This system would allow the legislative body to mirror the actual distribution of opinions and interests in society. Hence, the *concept* of proportional representation (P.R.) is based upon giving priority to the *value* of accurately representing the distribution of opinions in society in the distribution of seats in the politically significant house (usually the lower one) of the legislature. As one of the well-known advocates of P.R. puts it,

> we must first agree on what an election is for . . . an election must involve giving electors a choice and causing that choice to have an effect on which persons are elected [Lakeman, 1986].

Earlier, she and a colleague had written that "producing an image of the feelings of the nation [is] the first of our aims which an electoral system should fulfill" (Lakeman and Lambert, 1955).

It should be noted that the normative presumption so self-evident to Lakeman and other P.R. advocates, that the aim of elections is to mirror as closely as possible the distribution of opinions and interests of society in the people who are elected to the legislature, may conflict with alternative, equally plausible assumptions. For example, one may presume that the purpose of democratic elections is to manifest the opinions and interests of society in the policy choices adopted by the government or even the composition of the government itself rather than manifest these opinions and interests in the personnel that occupy the legislature. These two goals are not necessarily mutually reinforcing.[7]

To illustrate the possible conflict between these goals, an electoral system that produces a close approximation to a mirror image of the distribution of opinions and interests in a complex society will frequently produce a fragmented party system. The aggregation of interests, after all, is a function that must be performed; it does not occur spontaneously. The process of aggregation of interests is one aspect of what Sartori calls the manipulative effect of a "strong" electoral system. Pure P.R. would be a no-effect system (Sartori, 1986). In such a fragmented party system, governments must be formed by an intensive and often lengthy bargaining process among the leaders of parliamentary parties, groups, or factions. The outcome of that bargaining process in terms of the composition of the government and its public policy directions is not only *not* a product of but may have little relation to the outcome of the election.

The concept of P.R. is never manifested in its pure form but rather in one of several distinct electoral systems. These systems implement the value of P.R. to a greater or lesser extent and have different actual impacts on the outcome of elections. The most frequently used system is list voting, utilized because it enhances the control of existing parties over their candidates. The most frequently advocated system is the Hare system of the single transferable vote, advocated because, among the major systems, it most closely approximates realizing the value of proportionality and most clearly favors weaker parties. It may also appear attractive to some because it involves voting for individuals rather than for party labels, thus weakening the power of parties. Reformers, who by definition compose the advocates of a switch from plurality to P.R. elections, frequently are antiparty, viewing parties as elite-dominated institutions that distort a populist conception of the general will.

Established parties generally have the controlling input into the choice of electoral systems; hence, it is not surprising that the list voting system is the most frequently adopted system. List voting is done by party label with the party determining an individual candidate's position on the list and, hence, that candidate's chances of electoral success.

Studies have appeared attempting to assess the various formulas for P.R. in terms of the degree of proportionality that they actually achieve.[8] The first glaring fact that emerges from looking at these analyses is the amount of disagreement that exists among them with respect to ranking the proportional systems in terms of the degree of proportionality achieved. The differing conclusions may be due in part to the differences between pure theoretical and applied forms of the P.R. formulas, in part to differing ways of measuring proportionality, and in part to the differing impact of a given electoral formula on differing existing party systems.

This more recent attention to the impact of the variation among actual formulas or proportional representation adds a note of sophistication to the earlier and now almost discredited indictment of proportional representation by people such as Hermans, Milnor, and their followers, an indictment that charges that proportional representation promotes both a proliferation in the number of parties and a more rigid, ideological, or extremist stance by parties, both of which, in turn, lower the probability of forming effective or even responsive governments in parliamentary democracies.

The argument was usually framed in terms of the logical effect of the principle of pure P.R. rather than in terms of an empirical test of the consequences of actual electoral formulas in use. Hence, while Hermans in particular was suggesting an explanation for the weakness of some parliamentary democracies in the face of a fascist or Nazi challenge, he did not construct a predictive explanation in the sense discussed in Chapter 2.

Based on the logic of what P.R. should do, Herman's work (and that of other opponents of P.R.) is more accurately characterized as polemical than explanatory in nature.

In a more recent essay, Hermans avers an awareness that party systems are the product of a multiplicity of variables and specifies three of them. However, he omits mention of significant others, such as culture, and makes no real effort to incorporate these variables into a multivariate causal model generating testable propositions (Hermans, 1984). He provides empirical data on an illustrative rather than a systematic basis.

A polemic purpose similarly characterizes the work of leading exponents of P.R., such as Lakeman. There is no question that the plurality system distorts the will of the voting public in the sense of the personnel in the legislature mirroring the distribution of significant opinion in society. The data and the logical arguments she presents on this point are superfluous; they are arguing that which is given. What is not given or self-evident but what both Lakeman and Hermans assume is self-evident is the purpose of an electoral system. The difficulty is that which is self-evident to the one is diametrically opposed to that which is self-evident to the other on this point. Is the purpose of an electoral system to mirror the spectrum of opinion, or is it supposed to provide a stable majority capable of governing?

Hermans, to his credit, discusses the differing perspectives on the nature of representation on which he has based his conclusions about the purpose of an electoral system. But he and Lakeman are ultimately in conflict over value priorities.

For Hermans and his followers, the stability and effectiveness of democracy take precedence over a perception of fairness in the distribution of political input. Lijphart and Grofman assert that both sides to the controversy agree on the empirical consequences of electoral systems and agree that proportionality and stability are both desirable goals (Lijphart and Grofman, 1984). The disagreement, rooted as it is in differing value priorities, goes beyond that. Critics of Hermans and Milnor persuasively claim that they overstate the causal impact of electoral systems on party fragmentation. Numerous party systems, such as those of Belgium and Sweden, remained quite stable for years after the adoption of P.R. It seems more defensible to claim that the various P.R. formulas, to a greater or lesser extent, *permit* the fragmentation of a party system when such party-system fragmentation reflects sociocultural fragmentation. Thus the Belgian party system that for so long was held to be an example of a party system that remained relatively aggregated and stable despite P.R. did fragment when the cultural linguistic cleavage, so long politically dormant, emerged in the mid 1960s (Lorwin, 1966; Hill, 1974). By the early 1970s, the three party system that had remained stable for decades had been transformed into a six party system without a dominant party. Similarly, the party system of the Netherlands fragmented from what had been a stable five party system into the highly fragmented system in which fourteen parties had seats in the *Tweed Kamer* as of 1974 in the force of the fissiparous cleavage structure of Dutch society in the early 1970s.

This modification of the Hermans thesis does not abrogate Hermans' claim that such fragmentation might be avoided by adopting an Anglo-American plurality election system if one accepts the converse proposition advocated by and associated with Maurice Duverger, that the plurality electoral system favors the two party system. Of all the hypotheses he advances in his *magnum opus*, "this approaches most nearly to a true sociological law" (Duverger, 1963). For reasons that have been fully explored in textbooks too numerous to mention, the Anglo-American plurality electoral system so severely penalizes weaker parties as to make the electoral success of third or weaker parties on a national scale highly improbable. These penalties create a psychological climate in which votes for smaller parties appear ineffective and wasteful; hence, the plurality system not only distorts the proportional correspondence between votes and seats but further reduces the actual vote for smaller parties.

Therefore, while the electoral system does not directly cause the degree of party system fragmentation, it is statistically, although imperfectly, related to such fragmentation through the intervening variable of the degree of cultural fragmentation.

Moreover, research has further corroborated that the latter part of Hermans' implicit causal model (Figure 5.1), that party system fragmentation is statistically related to indices of cabinet stability in parliamentary systems although, as the present author has shown, the strength of that relationship varies with the conceptualization of party system type (Taylor and Herman, 1971).[9] It thus seems fair to conclude that the consensual discrediting of the basic idea of Hermans and his followers was premature in that it is probably possible to engineer party system aggregation and, in turn, a higher degree of cabinet stability by the adoption of an Anglo-American plurality electoral system. The problem with this simplistic solution is its cost in terms of values that conflict with the value of cabinet stability.

The proponents of alternative electoral systems are not, therefore, arguing about the empirical consequences of one electoral system over another so much as they are about the most important purposes of a party system. Hence, the literature in this area, as in so many areas of comparative politics, boils down to a normative issue: ranking the value of stable, effective government against the value of articulating all significant interests and strands of opinion in the national decision-making process.

PARTY IDEOLOGY OR PROGRAM AND PARTY SYSTEM PERFORMANCE

Assuming the null hypothesis of the increasingly probable proposition discussed in the first section of this chapter—to wit that parties and party systems do not make a significant impact on what policies societies do or do not adopt on the major salient issues of the day—the dimension of party program or ideology has generated a substantial literature that identifies the ideological dimension as the source of much party behavior and its impact. Otherwise put, the literature seems to assume the following causal model: the principles or ideology that define a party determine the programs that a party advocates, and the policy choices made by a political system emerge from the electoral competition among alternative party manifestos and their advocates. The dimension of party program or ideology includes a number of distinct variables: whether the party bases its appeal on principles or programs whose advocacy or realization takes precedence over the goal of vote maximization (the distinction between parties of principle and those of expediency); the ideological distance between parties in a system (the degree of polarization); the content of party ideology (left to right) and its compatibility with the salient issues of society (the materialist to postbourgeois value transformation discussed above).

The first of these aforementioned variables is a function of the oft-discussed role of ideology or principle itself in modern politics. The so-called decline-of-ideology thesis has already been discussed in this chapter; it refers to the proposition that the major thought systems that have structured political competition in the Western world have lost their salience because the problems and issues that generated those thought systems have largely been resolved. The great religious (and antireligious) philosophies have been rendered almost peripheral to the lives of the masses by the progressive secularization of modern life. The ideologies of the class struggle originating out of social dislocations of early industrialization no longer apply to the affluent, increasingly skilled and specialized, and largely unionized labor force. Classical liberalism struggled for a political equality that has largely been achieved.

One of the most venerable and most frequently cited essays on the subject of political parties is the late Otto Kirchheimer's essay, "The Transformation of Western European Party Systems" (Kirchheimer, 1966).[10] Reflecting the decline-of-ideology thesis, Kirchheimer suggests a trend in such party systems from parties basing their appeals on specific class or sectarian interests or outlooks to broadly aggregated parties standing for no discernible principles or programs trying to appeal to the broadest and most diverse possible constituency. Kirchheimer's data is of the illustrative variety, largely consisting of examples drawn from parties whose *raison d'être* has substantially been rendered moot by the issue and value transformation of the Western world. The clearest example of such a deideologizing transformation may be the pro-free-enterprise program adopted by the formerly quasi-Marxist (at least in terms of self imagery) German Social Democratic Party in 1959. The deconfessionalization of Christian Democratic Parties throughout Europe in the 1970s constitutes another example. The Gaullist U.N.R., based upon allegiance to a personality, never did stand for anything specific in the way of program or ideology. In relying on such illustrations, Kirchheimer chooses to ignore numerous other parties that clearly are not catchall. He never suggests criteria for disconfirming the claim that a trend does, in fact, exist in the catchall direction. In fact, evidence suggests that Western party systems are not aggregating over the last two decades, a finding that casts doubt on Kirchheimer's widely acclaimed thesis that catchall parties are the wave of the future (Mayer, 1980a; Shamir, 1984).[11] (See Table 1) These findings once again remind us of the danger of relying too heavily on essentially impressionistic conclusions.

Beyond Kirchheimer, precious little research has appeared delineating trends in program and ideology, despite the burgeoning literature on transformation of social cleavages and values. Possibly, the greater difficulties involved in gathering data and in measuring the inherently soft concepts in this area have contributed to this lacuna. Serious questions for inquiry in this area suggest themselves. Foremost is the extent to which new or traditional parties have presented programs for or based their electoral appeals on postbourgeois concerns. Second is the extent to which parties are perceived by the voting publics in various systems as representing such concerns. Is there, for example, a difference among the parties in each system in the extent to which they speak for or are perceived to speak for women's issues, armament or war-peace concerns, or tolerance of counter-culture life-styles?

Third is the importance of principle or ideological baggage as a guide to or predictor of policy choices or party behavior. How much discrepancy exists between what parties say they will do if their people are elected and the policy choices adopted by the winners after the election? The research and scholarship on the important topic of electoral change in industrial democracies has focused thus far on the behavior, attitudes, and values of the voter. A need exists to move beyond impressionistic assertions with respect to the response of the parties to the now well-documented trends among the voters. Systematic analyses of party platforms and programs and of campaign speeches or statements by major candidates would serve as a useful complement to the wealth of existing data on voter attitudes and behavior toward revealing how well parties fulfill the function of providing the linkage or serving as a broker between the needs and demands of the voting public and public policy.

Beginnings in this direction have been cited by Richard Rose with respect to election or party manifestos in Great Britain (Rose, 1984). Two major studies by David Robertson and Monica Chalet both clearly indicate the major parties moving toward what Rose calls "the consensus model," a model in which the principled and/or programmatic disagreement between the major parties is minimized. While these data from Britain constitute an important contribution in this regard, comparable data from other competitive party systems are scarce.

Substantial progress has been made in the analysis of the content of ideologies with respect to coherence and dimensionality. Scholars have been increasingly pointing out, for example, that the traditional left-right dimension is inadequate for the characterization of political positions. This kind of distinction is at the heart of Inglehart's revolution in values. In general, scholars have been increasingly sophisticated in classifying principled or ideological positions.

Research shows, however, that ideology plays a very limited role in determining voting choice for the vast majority of people. Rose shows, for example, that, in the United Kingdom, not only do a substantial majority of voters agree on a majority of issues but almost half of the voters do not percieve "important differences (presumably of principle and program) between the parties (Rose, 1984). The voting literature, predominantly American but not exclusively so, consistently finds that the data support the conclusion that party identification is the most important predictor of electoral choice and that this identification is acquired early in life with a high degree of permanence, usually from the party identification of one's parents (Campbell, Converse, Miller, and Stokes, 1960; Budge, Crewe, and Fairlie, 1976). In any event, the pattern of voting choice is, to a large extent, determined before one attains an awareness, let alone an understanding, of political principles and ideology.

Given that party program or ideology are very weak predictors of policy choices that a party elite will make when it controls the government and that neither program nor ideology plays a very significant role in determining electoral choice, parties are not fulfilling the ideal role of offering voters meaningful and effective choices among alternatives of public policy. Hence, it seems that Anthony King's "skeptical reflections" (King, 1969) about the utility of parties for the processing of issues are, to a large extent, justified. King suggested that since parties have not been offering positions and alternative positions on the major issues dividing Western industrial societies, such issues have been, to a large extent, addressed, if not resolved, outside the arena of interparty competition.

Not only is party ideology a weak predictor of policy choices made by governments and a weak determinant of voter choice, but it is also a weak determinant of intraparty organization and politics. On a theoretical level, parties with an egalitarian ideological baggage—usually parties of the left—have emphasized rank and file control of party leadership—internal party democracy. Robert McKenzie's now-classic study of the major British parties in this regard concluded that, despite such theoretical differences between the egalitarian Labour Party and the elitist Tories, the Labour Party elite was not nearly as accountable to rank and file control as their ideological baggage would lead one to expect, nor were the Conservative Party elites as insulated from such control as their ideological baggage would lead one to believe. The subsequent adoption of elections by the Tories as a means of choosing their leaders beginning with Ted Heath supports McKenzie's judgment about that party. Samuel Beer, in his study of *Modern British Politics*, implies that McKenzie has overstated the structural similarity between the parties (McKenzie, 1963; Beer, 1982). McKenzie was focusing on tenure of office as the index of the autonomy of leadership while Beer places more emphasis on the impact of the party back bench on party programs. Even by that criterion, however, differences between the British parties are largely a matter of judgment rather than being self-evident. The implicit conclusion to be drawn from such studies is that intraparty organization is more a function of the structure of the system in which the party operates than of individual party ideology.

Here again, the data being discussed are drawn from the British political system, one of the most thoroughly described and analyzed settings in the political universe. Such analyses and data are scientifically useful, however, to the extent that they are applicable to settings beyond that body of data from which they are drawn.

The foregoing concerns about the failure of political parties in Western democracies to provide meaningful alternatives for the salient public policy issues presumes that the *raison d'être* of parties is to provide and promote such policy solutions rather than that parties devise programs or discuss principle primarily as an instrument to their real goal of maximizing votes or of winning elections. The seminal work of Anthony Downs has influenced the thinking of comparativists on this matter for decades. Downs created an elaborate model of rational behavior for two- and fragmented multiparty systems (Downs, 1957). *Rationality*, conceptualized as the most efficient strategy for goal attainment (getting the greatest output for the smallest input), is a necessary assumption for a predictive model, since irrational behavior is, by definition, haphazard and unpredictable.

As with any rational model, rationality depends on the goals and values of the actor, and Downs explicitly assumes that the overriding goal of parties is to maximize their votes or to reap the rewards of office (Downs, 1957). *Party ideologies* (conceptualized here as encompassing both principles and programs) are viewed by Downs as instrumental to the fundamental goal of winning elections, and the parties will provide significantly distinct alternatives of programs or ideologies only insofar as no one such alternative is manifestly more effective and popular than the others (Downs, 1957). Thus, in an aggregated party system, the Downs model predicts that the ideologies of parties of both the left and right will converge toward the majority in the center.

Some scholars, as well as events, bring this assumption of Downs' into question. As far as events are concerned, political success in the major democracies is not as manifestly monopolized by the pragmatic centrists as previously presumed. The victory of Margaret Thatcher in Great Britain, the leftward tilt of the British Labour Party, and the "Reagan revolution" in the United States are among the events that may be adduced to support a contention that polarization and the ideological distance between parties may be waxing, rather than waning, in some situations. Moreover, Henry Chappell and William Keech have devised a theoretical model of party competition based upon an assumption of imperfect information for the voter and a presumption that parties seek office to implement programs and principles, rather than the converse Downsian assumption that they use such ideologies essentially as an instrument to gain office *per se* (Chappell and Keech, 1986). The empirical support for the model, however, is limited in this case to three voter experiments. Putnam's survey research also lends empirical support to the evidently plausible proposition that principle does motivate the political behavior of elites to an extent that varies from one individual to another, depending on the person and the cultural context (Putnam, 1971).

It may be reasonable, therefore, to presume, in the absence of much-needed further research on this question, that, to a varying extent, some elites and parties do care about formulating and selling alternative courses of public policy. However, party elites are also clearly cognizant that there may be electoral consequences of taking clear positions on policy issues. As Russell Dalton (1984, p. 130) has pointed out with respect to West Germany,

Parties are naturally hesitant to take clear stances on the new dimensions of conflict until the costs and benefits are clear, and the electoral consequences of the New Politics are not yet clear to see. First, the number of citizens exclusively concerned with new politics issues is still quite small; thus their present weight is still quite limited.

Hence, a kind of vicious circle of old politics would seem to operate. It may be difficult to mobilize large numbers of voters around postbourgeois cleavages if parties fail to offer clear alternatives on such issues. However, parties may be unwilling to offer clear positions on such issues unless they are convinced that large numbers of voters are so mobilized.

It has proven difficult for parties that have been around for a long time to change the way that they are perceived by the electorate. Even if parties should de-emphasize the old materialist issues and offer meaningful alternatives on postbourgeois issues, this shift may not be clearly perceived by the average voter, who, research has shown, has tended to make electoral choices on the basis of a party identification acquired early in life and persisting without regard to changing issue concerns. These traditional bases for electoral choice have been brought into question by recent research into the basis of electoral cleavages.

POLITICAL CLEAVAGES AND PARTISAN ALIGNMENTS

The foregoing section addresses the role and impact of principle and program in the behavior and effectiveness of political parties. As the concluding sentences in that section indicate, the ideologies or programs of parties and the way that parties utilize them are, to a large extent, a function of the way that ideologies or principles are perceived by and, therefore, affect the voting public. Although there may be something of a paucity of data on the ideologies, programs, and electoral appeals of parties, no such lacuna exists with respect to the perceptions of the electorate, their partisan alignments or lack thereof, and their consequent electoral behavior.

Research in this area has provided a significant and relatively recent example of conventional wisdom being contradicted by a systematically accumulated body of data. An impressive earlier body of data—from the first electoral research following World War II—led to the aforementioned conclusion that party identification was the best predictor of voting behavior, a conclusion that had been so widely accepted for so long that it had acquired the status of conventional wisdom. This party identification was acquired early in life, frequently from one's parents; it was diffuse in the sense that it was highly independent of one's preferences on specific issues; and it was pervasive in that most people reported that they identified with or thought themselves a member of a particular party (Rose, 1984). The phenomenon of such a pervasive, diffuse party identification was thought to be manifested throughout the Western world, although others have questioned whether party identification independent of voting choice is as applicable a concept in Europe as in the United States.

A growing corpus of research has been documenting a trend in the past decade and a half to two decades, a trend away from the strength and/or pervasiveness of such party identification (Dalton, 1984b; Campbell and Stewart, 1984). Known as dealignment, this process refers to a decreasing tendency among voters in mature industrial democracies to report a sense of partisan attachment to a political party that is, at the same time, independent of yet predictive of electoral choice or a tendency for the strength of such attachments to be declining. The tendency for the strength of such attachments to be declining has been called "dealignment of degree." It has been suggested that this dealignment stems from several factors.

First, partisanship has been, to some extent, a cost-saving method of making quasi-rational choices in the context of limited information. Time, effort, a high level of literacy, and a fair amount of political sophistication are required to possess the knowledge and information to make rational electoral choices based upon the current issues, the records of candidates, and the self-interest of the voter. These qualities that have been scarce among the general population, even in the industrialized world, have increased significantly in recent years. Hence, the need to rely on party labels has diminished for the more educated and sophisticated voter. Thus, Dalton offers the concept of "cognitive mobilization" to refer to an active interest in and the skill to participate in politics without the benefit of the cost-savings cues of partisan labels. One may possess these skills and still feel closely identified with a party on the basis of a rational application of such knowledge and information, an individual that Dalton labels a "cognitive partisan."

The significant category for Dalton is what he calls "apartisan," that group possessing the knowledge, information, and skills for rational political involvement but eschewing partisan attachment. This latter category is composed more of younger citizens who tend to be more educated and raised in an atmosphere of the declining importance of parties. Dalton identifies a new middle class of salaried white-collar employees and government workers which differs from the old middle class of business owners and the self-employed (Dalton, 1984b). This new middle class would seem to comprise a good portion of the technocracy that dominates postindustrial societies and, being essentially outside the traditional business leader-salaried worker class structure, this new class is possibly a prime repository of Inglehart's postmaterialist values. Hence, it is not surprising that Dalton found that members of this group are likely to be apartisan. Dalton does not specifically tie these findings into the nature of the party structure, but if, as was suggested above, the traditional party systems in advanced industrial democracies have not adapted to postmaterialist issues and cleavages, then it is to be expected that young voters whose socioeconomic roles and interests are outside the cleavages of industrial (as opposed to postindustrial) society would tend to feel attachments to traditional parties less frequently and less intensely than older voters.

Measurement of the dealignment phenomenon has been both

direct and indirect. Direct measurement must, of course, come from survey data. This dealignment phenomenon has also been indirectly inferred from such electoral data as the growing instability of electoral outcomes. However, electoral instability is sometimes the very phenomenon that dealignment is adduced to explain, producing a circular or tautological argument. Such dealignment on an individual level—growing interchange of voters between parties or a declining percentage of stable voters—is taken as an indication that such dealignment has occurred.

Although the dealignment literature is another "growth industry" in comparative politics, the discipline has not produced a unified and unambiguous set of conclusions on the nature and extent of that phenomenon. Neale Tate, for example, finds that dealignment in five Western democracies peaked (or bottomed out, depending on one's perspective) in the 1970s; then the decline in partisan attachments began to be reversed, and such attachment actually grew in amount and intensity (Tate, 1980). As is so frequently the case in social research, choices in the mode of measurement and of the data base affect the consistency of the findings from one study to another. Moreover, the dealignment pattern appears more clearly in some settings than in others. What may be occurring in some settings is more of a realignment than a dealignment, with minor parties gaining some of the strength lost by the major parties, the parties in which the decline in the intensity and pervasiveness of partisan attachments seems most pronounced. Thus, the concept of dealignment lacks some consistency in its precise empirical entailments from one setting to another. Hence, what Przeworski and Teune called the problem of "equivalence" and what Sartori called "the travelling problem" can become a concern even with research carried out within a class of relatively similar systems such as industrial democracies (Przeworski and Teune, 1970; Sartori, 1970).

The literature is just beginning to explore the implications of dealignment for the future of the party systems of industrial democracies. Primarily, the analysis of this question has focused on American parties. The specific question is whether this dealignment trend portends the demise of Western party systems as we have known them or at least detracts from the effectiveness of such party systems in performing their putative functions for the maintenance of industrial democracy. An affirmative answer to this question constitutes the so-called "decline-of-parties" thesis.

Joseph Schlessinger has challenged the decline-of-parties thesis with respect to the American context. Schlessinger argues that American parties still perform their function of providing meaningful alternatives of political orientation as well as or better than they ever have (Schlessinger, 1985). American parties, he argues, have grown more cohesive or ideologically more coherent in the face of a declining incidence of partisanship. In essence, he argues that American parties have moved away from Kirchheimer's catchall model.

This argument, it is important to note, does not dispute the decline-of-partisanship data. Rather it is an interpretation of those and other data that American parties, far from declining into irrelevency, remain healthy institutions. Schlessinger's argument is applied to the American context; he makes no effort to speculate on its applicability to other industrial democracies.

There is evidence, however, to cast doubt on the health of major parties in other Western nations with respect to their ability to structure the electoral choices for a significant segment of their populations. Data suggest that major parties in several such Western democracies have suffered significant declines in both partisan identification and electoral support. Harold Campbell and Marianne Stewart, for example, find that while the actual numbers of people (or percentages of the population) expressing partisan identification with British political parties have not changed significantly over the years, the strength of such identification, expressed as a matter of degree rather than as an either/or phenomenon, has declined significantly (Campbell and Stewart, 1984). The parties of the left, such as Labour or Social Democratic parties, have suffered the greatest losses, both in terms of absolute numbers and in terms of degree, due to their inability to mobilize their natural clientele of lower class and less-educated individuals in this era of postmaterialist values. In addition, confessional parties in some settings, notably the Netherlands but discernable elsewhere too, have been unable to eschew their partisan image in an era of growing secularization and have lost significant electoral support. In the Dutch case, the merging of the three confessional parties into the Christian Democratic Appeal seemed to arrest the electoral decline that the three confessional parties had suffered individually; however, these three major parties had already suffered such devastating electoral losses as to be relegated from a major political status—whereby they had participated in or dominated every governing coalition—to a minor political status—whereby they have been excluded from most recent governments. The merger did not bring about a recovery of their earlier electoral strength (Irwin and Dittrich, 1984).

To the extent that a decline of partisanship, in either pervasiveness or intensity, has been occurring with the major parties that normally comprise or at least dominate governing coalitions, the party system is not functioning well as a set of cues for structuring electoral choice in the context of scarce and expensive information (Downs, 1957). Thus, dealignment not only means that parties will not function as well to structure electoral choice, but it also indicates a prior perception among the voting public that the conflict among parties is not terribly relevant for determining the outcome of issues of importance to them.

Voters have apparently been perceiving, to an increasing extent, that it does not make much difference which parties gain or lose seats in the election or make up the government because the outcome of issues is determined outside the party system—in the efforts of organized groups, such as the "pro-life" and "pro-choice" forces in the United States; in the efforts of more anomic movements, such as the anti-nuclear weapons movements in Europe and in the Anglo-American nations; in neo-corporatist institutions as discussed in the preceding chapter; or in the higher civil service. If people do not particularly care which parties win the electoral struggle, they will not invest scarce resources in that struggle. They may work for individual candidates who pass muster on some litmus test principle but such candidates would then be independent of their party for their political fortunes across the spectrum of all other issues.

Even if Schlessinger is right about American parties in his assertion that they are, in fact, more coherent and better able to formulate policy alternatives than ever, they will still be unable to structure electoral choice for the mass of voters who *perceive* party label as increasingly irrelevant. Voters, after all, act on their perceptions.

Accordingly, Irwin and Dittrich argue (with respect to the Netherlands but, like any worthwhile insight in comparative politics, more generally applicable) that with the dealignment phenomenon, any outcome is possible with respect to party fortunes (Irwin and Dittrich, 1984). Greater gains or greater losses may befall parties in situations in which voters are undecided until right before the election; hence, campaigns assume even greater importance for the parties than in more stable situations where most voters were committed and election results highly predictable. It is being argued in this chapter, however, that while parties may stand to win or lose greater numbers of votes and seats in a given election, these votes have a diminished significance for voters who perceive that these outcomes do not substantially determine the outcome of issues salient to them.

The dealignment or decline-of-partisanship phenomenon is uneven in its manifestation and impact in various industrial democracies. In some nations, it may be a realignment. But this much is clear: party systems in Western democracies are, to a greater or lesser but still significant extent, in a state of flux; the political cleavages that characterized the Western world since World War II and even, to a large extent, before that are no longer axiomatic. It also seems clear that where realignment is a more accurate term than dealignment, the realignment process is in the process of becoming. A new set of stable party cleavages that accurately reflect a changing but not yet stabilized system of societal cleavages has not yet emerged. This fluctuation renders party systems and the electoral struggles in which they engage increasingly irrelevant to the core subject of politics—the determination of the allocation of values.[12] It thus appears that the answer to the question posed by Richard Rose, "Do parties make a difference?" is a disappointing, "Not much."

CONCLUSIONS

It has been shown that political scientists have taken advantage of the inherent quantifiability of the subject matter to amass an impressive corpus of precise data on the topics of party systems and electoral choice. In comparative politics, as in political science in general, we have more precisely delineated the patterns and trends on these topics than in any other areas of the field. We have delineated trends in the nature of the party systems themselves, such as fractionalization or degree of hegemony or rate of turnover. Even here, however, the data are subject to interpretation in some respects. For example, Kirchheimer's oft-cited trend toward catchall parties is not universally apparent.

Most impressive has been the growing corpus of data on voting behavior and on the politically relevant attitudes of voters. Important trends in this area highlight the new and recent discoveries in comparative politics. The literature on realignment and dealignment suggests that the social bases of partisan identification and electoral support are in a state of fundamental flux.

The facts tell us what has happened with a fair degree of precision. The conclusions about the causes and the impacts and implications of these developments are based on a great deal of inference. We have seen some scholars attribute dealignment to the growth of education among the electorate. Clearly, in the settings in question, both the spread of education and the decline of partisan alignment are supported by the data, and the inference of a causal nexus between education and dealignment does not offend one's logical sensibilities. Yet, this inference begs the question of why in other settings with as much advance in education the data support the conclusion that realignment rather than dealignment has taken place. This chapter has suggested that the breakdown of the old partisan alignments, which could produce either realignment or dealignment, is related to the failure of the party systems that emerged following World War II to adapt to those sociocultural changes that have been identified with the research of Ronald Inglehart. What remains to be done is to identify the circumstance in which the breakdown in the old partisan attachments result in realignment rather than dealignment and vice versa.

Comparative political analysis in the postwar era has been characterized, to a large extent, by the development of grand, almost "neo-scholastic" (LaPalombara, 1970) theory, impressionistic theorizing at the highest level of generality and abstraction with very imprecise empirical content. The study of political parties, conversely, has been characterized by the acquisition of a large corpus of precise data that developed more quickly than a theoretic framework to render such data meaningful. Years were spent gathering data on interparty electoral conflict and intraparty program, ideology, and organization before scholars began raising the question of the extent to which such data on parties contributed to an explanation of the resolution of issues and the content of public policy.

Fortunately, as has been noted throughout this chapter, scholars have, in recent years, begun to address this lacuna in political theory from several perspectives: the growth of catchall parties, the development of neo-corporatism and the administrative state, and the value revolution in Western societies that has rendered party cleavages increasingly noncongruent to societal cleavages. This last phenomenon has rendered the relationship between parties and their target or traditional clientele increasingly problematic.

Research on such questions is still somewhat inconclusive and much more needs to be done. Especially lacking is data on the adaptation of party program and electoral appeal to the revolution in societal cleavages and salient issues. However, research in the field of comparative political parties has clearly moved beyond the sterile collection of electoral data and has been asking some of the useful questions. In that, the trends in this field are more promising than they have been in the recent past.

NOTES

1. *Equivalence* is used here in the sense that it is employed in Przeworski and Teune (1970).
2. These roles or functions have been specified in numerous sources in the literature. For example, see McDonald (1955) and Neumann (1955). Of course, Professor Almond would be a leader in approaching the treatment of parties from a set of putative functions. See Almond and Powell (1984).
3. Several works have dealt with this topic extensively but not exclusively, e.g. Beer (1982).
4. Dalton, Flanagan, and Beck (1984) contains much of the significant work on this question.
5. For instance, Lawrence Mayer and Roland Smith find that emerging feminist attitudes are not reflected in electoral choice in three European democracies. See Mayer and Smith (1985).
6. See Hill (1974) for an excellent analysis of change in the Belgian system. Hill's analysis is now dated, and it is curious that Belgium, presenting such a unique party system and such a unique political response to extreme cultural and linguistic segmentation, has not evoked more recent analyses.
7. These conflicting values are close to, but not identical with, Dieter Nohlen's "Two Incompatible Principles of Representation." The alternative principle is that an election system is supposed to identify and represent a majority.
8. Lijphart (1986) provides a summary of several of these analyses.
9. See Taylor and Herman (1971). By modifying the indices of party system type to distinguish the aggregation of the government from that of the opposition, Lawrence Mayer obtained a substantially higher statistical relationship between party systems and stability than did Taylor and Herman. See Mayer (1980).
10. Kirchheimer's "The Transformation of Western European Party Systems" originally appeared in LaPalombara and Weiner (1966). This essay was one of only three of sixty-seven pieces in the third edition of the popular Macridis and Brown reader to survive through the current sixth edition.
11. Mayer (1980b) finds that party systems have become more fragmented and less aggregated, contrary to Kirchheimer's thesis. Shamir (1984) finds that the fragmentation of party systems varies widely over time and not linearly in a given direction across time and space.
12. Easton (1971) defines *politics* as the "authoritative allocation of values." The idea of politics as allocation runs through the Lasswell and Kaplan view (1936). Also see the critique of this allocative perspective of politics by Mitchell (1961). Miller has long advocated a rational-choice perspective for viewing politics.

REFERENCES

Almond, Gabriel and G. Bingham Powell. 1984. *Comparative Politics Today: A World View*, 3rd ed. Boston: Little, Brown.

Beer, Samuel. 1982. *Modern British Politics: Parties and Pressure Groups in the Collectivist Age.* New York: W. W. Norton.
Bell, Daniel. 1962. *The End of Ideology.* New York: The Free Press.
Budge, Ivan, Ivor Crewe, and Dennis Fairlie. 1976. *Party Identification and Beyond.* New York: John Wiley.
Campbell, Angus, Phillip Converse, Warren Miller, and Donald Stokes. 1960. *The American Voter.* New York: John Wiley.
Campbell, Harold and Marianne Stewart. 1984. Dealignment of Degree: Partisan Change in Britain, 1974–1983. *Journal of Politics* 43 (3, Aug.): 689–719.
Chappel, Henry and William Keech. 1986. "Policy Motivation and Party Differences in a Dynamic Model of Spacial Competition." *American Political Science Review* 8(3, Sept.):881–899.
Dalton, Russell. 1984a. "The West German Party System Between Two Ages." In *Electoral Change in Advanced Industrial Societies,* edited by Russell Dalton, Scott Flanagan, and John Beck. Princeton, NJ: Princeton University Press.
Dalton, Russell. 1984b. "Cognitive Mobilization of Partisan Dealignment in Advanced Industrial Democracies." *Journal of Politics* 46(1, Feb.):264–285.
Dalton, Russell. 1988. *Citizen Politics in Western Democracies.* Chatham, NJ: Chatham House.
Dalton, Russell, Scott Flanagan, and John Beck. 1984. *Electoral Change in Advanced Industrial Democracies.* Princeton, NJ: Princeton University Press.
Downs, Anthony. 1957. *An Economic Theory of Democracy.* New York: Harper and Row.
Duverger, Maurice. 1963. *Political Parties,* translated by Barbara and Robert North. New York: John Wiley.
Easton, David. 1971. *The Political System: An Inquiry into the State of Political Science,* 2nd ed. New York: Knopf.
Grofman, Bernard and Arend Lijphart. 1986. *Electoral Laws and Their Political Consequences.* New York: Agathon Press.
Harding, Steve. 1986. *Contrasting Values in Western Europe.* New York: Macmillan.
Hermans, F. A. 1941. *Democracy or Anarchy: A Study of Proportional Representation.* Notre Dame, IN: University of Notre Dame Press.
Hermans, F. A. 1984. "Representation and Proportional Representation." In *Choosing an Electoral System: Issues and Alternatives,* edited by Arend Lijphart and Bernard Grofman. New York: Praeger.
Hill, Keith. 1974. "Belgium: Political Change in a Segmented Society." In *Electoral Behavior: A Comparative Handbook,* edited by Richard Rose. New York: The Free Press.
Inglehart, Ronald. 1947. *The Silent Revolution: Changing Values and Political Styles Among Western Publics.* Princeton, NJ: Princeton University Press.
Irwin, Galen and Karl Dittrich. 1984. "And the Walls Came Tumbling Down: Party Realignment in the Netherlands." In *Electoral Change in Advanced Industrial Democracies,* edited by Russell Dalton, Scott Flanagan, and John Beck. Princeton, NJ: Princeton University Press.
King, Anthony. 1969. "Political Parties in Western Societies: Some Skeptical Reflections." *Polity* 11(2, Winter):111–141.
Kirchheimer, Otto. 1966. "The Transformation of Western European Party Systems." *Political Parties and Political Development,* edited by Joseph LaPalombara and Myron Weiner. Princeton, NJ: Princeton University Press.

Lakeman, Enid. 1984. "The Case for Proportional Representation." In *Choosing an Electoral System: Issues and Alternatives*, edited by Arend Lijphart and Bernard Grofman. New York: Praeger.

Lakeman, Enid and James Lambert. 1955. *Voting in Democracies*. London: Farber and Farber.

LaPalombara, Joseph. 1956. "The Decline of Ideology: A Dissent and Interpretation." *American Political Science Review* LX(1, Mar.):5–16.

LaPalombara, Joseph. 1970. "Parsimony and Empiricism in Comparative Politics: An Anti-Scholastic View." In *The Methodology of Comparative Research*, edited by Robert Holt and John Turner. New York: The Free Press.

Lasswell, Harold and Abraham Kaplan. 1936. *Politics: Who Gets What, When, How*. New York: McGraw Hill.

Lijphart, Arend and Bernard Grofman. 1984. *Choosing an Electoral System: Issues and Alternatives*. New York: Praeger.

Lijphart, Arend. 1986. "Degrees of Proportionality of Proportional Representation Formulas." In *Electoral Laws and Their Political Consequences*, edited by Bernard Grofman and Arend Lijphart. New York: Agathon Press.

Lipset, Seymour. 1963. "The End of Ideology." *Political Man*. New York: Doubleday Anchor.

Lorwin, Val. 1966. "Belgium." In *Political Oppositions in Western Democracies*, edited by Robert Dahl. New Haven, CT: Yale University Press.

Mayer, Lawrence. 1980a. "Party Systems and Cabinet Stability." In *Western European Party Systems*, edited by Peter Merkl. New York: The Free Press.

Mayer, Lawrence. 1980b. "A Note on the Aggregation of Party Systems." In *Western European Party Systems*, edited by Peter Merkl. New York: The Free Press.

Mayer, Lawrence and Roland Smith. 1985. "Feminism and Religiosity: Female Electoral Behavior in Western Europe." *West European Politics* 8(4, Oct.): 38–49.

McDonald, Neil. 1955. *The Study of Political Parties*. New York: Random House.

McKenzie, Robert T. 1963. *British Political Parties*. New York: St. Martin's Press.

Michels, Roberto. 1915 and 1959. *Political Parties*. New York: Dover Editions.

Miller, Warren and Teresa Levitin. 1979. *Leadership and Change*. Boston: Winthrop Publishing Company.

Milnor, Andrew. 1969. *Elections and Political Stability*. Boston: Little, Brown.

Mitchell, William. 1961. "Politics as the Allocation of Values: A Critique." *Ethics* LXXI(1, Jan.):79–89.

Neumann, Sigmund. 1955. *Modern Political Parties*. Chicago: University of Chicago Press.

Nohlen, Dieter. 1984. "Two Incompatible Principles of Representation." In *Choosing an Electoral System: Issues and Alternatives*, edited by Arend Lijphart and Bernard Grofman. New York: Praeger.

Ostrogorski, M. 1964. *Democracy and the Organization of Political Parties*, abridged by Seymour Lipset. New York: Doubleday.

Przeworski, Adam and Henry Teune. 1970. *The Logic of Comparative Social Inquiry*. New York: John Wiley.

Putnam, Robert. 1971. "Studying Elite Political Culture: The Case of Ideology.' *American Political Science Review* LXV(3, Sept.):651–681.

Rose, Richard. 1963. "Complexities of Party Leadership." *Parliamentary Affairs* 16(3, Summer):257–273.

Rose, Richard. 1984. *Do Parties Make a Difference?*, 2nd edition. Chatham, NJ: Chatham House.

Sankiaho, Risto. 1984. "Political Remobilization in Welfare States. In *Change in Advanced Industrial Democracies*, edited by Russell Dalton, Scott Flanagan, and John Beck. Princeton, NJ: Princeton University Press.

Sartori, Giovanni. 1986. "The Influence of Electoral Systems: Faulty Laws or Faulty Method?" In *Electoral Laws and Their Political Consequences*, edited by Bernard Grofman and Arend Lijphart. New York: Agathon Press.

Schlessinger, Joseph. 1985. "The New American Political Party." *American Political Science Review* 79(4, Dec.):1152–1169.

Shamir, Michael. 1984. "Are Western Party Systems Frozen?" *Comparative Political Studies* 17(1, April):35–81.

Spiro, Herbert M. 1959. *Government by Constitution*. New York: Random House.

Tate, C. Neal. 1980. "The Centrality of Party in Voting Choice." In *Western European Party Systems*, edited by Peter Merkl. New York: The Free Press.

Taylor, Michael and V. M. Herman. 1971. "Party System and Government Stability." *American Political Science Review* LXV(1, Mar.):28–37.

CHAPTER SIX

Micro-Level Analysis: Culture, Violence, and Personality

The modernization of comparative politics involved a fundamental refocusing of the field from an essentially descriptive focus to an explanatory one. As discussed in Chapter 2, a considerable amount of effort by the preeminent scholars in the field was directed toward the construction of highly abstracted and often formalized models or quasi-models of the political process, a body of literature that failed to produce a single explanation with predictive power of any specified class of political phenomena. Another, more promising concomitant of the modernization of the field of comparative politics was the conceptual expansion of the scope of the field by incorporating into comparative political analysis clusters of variables that had previously been dismissed as outside the boundaries of the field. This expansion was an inevitable concomitant of the adoption of the explanatory focus for the field because, if one seeks to explain phenomena, one must include in one's analysis those phenomena that have a significant impact on one's objects of explanation or explicanda. A field of analysis that had as its goals the explanation of a class of phenomena cannot impose upon itself arbitrary boundaries of relevance.

Micro-Level Analysis: Culture, Violence, and Personality

This book assumes that political behavior and/or processes constitute the legitimate explicanda for modern political analysis. Such behavior or processes do not occur in a vacuum but, rather, are imbedded in a sociocultural context. Hence, the explanation of such phenomena inexorably leads to an analysis of those variables that comprise that context. Since many of these sociocultural variables are micro-level ones, the formulation of explanatory theory necessarily leads to analysis at the micro level as well as the macro level of generalization about whole systems that Przeworski and Teune have argued is part of the essence of comparative social inquiry (Przeworski and Teune, 1970). For this reason, the concept of political culture has received widespread attention in modern comparative analysis, both as a potential source of variables with significant explanatory power and as a link between these two levels of analysis (Mayer, 1972).

Political culture is only one of several dimensions of micro-level analysis that has been utilized in the comparative field. Micro-level concepts, by definition, refer to dispositional attributes that inherently contain an element of softness that necessitates certain compromises with rigorous adherence to the standards of scientific epistemology. By *softness*, the present author means that a degree of inference is involved in moving from hard or directly observable data to the conclusion that an attribute exists to a given extent. Indicators in this area are necessarily indirect and, therefore, raise questions of validity. Dispositional terms refer in their most clinical conceptions to neurological and chemical states of the human body. In their more metaphysical conceptualizations, dispositional terms may refer to what B. F. Skinner derisively calls "indwelling agents" (Skinner, 1972) and totally lack direct empirical content. Terms such as *pride, fear, ambition,* or *alienation* do not refer to directly observable phenomena.

After all, only behavior (defined broadly to include what people say) can be directly observed with respect to human beings. Dispositional states must be inferred from such behavior or patterns thereof. By definition, inference, the movement from sensory data to a conclusion with a certain amount of interpretation, involves subjectivity. Concepts measured by indirect data or indicators are vulnerable to questions of validity—do the indicators actually measure the concept they purport to measure? However, as pointed out in Chapter 2, the use of such indirect indicators is not only a perfectly legitimate tool in social research but, given the inherently soft nature of most of our important concepts, is a vital tool of social inquiry. The questions of validity that are raised by the use of such inferential or indirect indicators are difficult but frequently manageable.

The epistemological problems inherently emanating from the use of dispositional concepts are exacerbated when those concepts are from what may be broadly referred to as the *psychoanalytic tradition*, that set of perspectives that descends from the thought of Sigmund Freud. The psychoanalytic perspective varies greatly in its conclusions about human personality from one theorist to another; however, it is defined by the common presumption that human behavior—what people do and say—is determined by deep-seated needs and drives of which the actor is unaware. The especially serious nature of the epistemological problems that accompany the increasingly popular use of psychoanalytic concepts will be discussed below.

This chapter will, therefore, argue and attempt to demonstrate that micro-level research in political science inevitably entails compromises with rigorous epistemological standards. Yet, this chapter will argue that such compromises are essential because dispositional concepts appear to constitute an unavoidable part of any reasonably complete explanation of those political outcomes with which political scientists must deal. In particular, and as stated at the outset, political theorists have long been aware that a nation's political format and processes are inexorably imbedded in a cultural context that shapes their nature. Accordingly, for a long time, political scientists have attempted to incorporate into their analysis some conceptualization of that context, albeit in an unsystematic and impressionistic manner (Inkles and Levinson, 1954). The earlier conceptualization of contextual variables, frequently called "national character," tended to be more vague and less systematic than its modern version known as "political culture." Despite the inherent softness of cultural data and the epistemological problems that their use entails, this chapter will argue that some of the more promising research in the field of comparative politics concerns cultural variables.

THE CONCEPT OF POLITICAL CULTURE

Political culture remains a rather imprecise term for a cluster of variables that vary from one scholar to another with respect to which variables are included and how they are conceptualized. This imperfect consensus on what is included in the concept, how those variables are interpreted, and what indicators might be specified for them creates problems for the goal of cumulative theory building. Furthermore, the concept of political culture is especially vulnerable to the problem of equivalence discussed first in Chapter 2 and then at various other points in this book. *Cultural concepts,* by definition, refer to part of that which is idiosyncratic about political or social systems, and the cultural meaning that may be assigned to particular behaviors is likely to be especially system-specific. This variation in the meaning of behaviors will become clearer as specific cultural variables are discussed.

The concept of political culture takes on particular importance for comparative political inquiry because it provides a potential link between the micro and macro levels of analysis. It will be recalled that a comparative problem in social science is one that includes the two levels of analysis. *Cultural variables* essentially refer to the dispositional sets of individuals. These essentially micro-level attributes are converted to system-level variables when they are labeled as the attribute of a political system on the basis of a conclusion that these are the modal attributes among the individuals in that system. Thus, one may speak of a British attitude toward authority, implying that this attitude predominates among British citizens while allowing that significant numbers of British citizens may not share this attitude. No one has attempted to specify any kind of threshold level of domination of a particular individual-level attribute before it can legitimately be labeled as a system-level attribute; hence, the specification of an attribute as part of a nation's political culture remains essentially judgmental, a conclusion about which reasonable men may disagree.

This adds an element of softness to the concept of political culture in addition to the softness that is inherent in all dispositional concepts. This added element consists of the dilemma that even when agreement is reached on the indicators (which answers to which questions) for a particular dispositional attribute, reasonable men may still disagree as to whether to attach that label to a given political system, even when all such men are exposed to the same hard data.

However, the existence of choice in affixing a certain attribute label (to a political system in the case of a cultural attribute) does not fatally flaw the use of that concept in the enterprise of cumulatively building a body of explanatory theory with predictive power. The key question with regard to the empirical base of cultural concepts is whether the criteria for making those choices and affixing those labels are precisely specified. For example, there have been several studies on the psychology of conservatism (McCloskey, 1958; Wilson, 1973). Each of these studies specified indicators for identifying those individuals to be subsumed by that concept, indicators that not only varied from one study to another but were vulnerable to various critiques. Those indicators, however, were specified with sufficient precision so that once the relevant data about any given individual were known (e.g., behaviors or statements), all observers, regardless of their attitudes toward the concept, would have to agree as to whether that case should be included in that category. Unless one accepts the ontological assumptions of Platonic essentialism, that there is a "true" meaning of concepts like *conservatism* in the transcendent realm, questions of the validity of the indicators become a matter of individual judgment. The bottom line for scientific epistemology is that propositions using cultural concepts may be empirically falsifiable as long as the specification of indicators is precise.

In order to render theory utilizing cultural conepts susceptible to cumulative development, the criteria for the specification of indicators must be consistent from one piece of scholarship to another. This does not mean that the indicators must be identical. Because the meaning of indicators is specific to a given sociocultural context, the principle of equivalence requires that the idiosyncratic attributes of these unique contexts be reflected in different indicators. The requirement of the principle of equivalence is that the essential meaning of the concepts being utilized remains consistent from one piece of research to another.

While there is no consensually accepted list of variables subsumed by the concept of political culture, and while the specific content of that concept varies somewhat from one scholar to another, it is still possible to delineate dimensions of the concept that regularly appear in the analysis of political culture. Sidney Verba defines political culture as "the system of empirical beliefs, expressive symbols, and values which define the situation in which political action takes place (Verba, 1965). Gabriel Almond, deriving his conceptualizations from his sociological guru—that exponent of sociological metaphysics, Talcott Parsons—says that culture comprises cognitive orientations, affective orientations, and evaluative orientations (Almond and Verba, 1965; Almond and Powell, 1966; Almond and Powell, 1978). Samuel Beer conceptualizes political culture as that aspect of a society's general culture that is concerned with how government ought to be conducted and what it should try to do (Beer, 1962). Beer then goes on to specify the components of political culture more specifically: political values subdivided into conceptions of authority and national purpose—what Almond would call evaluative orientations, belief systems or, in Almondian-Parsonian jargon, cognitive orientations (involving knowledge and information), and, finally, emotional attitudes and symbols (or affective orientations in the sociological jargon).

Thus, despite individual differences in the conceptualization of the concept of political culture, a pattern does emerge in that certain dimensions and variables regularly appear in most, if not nearly all, utilizations of the concept. Political culture may then be said to regularly refer to the following elements: attitudes or conceptions of how things ought to be, values or preferences, belief systems or perceptions of how things are, cognition or knowledge and information, and feelings about political objects.

The attitudinal dimension usually focuses on attitudes about authority, a qualitative variable that may be manifested as egalitarianism, deference, or submission. An egalitarian attitude toward authority emanates from the presumption that people are relatively equal in their capacity to make political judgments. The attitude is that political institutions ought to afford the most widespread feasible participation in the policy-making process, that political elites should be afforded minimum discretion in that process, and that popular control of such elites should be maximized. A submissive attitude presumes that some people are manifestly more able than others to make political judgments and, therefore, to govern. Accordingly, elites ought to be obeyed without question. A deferential attitude presumes that the capacity to make political judgment and to govern is not equally distributed; hence, elites ought to be afforded considerable discretion. However, elites are obligated to govern in the interests of the governed, and the obligation to obey authority is contingent upon a widespread perception that these interests are, in fact, being pursued. Elites still govern in this view, but they are accountable to the governed. Note that these attitudes constitute a mixture of a perception of reality (i.e., in this case, human nature) combined with a perception of how the relationship between the elites and the masses *ought* to be structured—an evaluative dimension.

Even if these definitions are accepted, a substantial area of interpretation remains in translating these conceptions of authority into precise survey questions and answers. Hence, equally skilled and informed scholars may still disagree on such important questions as to whether the up-till-now axiomatic British deference still characterizes that nation's culture (Beer, 1982).

Although intersubjective empirical research cannot determine the superiority of some values over others, such research can establish the degree of value consensus or dissensus in a society and the relationship between certain patterns in the substantive content of beliefs and specified political outcomes. It has long been regarded as impressionistically true that long-term political stability requires a basis of widely shared fundamental values, values that define the very essence or nature of a society. There has never been an attempt to specify what fraction of all values must be shared or how widely they must be shared in the general population, nor has anyone specified the criteria for determining which values are fundamental. However, logic does support the assumption that widspread conflicts over values that are generally regarded as fundamental should detract from the ability of the political process to resolve such conflicts by the process of bargaining and compromise that is at the heart of the democratic political process.

The dimension of belief systems also refers to the dichotomous variable that distinguishes an ideological from a pragmatic style in the processing of political issues.[1] An *ideological political style* refers to the propensity to choose among policy alternatives according to the criterion of their consistency with some broad or abstract principle or system of principles, irrespective of their actual impact on society. *Pragmatism* refers to the propensity to choose courses of action according to the criterion of whether they actually promote some end in view (i.e., they "work"), irrespective of their consistency with any principle or of their logical consistency. Pragmatic choices would be determined on a trial-and-error basis, a process in which logic plays a negligible role.

Actually, logic and principle play some role in the policy-making process of any political system, as do pragmatic considerations. The dichotomy between the two political styles refers to tendencies; actual political systems are located on a continuum between the pure types and approach these polar extremes to a greater or lesser extent. The British have been characterized by James Cristolph, among countless others, as being the epitome of a pragmatic people (Cristolph, 1965); yet, the British clearly adhere to a considerable body of principle such as the principles that define the essence of liberal democracy. A total lack of principle would result in chaotic and unpredictable behavior; a total commitment to principle would result in a loss of touch with the sensory world and a tendency to create or perpetuate issues and conflicts divorced from the current world of interests.

Ideology is one of those terms with widespread usage and imprecise content. The adherents to the decline-of-ideology school, such as Seymour Lipset and Daniel Bell (Lipset, 1963; Bell, 1973 and 1962), tend to conceptualize ideology in a narrower sense of a closed, comprehensive system of logically related principles while critics of the decline-of-ideology thesis, such as Joseph LaPalombara, employ the term ideology to refer, to any set of principles (LaPalombara, 1966). It is in this narrower sense that the phenomenon is seen as declining. The two different senses in which the term is used has also led to further disagreement, if not outright confusion, in writings in the past several years.

For example, it has widely been impressionistically presumed that ideologism was related to a lack of tolerance of opposition or deviance. Putnam, however, offers data that conclude that higher civil servants with an ideological style are not less tolerant than those with a pragmatic style (Putnam, 1971). However, he conceptualizes ideology in the broad sense of the use of abstract principles as a guide to choices among alternative courses of action, to generalize rather than to particularize, to utilize deductive thinking, and to make references to future utopias, rather than as a closed thought system. A system is closed to the extent that the conclusions derived from it are not sensitive to sources of information from outside that system. Therefore, the principles of a closed system are, by definition, resistant to change and regarded as final truths. Tolerance implies that one is willing to impart legitimacy to those who adhere to conclusions, perspectives, or principles at variance with one's own. Such tolerance only makes sense when one is willing to accept the possibility that such other perspectives or principles may have merit or truth, in other words, an attitude of skepticism.

Such an attitude is possible when one's claims are presented as statements of the interests of oneself or one's group or nation, rather than as based on truth or moral rectitude.

There is no logical reason why adherence to principle, in itself, should necessarily be associated with a rejection of the legitimacy of other points of view. Only adherence to a closed thought system necessarily entails such a rejection of other perspectives. Therefore, the question for predicting tolerance is not whether political conflict is structured by some principles. Principles are never completely absent from any political context. The question is whether those principles are part of a relatively closed thought system. The denial of legitimacy to alternative perspectives on social, political, religious, or normative issues should logically encourage a greater dislike of such opposition and a greater intensity of partisanship. These attitudes, in turn, could make the compromises that make the peaceful resolution of issues possible in a democracy more difficult to reach.

The literature has thus offered conflicting conclusions on the political impact of an ideological style, a conflict that emanates from a complete absence of consistency on how such widely used concepts are defined. As implied earlier, the inherent softness of terms like *ideological political style* does not preclude precision and consistency in how they are defined. The use of the term to refer to any set of principles as a guide to actions or policy choices renders it indistinct from the term *principle*. If being ideological merely means being principled, why do we need the term ideology? Hence, the use of the term ideology to refer to a closed set of principles would distinguish it from just any set of principles and, thus, render the term scientifically useful as that criterion was discussed in Chapter 2.

Beyond exacerbating the intensity of political conflict and rendering necessary political compromises more difficult to reach, an ideological political style may be further dysfunctional for political success as distractions from the search for workable solutions to actual complex problems. Ideologies are, by definition, abstract simplifications of reality and, thus, not very useful in reconciling competing claims based on actual interests.

Although the literature has thoroughly debated the impact of an ideological political style, it has paid considerably less attention to the factors that cause such a style to be more predominant in a culture than a pragmatic one. Possibly this lack of attention is due to the fact that such an explanation would have to be primarily a historic one, and modern comparative politics has been less than enthusiastic about surveying the history of modern nations, a task that was generally associated with the traditional or prerevolutionary comparative politics. Yet, by ignoring the search for patterns in the historic development of the modern world, many practitioners of modern comparative politics have eschewed a potentially rich source of explanatory theory. Although one cannot measure attitudes or even individual-level behavior, the record of events and system-level behavior is quite complete for the Western world. Some notable exceptions do exist, however, to this neglect, such as Raymond Grew's edited volume of essays on *Crises of Political Development in Europe and the United States* (written almost exclusively by professional historians) and Samuel Huntington's essay, "Political Modernization: America vs. Europe" (Huntington, 1966 and 1968).[2] Herbert Spiro, moreover, has discerned a pattern in the development of an ideological style from his examination of the historical record. He notes that when groups acquire their political consciousness while being excluded from participation in the political process, such groups tend to frame their demands in ideological terms (Spiro, 1959). Such groups, lacking power, cannot be held responsible for the consequences of their political positions, and, hence, they are under no compulsion to moderate such position in the face of political realities or competing claims.

The inability to agree on what is meant by the term ideology fueled one of those debates over the interpretation of known facts that can only occur in a discipline dominated by soft concepts. The debate over "the end-of-ideology thesis" can be traced to whether one accepts the broad or narrow conceptualizations of the term, as discussed above with reference to the Putnam thesis. Scholars like Lipset and Bell, who proclaimed the end of ideology as a salient force shaping Western politics, were referring to the great, relatively closed, comprehensive thought systems generated by the problems and social dislocation surrounding the industrial revolution, the role of institutionalized religion in the secular state, and the distribution of political authority. Bell, for example, refers to ideology as "an all-inclusive system of comprehensive reality" (Bell, 1973 and 1962), a conceptualization very close to the German term *Weltanschauung,* an oft-used and imprecisely translatable term that approximately means a total thought system or perspective from which one views the world and from which the answers to all social questions can be logically derived. Lipset suggested that the problems which the great ideologies addressed had largely been solved (Lipset, 1963), a view of ideology limiting it substantively to thought systems that deal with a finite set of issues. Hence, Lipset feels that ideologies are atavistic, not salient to the problems of today's world.

Ideology in the classic sense of a closed, comprehensive thought system may simply be incompatible with the imperatives of a postindustrial society, a society increasingly dominated by a technocracy and a commitment to the values and imperatives of modern science. Scientific inquiry presumes openness in the sense that scientific conclusions must be continually adjusted to an ever-changing body of evidence. Ideological propositions, by way of contrast, are, by definition, final and independent of such evidence. To the extent that the development of modern science entails the continual questioning of accepted wisdom and the ultimate rejection or modification of much of it, the widespread acceptance of modern scientific epistemology may, in itself, lead to the weakening and abandonment of the classic, closed, comprehensive ideologies.

Ideologism, in this classic sense, has been identified as a more common attribute of non-Western political systems (Pye, 1958; Kahan, Pauker, and Pye, 1955). This identification was impressionistic due to the absense of any criteria for measuring this attribute. However, to the extent that there is truth in this observation, such ideologism would render the process of modernization more difficult. There may be a limit to the possibility of maintaining rigid adherence to a classically closed ideology on the one hand and a modern society based on and utilizing the imperatives of modern science on the other.

The cathectic dimension of political culture that has received the most attention in the literature is a sense of belonging to or identification with the political system itself, a feeling that one had a direct interest in the well-being of the system or a tendency to think of the political system as *us* rather than *them*. The absence of such feelings is what is generally meant by the frequently employed concept of alienation.

As subjective as feelings are, they may be precisely defined and measured; therefore, their impact on sensory phenomena is a researchable question. People, after all, act on the basis of their feelings and perceptions rather than on the basis of some objective reality, and the content of such feelings and perceptions can be determined by survey research, provided that a valid survey instrument can be constructed.

Statements about alienation and its impact on the stability and success of political systems abound in the literature, but they generally fall into the category of conventional wisdom. While some attempts have been made to measure alienation, no criterion has yet been offered to determine the threshold level of alienation that will bring about the absence of stability or success of a system. Moreover, alienation is one of those concepts that present particularly acute problems of equivalence for cross-national research.

Nevertheless, such attempts as have been made to employ the concept of alienation in empirical research do contribute to our understanding of the political systems in question. It is useful, for example, to know that the AWOL and draft evasion rate among French Canadians was exceptionally high in World War II, a war in which vital Western values and, perhaps, the sovereign integrity of Canada itself were at stake (Wade, 1956). This rate reflected a widespread feeling among such French Canadians that this was not *their* war but "the English war" or "the Queen's war," indicating the depth of the cultural segmentation besetting the social stratification system of the nation.

Feelings are frequently expressed with symbols rather than

with such overt behavior as the aforementioned draft evasion. The acrimonious debate in the mid-1960s in Canada over the adoption of a new flag, a debate in which the sensibilities of the French Canadians had to be reconciled with those of the rest of the Canadians who felt an attachment to the Union Jack as a symbol of their English heritage, reflects the depth of subcultural alienation in that nation. Clearly, the monarchy functions as an affective symbol of unity in the British system, but it does not so function in French Canada (Elder and Cobb, 1983).

Finally, political culture includes a cognitive dimension. *Cognition* here refers to both knowledge and information. This dimension refers to how well informed people actually are about political objects. Cognition is distinct from having feelings or opinions about political objects; citizens are more likely to have strong opinions about issues than to be well informed about them.

Psychological involvement in politics—caring deeply about political outcomes—is itself distinct from political participation. The level of participation and the causes thereof have been thoroughly and skillfully analyzed (Nie, Powell, and Prewitt, 1969; DiPalma, 1970; Verba, Nie, and Kim, 1978), perhaps because participation presents relatively fewer problems of measurement. (Questions of equivalence may be raised with regard to any cross-national conceptualization of participation, however.) People may be psychologically involved in politics, even passionately so, without actually engaging in measurable participation. Conversely, measurable participation does not necessarily indicate psychological involvement. The growing corpus of data on political participation has not produced a consensus on the putative political impact of various levels of participation. It will be shown below that the earlier conventional wisdom on the desirability of high levels of participation for successful democracy has been brought into serious question by subsequent empirical research on the cultural requisites of democracy, a topic that has engaged a considerable proportion of the total research effort on political culture.

The foregoing has been intended to show that political culture has generally been imprecisely defined with respect to the broader dimensions of the concept, not to mention a lack of specification of empirical indicators. Without a broader consensus on the empirical content of the concept of political culture, it cannot be used as a predictive device; that is, one cannot predict trends and outcomes using political culture as the explicans. Rather, such a soft concept is generally used as a vague retrospective explanation of outcomes that have already occurred. The soft concept of culture serves as what Professor Huntington has called a residual category (Huntington, 1987), a vague concept referring to the body of factors that affect the outcome in question but which one's research has not identified.

THE CULTURAL REQUISITES OF DEMOCRACY

As stated in Chapter 4, democracy is one of the most highly valued concepts throughout the world, even though it seems to mean very different ideas to different people. Reflecting the values and concerns of the society in which they live, American scholars have devoted a considerable amount of attention to the establishment and maintenance of democracy as they understand that concept. This attention has been focused not only on those Anglo-American and European nations that have been the traditional home for Western-style democracy but also on the prospects for the dissemination of democratic institutions among the newly emerging nations of the less-modernized world (Huntington, 1984).

Given the growing concern for the success of liberal democracy in as much of the world as feasible, and given the growing popularity of culture as an explicans of political outcomes, it is to be expected that the comparative field should have been presented with a considerable body of literature on the cultural requisites of democracy. Given the aforementioned softness of the concept of political culture, it is to be further expected that much of this literature is of the speculative or impressionistic variety.

The best of this speculative literature does not offend one's sense of logic and is supported, to some extent, by the subsequent accumulation of data. The literature lacks conceptual precision and, therefore, does not lend itself to rigorous empirical testing; however, the conclusions offered are still consensually accepted. Seymour Lipset's now-classic essay on "Some Social Requisites of Democracy" posited a number of factors, some of which are cultural by the criteria developed in this chapter, that putatively support stable democracy (Lipset, 1959). While leading scholars today accept and even echo Lipset's substantive conclusions about these cultural requisites (Dahrendorf, 1980; Huntington, 1984),[3] these conclusions are not stated in such a way as to permit empirical testing. Lipset, for example, primarily posits widespread legitimacy as a cultural requisite of democracy. However, he not only appears uninterested in how such legitimacy might be measured but does not attempt to posit criteria for determining the level of such legitimacy that would be required for stable democracy. Details such as the question of how to weight the intensity versus the pervasiveness of legitimacy or the absence thereof are not even considered. Clearly, outcomes such as cabinet or constitutional stability are overdetermined in the sense that they are products of numerous factors, some of which are idiosyncratic to a particular system or set of systems; hence, the level of legitimacy necessary for the survival of a system will vary from system to system. One can only conclude that a given level of legitimacy is sufficient for the survival of a system in a particular setting when the system has in fact survived. There is thus an element of tautology that is inherent in positing an adequate level of legitimacy as the explicans of a political outcome; the adequacy of the level of legitimacy in a particular setting can only be established by the outcome that was to be explained. It is hard to see how the threshold level of legitimacy can logically be determined *a priori* to that outcome, making a predictive rather than a retrodictive explanation possible.

Philosophers of social science have long acknowledged that, given the necessarily incomplete nature of the explanations they could possibly produce, a probabilistic rather than a deterministic predictive capacity was the best to which they could aspire (Brodbeck, 1968). While social scientists acknowledge the inability to specify and analyze all the variables that have a causal impact on the explicanda, they do aspire to specify some of the necessary factors in the explicans, thereby producing a probabilistic explanation. Lipset, however, goes beyond the point of acknowledging the necessarily incomplete nature of his explanation and argues that even a strong correlation between his social requisites and stable democracy cannot be logically expected because "unique events may account for the persistence or the failure of democracy in any given society" (Lipset, 1959). Therefore, Lipset is saying that democracy can exist despite conditions that are, *ceteris paribus*, adverse to that form of government and that democracy may fail to survive or even appear in the first place despite the presence of any number of factors that are, *ceteris paribus*, conducive to democracy. As stated, Lipset's proposition about the requisites of democracy is consistent with any combination of social variables and political formats in any number of observed political systems. It does not explain why democracy exists in one place but not someplace else. Since any outcome or combination of outcomes can be ascribed to that residual category of "unique factors," the Lipset proposition is not falsifiable and cannot afford us the ability to predict the emergence or persistence of democracy in a given social setting with any knowable probability of being accurate.

The foregoing extended discussion of Professor Lipset's article is not intended to denigrate the heuristic contribution of what was, at the time, a rather ground-breaking incursion into what had been relatively unexplored ground. Rather, the discussion is meant to delineate attributes that continue to characterize the body of speculative theory about the cultural requisites of democracy. Harry Eckstein, for example, has produced a rather extensive body of literature in this regard based on something called congruence theory, the essential proposition of which is that stable democracy requires that the pattern of authority relationships in a political system must be more or less congruent with the corresponding authority patterns found in the social groupings in that society (Eckstein, 1966, 1969 and 1973).[4]

Although seriously advanced in several prestigious scholarly sources or outlets, Eckstein's "congruence theory" not only suffers from the vice of vagueness or imprecision so common to exploratory theorizing in that Eckstein shows no interest in how his critical concepts might be measured, but it is further rendered scientifically useless by Eckstein's lack of interest in specifying criteria for the degree of convergence that must be obtained for stable democracy to persist. Moreover, there is no logical reason why Eckstein's theory should be regarded as self-evident.

In the first place, despite their widespread use, no one has yet specified indicators for such concepts as deference or egalitarianism, concepts that are crucial to a theory based on authority patterns. The classification of any given system on the basis of such concepts remains unavoidably judgmental and, hence, subjective. In the second place, there is no conceivable way one can objectively specify a threshold for the degree of convergence that must be obtained for stable democracy. Eckstein himself has acknowledged that, since perfect convergence cannot be obtained, it is more important to obtain the greatest degree of convergence in those social relationships closest to the level of the state. Since some degree of divergence or incongruence must be expected in any system, the criteria of scientific epistemology demand that one specify what degree of such incongruence—independently defined and measured—must be reached before the failure of democracy is predicted. In the third place, it is not self-evident on a logical level that such incongruence should result in a failure of a stable democracy. Eckstein relies on the psychological concept of strain produced by a shifting of roles to make his case that if, for instance, one confronts a norm of absolute obedience in all of one's social relationships during the formative years, one will find it impossible to hold political authority responsible in one's political role. But it is not self-evident that people are incapable of submitting obsequiously to authority in one role or context while asserting their equality and rights in another. Citing the now almost hackneyed example of the failure of the egalitarian Weimar Constitution in the authoritarian German society will not do. Aside from the obvious fact that the collapse of Weimar was due to an enormously complex array of forces and circumstances—some of which, like Adolph Hitler, were quite idiosyncratic, it is not clear that the German attitude toward authority was *sui generis* in the context of central Europe of that time.

The foregoing two examples of speculative theorizing about the cultural requisites for stable, effective democracy were illustrative of a genre of work that has been all too common in this area. Speculative theorizing that is not accompanied by some attempt at least to assess its compatability with data in some preliminary fashion is likely to lead to theory that is inherently untestable. It will not do to suggest some elitist division of labor between the creative theoreticians and the "bronze" caste of ordinary academics who must see to the mundane task of applying these creative enterprises to the sensory world. The field has seen too many inherently untestable exercises in what LaPalombara has derisively called the new "scholasticism" (LaPalombara, 1970) to have much confidence that conceptualization without attention to its empirical content will be susceptible to receiving such content. Concepts in empirical research cannot be created in the abstract but must be adapted and adjusted to the imperatives of specifying indicators.

Fortunately, a growing body of research in the area of the cultural requisites of democracy has rooted in an impressive collection of data. The relatively recent phenomenon of an extensive body of comparative survey data—much of it collected under the auspices of the Inter-University Consortium for Political and Social Research (I.C.P.S.R.)—has provided much of the empirical basis of this growing body of research.

Almond and Verba's *The Civic Culture* is clearly a landmark study, not only in their substantive conclusions that permanently reshaped conventional wisdom on the cultural foundations of successful democracy but in the ground-breaking methodological foray into the hitherto largely uncharted area of cross-national survey research. Their five-nation cross-national survey produced a data set whose impact extends well beyond the specific study that was its impetus, a data set that is, perhaps, the most reworked and cited in the entire field and that, therefore, is the empirical basis of numerous other studies.

One of the rewards of empirical research, it has been suggested a number of times in this volume, is the satisfaction of disproving conventional wisdom. Conventional wisdom, up to that point in time, as taught in countless thousands of high school and other introductory-level American government courses, included what Almond and Verba call the rational activist model, that successful democracies are populated by citizens who are well informed about politics, who understand how to translate their interests into policy alternatives and support for political candidates, and who actively participate in politics to maximize their interest.

One of the main themes of the book is the demonstration that this rational activist model has little correspondence with empirical reality. It is, by now, widely demonstrated that not only is meaningful participation beyond the minimal and routine act of voting confined to a very small segment of the population, but even the knowledge and information on which rational political choices must be based are similarly confined to a relatively few. Hence, the assumption of traditional democratic theory that the tenure of political elites will be jeopardized if they do not govern in the public interest is brought into serious question. How can the general citizenry hold the government accountable to act in their interest if that public cares little and knows less about what that government is doing and with what effect?

The data presented by the *Civic Culture* study indicate that, at that point in time, although the level of knowledge and participation is higher in the successful democracies than in the less-successful ones, those levels were very low even in the Anglo-American democracies. (Later data indicate those levels have risen significantly in recent decades as discussed below). Hence, in the original *Civic Culture* study, the classic rational-activist model cannot account for the distinction between the successful and less-successful democracies. Rather, the distinction is made with respect to the widespread belief in that model of the successful democracies, a belief shared by elites and masses alike.

As the authors of the book put it, the elites, believing that the masses will be looking over their shoulders, act as if that were true. Thus, respondents in the Anglo-American democracies were much more likely than those in the less-successful democracies to express the value that citizens ought to participate in politics and the opinion that they could do so effectively. This mixture of "balanced disparities" provides both the check on government discretion entailed by democratic theory and the insulation of elites from the day-to-day currents of public opinion entailed by the principles of stable, effective government.

The core finding of *The Civic Culture* (Almond and Verba, 1965) that Western publics are uninvolved and uninformed must be amended and qualified by more recent data summarized and analyzed in an important study by Russell Dalton (1988). By a process that he calls *cognitive mobilization*, Dalton claims that Western publics increasingly have the knowledge, information, and inclination to make political decisions for themselves. The growth of the average level of education among these publics, the expanded role of the mass media, and a growing level of politicization are factors named by Dalton as contributing to this process of cognitive mobilization. These publics tend to be issue-focused, however, in that individuals tend to specialize in following one or a few issues of special salience to their lives and values. In their own issue specialty, these *issue publics* demonstrate a "suprising level of political sophistication" (Dalton, 1988).

Dalton's volume illustrates what can be accomplished in applying theory to data. Here is another case in which the systematic analysis of relevant data either qualifies or contradicts conventional wisdom. The earlier data on the political ignorance and apathy of Western publics had been widely repeated as a given in the analysis of liberal democracy. These data on the increasing politicization and sophistication of Western publics add support for the *crisis-of-democracy* thesis discussed in Chapter 4, the thesis that alienation and a consequent loss of legitimacy are affecting Western political systems because, being "overloaded" with demands from newly politicized citizen groups, these systems are unable to satisfy these demands and process their issues (Crozier, Huntington, and Watanuki, 1975).[5]

The *Civic Culture* study also produced support for one cultural attribute long held to be one of the major prerequisites of political democracy: tolerance and legitimacy of opposition. Respondents in the Anglo-American systems were far less likely to characterize their political opponents in pejorative terms than those in the other systems and especially in Italy where the ideological distance between major contenders is particularly high. Another dimension in which the authors of the five-nation study found that there was a clear distinction between the more and the less successful democracies is in the level of affect or diffuse support for the system itself. This dimension was operationalized as questions about pride in the system, with the objects of such pride being expressed as either the political institutions or aspects of the society in general. The citizens of the Anglo-American democracies exhibited a much greater tendency to express pride in the political institutions of their respective nations than did the citizens of Germany, who were more likely to confine their affect to the more general concept of nationhood, and those of Italy, who were alienated from both the political and the social system. From this finding, it may be implicitly inferred that generalized or diffuse support of the political system is, in fact, a distinguishing hallmark of "successful" democracies.

This study pointed the way for other studies utilizing cross-national survey data and, as such, has become a classic landmark study, as noted above. The lessons learned from this pioneering effort at cross-national survey research informed subsequent projects based upon cross-national surveys. Thus, despite the study's deserved place as a classic in the field, criticisms have been levied at the study in recent years, criticisms both of substance and of method (Almond and Verba, 1980).

The basic theoretical proposition, that there is a causal nexus between "the civic culture" and stable effective democracy, is presented with less than rigorous scientific standards. In the first place, there is a great deal of imprecision in the specification of the dependent variable. The classification of the five nations along this dimension is strictly judgmental and independent of any clear criteria (Lijphart, 1980).[6] In the second place, culture is presumably a persisting and deep-seated phenomenon; hence, those nations that are successful democracies as a product of exhibiting the civic culture to a greater extent should continue to be relatively successful for some time, while those nations that are characterized as low on the civic culture dimension will continue to be less-successful democracies. Yet, one of the most successful democracies in Almond and Verba's study is consensually characterized as in steep decline, while one of their less-successful democracies has become a paragon of stable, successful democracy. This fact suggests that the degree to which a nation is a stable, effective democracy is the product of a more complex array of factors than *The Civic Culture* would have us believe. The facile conclusion that the degree of success or stability of a democracy is a product of its cultural patterns presumes that the direction of causality inferred from the observed relationship between culture and the political outcome is self-evident. Yet, some scholars argue that it is also plausible to argue that the observed cultural patterns are a product of the political format or that, at least, the causal relationship is reciprocal (Lijphart, 1980). It will be recalled that a scientific explanation should clearly fit the available data better than alternative explanations; yet, the reciprocal-relationship theory provides at least as good a fit to the data as does Almond and Verba's thesis of the civic culture as the explicans and stable democracy as the explicandum. Actually, the reciprocal-relation theory or even culture as the dependent variable may seem to be a better fit to the more recent data than the theory of culture as the independent causal variable and political structure as the dependent variable. In the update to the study, *The Civic Culture Revisited,* Conradt finds that attributes of the civic culture are significantly increasing in Germany, while Kavenaugh finds such attributes declining in Great Britain (Conradt, 1980; Kavenaugh, 1980). Political culture, therefore, becomes a dependent variable, apparently altered by change in political structure or outcomes. It has been assumed by conventional wisdom that political structure or format cannot survive unless it is congruent with political culture, an assumption that received its clearest specification in Eckstein's aforementioned congruence theory. The understood proposition is that if noncongruence exists, political structure will change to fit the culture. For example, a democratic political format will fail and will be replaced by an autocracy if such a format were placed in an authoritarian cultural context, as in the classic case of the Weimar Constitution in Germany. However, the data by Conradt, Kavenaugh, and others appear to suggest that cultural factors are themselves evolving, apparently to adjust to structural or political realities.

More importantly, the inference of causation is flawed by the failure of the authors to specify whether they consider the civic culture to be a necessary or a sufficient precondition of stable democracy, or both, and the extent to which a nation may deviate from the civic culture and still persist as a stable democracy. Unless the cultural parameters of stable democracy are specified at some precise tolerance level below which the character of such a system cannot be maintained, one cannot, in principle, disprove the assertion that such a culture is either a necessary or sufficient condition of stable democracy.

In the third place, the civic culture is itself specified with less than scientific rigor. The concept consists of several distinct attributes, such as cognition, sense of civic competence, sense of an obligation to participate, sense of pride in the system, and tolerance of different points of view. The relative importance or weight of these distinct attributes in the overall designation of having the civic culture is never addressed, let alone precisely specified. The specification of the cultural attributes of a nation as a system-level characteristic from the ego responses of individuals represents an unwarranted inference that Erwin Scheuch calls the "individualist fallacy" (Schuech, 1969).

In sum, beyond the impressionistic conclusions as to which nations most approximate the civic culture, one is unable, from the data presented, to reach a conclusion as to the precise extent that a given nation possesses that culture. What the Schuech criticism is implying is that Almond and Verba must mean that the civic culture is more than the mere sum of the answers to the question being asked in the survey; it is an organic whole for which the specific responses function as indicators with the rules of correspondence left imprecise.

CULTURAL CHANGE IN THE POSTINDUSTRIAL WORLD

The idea of political culture as an evolving phenomenon adapting to changes in the social and political structure has produced some of the most interesting and significant literature in comparative politics in recent years, the growing body of literature surrounding Ronald Inglehart's thesis of "The Silent Revolution."[7]

Beginning with a plausible assumption that certain types of values characteristically take precedence over other values in the sense of becoming more salient to groups of people at a given time and place is not helped by the elaborate reference to the epistemologically shaky work of Abraham Maslow. As this chapter will argue below, Maslow represents that area of psychology that infers subconscious needs and drives to explain human behavior, motivations for which there is no direct empirical evidence and which are not self-evident to all reasonable men. Maslow is attempting to propound a manifestly normative set of priorities as intrinsic truth. His highest value, the "self-actualized" personality, is defined as "psychological health" that is "correct, true, real" as opposed to psychopathology (Maslow, 1970). In order to cloak his disquisition on superior values with academic respectability, Maslow resorts to the frequently used tactic among his cohorts in the psychoanalytic tradition of co-opting the value-positive term *science* to describe the antithesis of what that term has traditionally been understood to mean [as that term has been discussed in Chapter 2]. This co-optation involves the claim that he uses a different kind of science, something he calls "humanistic and holistic conceptions of science . . . in blunt contradiction to the classical, conventional philosophy of science still too widely prevalent, and they offer a far better substitute for scientific work with persons"(Maslow, 1970). Of course, the claim of psuedo-scientists like Maslow that "'Pure' science has no more intrinsic virtue than 'humanistic' science" (Maslow, 1970) is contradicted by the fact that the scientific method, by definition, produces results that are intersubjectively demonstrable. The psychological health of Maslow's "self-actualizing" personalities [even assuming that concept could be precisely defined] is not so demonstrable. However one may choose to characterize the impressionistic ramblings of Platonic metaphysicians like Maslow who arrogantly presume they can intuit essential and transcendent truth, they certainly are not science. The extensive references to this work by Inglehart as a body of putative psychological findings on which he can build detracts from the academic respectability of what is otherwise a provocative and scientifically sound body of research.

Perhaps one of the first lessons that needs to be learned by comparativists is to recognize academic charlatans despite their scientific pretentiousness. Too much effort has been spent borrowing indiscriminately from scientifically marginal disciplines such as psychology or, more particularly, sociology and cultural anthropology, effort that has really contributed little to the implicit goal of building a body of scientifically sound, explanatory theory. Much of the early work of the Comparative Politics Committee of the Social Science Research Council with its heavy reliance on the Parsonian school of sociology exemplifies this misplaced effort.[8]

Despite his misguided reliance on the conclusions of Maslow, the work of Inglehart has done much to reshape the thinking of scholars about the actual nature and operation of industrial democracies and especially about the nature of political conflict in such nations. The evidence is impressive that such an intergenerational change has, in fact, occurred throughout Western Europe, the significance of which expands beyond the irrelevance of party-system cleavage discussed in the preceding chapter. The value change has altered the traditionally understood meanings of left and right in political conflict and the relationship of those orientations to such individual attributes as socioeconomic status and education. The very kinds of people who were probable adherents of the left on the bourgeois or materialist value dimension—the less-educated, blue-collar classes—are precisely those who are least likely to possess the attributes associated with the left on the postmaterialist value dimension—the better-educated middle to upper classes.

Of course, the validity of the claim that the research demonstrates a fundamental shift in the society's basic orientation toward politics is a function of the validity of the indicators by which the value orientations of the respondents are measured. Since the premise here is that these are deep-seated attributes of the personality of which the respondent is unaware, one cannot directly ask the respondent to assess his or her own values as on a self-anchoring scale. Rather, one must assume that these values will manifest themselves in attitudes about other matters. Therefore, Inglehart offers an instrument containing four policy goals from which the respondent was asked to choose the two most important to him or her. From this choice, Inglehart infers a far-reaching conclusion about the kind of values that are salient to the respondent over a wide range of issues. While not offensive to common sense, the inference does entail enough interpretation as to allow a question of validity to be raised. For example, one of the policy choices is "Maintaining order in the nation." Choosing this goal is inferred to indicate an acquisitive or materialistic set of value priorities because, Inglehart explains, ". . . a concern with domestic order is presumed to relate, above all, to the protection of property" (Inglehart, 1971). Yet, a concern with the maintenance of order can also be viewed as indicating the noneconomic value of controlling political dissent or suppressing countercultural activity; hence, the validity of this item as an indicator of the prevalence or salience of materialistic values in the respondent is not self-evident to all reasonable men. The problem is one of effectively balancing the conflicting values that are inherent in the inference of subconscious personality dimensions, the values, on the one hand, of producing items on the survey instrument or interview that appropriately disguise from the respondent the attribute being measured and, on the other hand, of validly indicating the presence of the attribute to the satisfaction of most reasonable people.

The validity of the classification of individuals as either acquisitive or postmaterialist personalities is the presumption that underlies the entire substantial body of literature discussing the political implications of Inglehart's postbourgeois social cleavages. The claim that the survey instrument is a valid measure of one's value orientation may be supported in several ways. *Face validity* means that the measure is consistent with common sense impressions. As noted above, while Inglehart's measure does not offend common sense, it is not self-evidently valid either. *Criterion validity* means that the results are empirically related to other variables to which they should be related. In Inglehart's study, the relationships between one's value orientation and other factors constitute the main body of the research; they are not self-evident expectations inherent in the nature of the value orientations themselves. Therefore, the criteria to independently establish validity are not clear. In fact, Inglehart's research makes no serious attempt to independently assess the validity of his measure of value orientations. He just assumes it, as he assumes the questionable truth claims of Maslow.

In a more substantive sense, one may question the dichotomizing of the concept of value orientation. It is not unlikely that such a facet of one's personality is a matter of degree rather than a matter of bifurcated, mutually exclusive categories. People probably are more or less acquisitive or postbourgeois rather than either one or the other. Moreover, people may be predominantly acquisitive or materialistic on one kind of question or issue and concerned with symbolic or life-style issues on another set of issues. Any classification of complex human personalities into dichotomous categories is almost certainly a major oversimplification. Simplification, however, is a useful tool for analytical purposes, as long as it is recognized that it is not a description of reality.

Despite the foregoing questions about the premises of Inglehart's research, the theory is one of the most creative and important in the field in recent years. The data support his claim that such value orientations are a function of the economic context in which one spends one's formative years and, hence, are not malleable to external events or stimuli. Inglehart is able to demonstrate that the category in which one is placed on this value orientation dichotomy does predict some important behaviors and attitudes, such as voting choice or party preference. More importantly, despite the foregoing qualifications, the data overwhelmingly point to very fundamental changes that are going on with respect to the social cleavages in Western industrial democracies, changes that researchers who wish to understand such systems and politicians who seek to govern such systems can ignore only at considerable peril. Inglehart shows that age cohort effects (operationalized by assigning a constant to each cohort for the time period being analyzed) account for an impressive 87% of the variation in the value dichotomy across time and between cohorts, while the effects of life cycle do not explain additional variation (Inglehart, 1985). Hence, it is clear that the context in which one spends one's formative years, rather than the age of the individual, shapes one's value orientation and, therefore, that the value change discerned by Inglehart is a permanent part of the structure of Western societies.

THE CULTURAL BASIS OF MODERNIZATION

Despite a number of works purporting to address this topic directly, the cultural basis of modernization has been a relatively neglected topic in comparative politics. Of course, there has been an enormous literature attempting to conceptualize and measure either political development or modernization and often discussing the political and theoretical implications of various conceptualizations of development (Almond, 1970; Huntington, 1968; Deutsch, 1961; Pye, 1966).[9] Another body of literature assesses the prospects of development in a democratic or Western direction (Kautsky, 1962; Huntington, 1984). The main thrust of the literature concerned with the explanation of levels of underdevelopment has been the dependency literature discussed in Chapter 4, a literature that ascribes the causes of underdevelopment to the imperatives of capitalism. In Chapter 4, it was suggested that the dependency theory has failed to take account of alternative explanations of underdevelopment, explanations based upon the attributes of the underdeveloped systems themselves. Chief among such internal explanations may be the cultural attributes of many of these less-developed systems.

The cultural requisites for modernization have been addressed by a number of scholars, albeit in an impressionistic, nonempirical manner. David Apter, for example, clearly has held that modernization involves not only structural but also normative or ideological dimensions (Apter, 1965). Specifically, Apter suggests that "consumatory" (sacred and ultimate) values dominate the less-developed systems while "instrumental" or secular values dominate the modern or industrial systems. What Apter only suggests without fully exploring its implications is the extent to which his consumatory values actually impede the modernization process. Daniel Lerner has described the modernization process as involving a fundamental shift in the orientation of individuals toward the political world, an expanding of one's horizons including a sense of belonging to a larger community and an expanded sense of the possible values to which one might aspire (Lerner, 1958). Lerner further identifies a modern personality as one having such attributes as an ability to identify with the needs and roles of others and to have opinions about political issues beyond the day-to-day concerns with one's daily life. Hence, the intrusion of some modern institutions, such as education and the media, generate the growth of a modern culture, which, in turn, facilitates the further growth and perpetuation of a modern society.

Lucien Pye's work on the relationship between culture and political development in Burma is another creative and insightful exploratory study that rests on an insecure empirical foundation, a fact attributable, to a large extent, to the reliance Pye places on the work of the psychoanalytic personality theorist

Eric Erikson. Erikson modifies the Freudian theory of sexual repression forming the basis of human motivation by positing the concept of ego identity as the unconscious basis of human striving (Erikson, 1950). The realization of this putatively basic human need is dependent on childhood experiences in the deep recesses of the memory, as with other psychoanalytic theorists. In the case of the Burmese leaders, they experienced unpredictable emotional relationships with their mothers who fluctuated in their attitude toward their child in an unsystematic way between extreme warmth and cold disinterest, an attitude apparently unrelated to the child's behavior. This maternal behavior leads the child to an expected aggressive and unpredictable behavior on the part of the generalized other and to a lack of trust in one's fellow man that is the basis of a modern and open system. Thus, Pye reports that Burmese "political parties operate on the basis that the opposition exists only to be crushed, and whichever party gets in power sets about this task as systematically as it can" (Pye, 1962), an attitude of political intolerance that is out of congruence (in the sense that the term is used by Eckstein) with the institutions of a competitive party system imposed on the traditional Burmese culture. The failure of Burmese elites to reconcile their sense of identity between the conflicting imperatives of tradition and modernity results in a failure to transmit a sense of collective identity to the Burmese people.

The need to solve a crisis of national identity is a theme that runs through the writings of Pye and his colleagues on the Comparative Politics Committee of the Social Science Research Council (Pye, 1966). This need is posited axiomatically in a large corpus of writings emanating from this group despite the fact that some apparently modern nations have manifestly failed to solve this crisis, nations such as Canada and Belgium; yet, such nations seem to persist and even function adequately by most measures of that concept. Moreover, no attempt is made to suggest how one might determine the extent to which an individual, let alone a system, has, in fact, solved this crisis and developed a sense of individual or collective ego identity. Without such an independently developed basis of measurement, so typical of works in the psychoanalytic tradition, the empirical foundation of the study becomes selective and illustrative rather than systematic. The case study interviews of selected Burmese politicians in the later chapters remind one of the interview data presented by Freud and his followers to support conclusions already reached. While the child-rearing practices reported by Pye can, in retrospect, account for a feeling of distrust towards one's fellow man, such experience could conceivably result in other behaviors and attitudes as well, such as withdrawal from social interaction. Moreover, we are never given any criteria for measuring the extent to which such experiences and their putatively consequent attitudes are prevalent enough to characterize the system as a whole or, for that matter, any given individual. What Abraham Kaplan called the "norms of correspondence" (Kaplan, 1964) are never specified with any precision; hence, there is no way to render the assertions of Pye falsifiable and accountable to the evidence.

David McClelland's work on the achieving personality, on the other hand, is an exemplary work of methodological creativity and sophistication that devises ingenious methods for measuring some rather soft personality concepts and also presents impressive evidence for the level of economic growth (and, presumably, of modernization itself) as a function of the predominance of psychological or personality factors in a society (McClelland, 1961). Advocates of dependency theory are anxious to dismiss work such as McClelland's as without merit, especially criticizing the degree of inference from his indicators or measures of his central concept, N-achievement, because the plausibility of such internal psychological explanations seriously weakens the more polemical and strident versions of dependency theory; however, McClelland and his associates make a strong case for the validity of their indicators and offer strong statistical evidence for their propositions. Empirical work involving soft concepts such as are commonly used in psychological research invariably involves inferences from indirect indicators that generate questions of validity. Not only did McClelland and his associates measure their key concepts with multiple indicators that yielded consistent results but they obtained an impressive measure of criterion validity that should give pause to those who would cavalierly dismiss McClelland's principle findings. McClelland's work shows that the standards of scientific epistemology can be followed in social research even when utilizing inherently soft psychological or cultural concepts. Unfortunately, no real attempt has been made to replicate this work or to follow McClelland's lead in searching for ways to measure psychological concepts that can account for varying levels of development. Much of the field was simply not interested in any explanations that were incompatible with the identification of a malevolent Western capitalism as the source of third world underdevelopment.

Yet, the impressionistic suggestions of scholars like Pye in the Comparative Politics Committee of the S.S.R.C. that there is a cultural component to the development process are difficult to dismiss. Specifically, Sidney Verba, in the concluding essay to the book he co-edited with Lucien Pye on the topic in question, suggests that there are cultural patterns that are logically inconsistent with the modernization process, patterns that are characteristically found in the less-developed systems. For example, Verba suggests that traditional belief systems discourage the process of change itself. More basically, he suggests that many traditional belief systems promote a fatalistic orientation toward the world in general and toward politics in particular, an orientation that presumes that events are beyond an individual's control (Verba, 1965). Such an orientation is accordingly not conducive to one's taking an active role in attempting to better one's sociopolitical environment or one's well-being. Furthermore, a widespread sense of identification with the symbols of the nation state may be one of the principle cultural prerequisites of a modern political system, according to Verba. This identification is impeded in the less-developed systems by an overriding identification with more parochial groups and symbols. Here again, the speculations of Pye about the relevance of Erikson's concept of ego identity are cited to illustrate and, to some degree, account for the failure of non-Western elites to disseminate a sense of psychological identification with the political system (Pye, 1965).

Modern societies presume another cultural pattern not generally discussed in the literature, a degree of secularization not generally found in the less-developed systems. Modernity implies the integration of modern technology into the system. This means not merely the use of such technology but the adoption of the values and methods of modern science. Science, in turn, entails a relatively open society, a society in which truth claims are sensitive to a constantly unfolding body of sensory data. A society based on faith—the persistent adherence to a body of beliefs or set of conclusions, no matter what the evidence—is not conducive to the development of scientific knowledge. It is no accident that the "Age of Faith," the Middle Ages in West European history, coincided with the nadir of the development of science and enlightenment in the West. The growth of scientific knowledge is not encouraged by a society that punishes for the crime of heresy or apostasy. In the West, the various attempts by the Church to stamp out such heresy, including the notorious Inquisition, exemplify the kind of closed society that can negate the growth and support of science. In the so-called second world, the Communist bloc nations, purge trials (such as those that occurred in the Stalinist era) clearly exemplify a closed society.

However, in the West, there has clearly been a process of secularization over the past several centuries in which the Church, or in which churches collectively, no longer maintain a great salience in the lives of most individuals, as was noted in the preceding chapter with respect to the declining fortunes of the so-called "confessional" parties. European history clearly shows that the scientific and technological revolutions coincided with the declining salience of faith and, precisely, in those areas in which the process of secularization was most clearly established.

In the Communist bloc systems, society has been nominally committed to a closed, comprehensive ideology, and the actions and policies of those systems have had to be justified in terms of that ideology. Despite the apparently closed nature of the Soviet system, one cannot say that that system is technologically underdeveloped. Thus, one may claim that the Soviet system seems to negate our proposition that modern technology requires a relatively open culture. Two points may be made in response to this apparent refutation of our proposition. One is that modern technology has not developed indigenously in the Soviet context but, rather, has been appropriated from the West through purchase or through espionage.

Secondly, it is not self-evident to all scholarly experts on the Soviet Union that that system is now characterized by an ideological political style. Rather than the entailments of a rigid Marxism-Leninism determining political and social choices, one or another convoluted reconstruction of a vaguely defined Marxism-Leninism has been adopted to justify what has been decided on more pragmatic grounds. It is not at all clear that the imperatives of the national interest, defined in traditional Russian terms, or the imperatives of a mature industrial society are seriously compromised by the constraints of Marxist ideology.

The impact of religions or other ideological systems on political development is, according to Donald Smith's perceptive analysis of this topic, a function both of the "systemic," or generic, attributes of the religions and of the "elements of historic particularity," or idiosyncratic factors of a particular nation (Smith, 1970). Thus, a degree of secularization or the weakening salience of a religion for the daily lives of the masses may modify the otherwise dysfunctional impact of that religion on political development. Hence, even assuming that all religions have such a dysfunctional impact on the modernization process, religion as such seems to have retained a far greater hold on the lives of the masses in the less-developed nations of the African, Asian, and Latin parts of the world than is the case in the industrialized West, a fact that can account for some of the slow rate of modernization in those systems.

It may be further suggested that the religious systems that dominate the non-Western world are particularly dysfunctional for modernization. Both Buddhism and Islam teach a fatalistic view of the world, that man cannot significantly alter his own destiny (Smith, 1970). Yet, one of the cultural requisites associated with successful government in the modern world is a widespread sense of competence, a perception that problems can be effectively resolved through appropriate civic action or social policy.

These non-Western religions tend to be organic, to use the terminology of Smith, one of the very few scholars who has even addressed the important topic of religions and modernization in the non-Western world. Organic religions, according to Smith, are those that are equated with society itself (Smith, 1970). The separation of church and state is not comprehensible to such a religious tradition; it is assumed that the state exists to serve the faith. Since religious faith, almost in its essence, embodies final, absolute principles, the inability to create autonomous secular institutions would weaken the ability of that system to generate meaningful social change. Professor Almond, among others, has told us that among the defining attributes of a developed political system are adaptive and responsive capacities (Almond, 1965). Huntington's modern institutions are also adaptable to the imperatives of changes in their context (Huntington, 1968).

The basic question that is being raised here is whether the technological attributes of modern society can be maintained in a context that is antithetical to the context in which these attributes were developed and to the imperatives of modern science. We have finally learned that democratic constitutions do not flourish when transplanted to a cultural context that is hostile to the values implied by such a constitutional format. It may be one thing to import technology in the short run to a closed cultural setting, as the Soviets may have done and which the Shah of Iran succeeded in accomplishing for a while. It may be something else to maintain that technology in the long run without the cultural attributes of modernity from which that technology emanated.

Comparative politics remains at the stage of speaking in general terms about the impact of cultural attributes, including those of religion. Much hard data is needed about the extent to which such putative cultural attributes actually characterize a political system and the strength with which the beliefs associated with a particular religion or ideology are actually held by the population or political elites in question. Scholars need to move beyond assertions about the principles that comprise a religion or ideology and their entailments if one is to have confidence in these scholars' assertions about the actual impact of such cultural attributes on the sociopolitical system. The principles of Roman Catholicism have not changed since the Middle Ages so much as has the hold of those principles on Western civilization. Culture, after all, refers not just to beliefs, attitudes, or values but to their dissemination in a particular society.

Furthermore, scholars need to move beyond assertions about the content of broad religious systems such as Islam and Buddhism to a recognition of the rich variety of subsystems within those broad categories. Eastern religions do not constitute monolithic wholes any more than does Western Christendom. The Theravada brand of Buddhism practiced in Thailand has left the Thai society much more amenable to modernization than is the case with societies that practice Zen and Mahayana Buddhism. Islam includes Shiites, Sunnis, and other sects that differ from one another as significantly as do the various Christian religions.

EXPLAINING AUTHORITARIANISM IN PSYCHOLOGICAL TERMS

The phenomenon of the Third Reich in Germany and its incalculable human consequences prompted a vigorous search for the reasons why a regime based upon ideas so abhorrent to much of the Western world found such easy acceptance in advanced industrial and putatively civilized nations such as Austria and Germany. Much of this effort was devoted to searching out psychological explanations of this phenomenon inasmuch as it was the widespread acceptance of Naziism, rather than Naziism itself, that was the subject of much of this inquiry. Although National Socialist Germany is a thing of the past, the more generic phenomenon of authoritarian dictatorship is not; hence, inquiries into the causes of the rise of Naziism continue to be currently relevant.

The quality of this research varied widely from that which has been regarded as easily dismissable by serious social scientists to that which has prompted serious comment, albeit much of it critical, by such scholars. The material that was directly based on a Freudian, Neo-Freudian, or other psychoanalytic approach has frequently been popular, sometimes makes intuitive sense, and makes interesting reading but has not been taken seriously as a scholarly explanation of Naziism.

For example, the work of Wilhelm Reich was widely popular for a while but has since been relegated to the worthless category by virtually all serious scholars. In one of the most overtly Freudian of the works under consideration, Reich focused on mass sexual repression as the explanation for the attitudes that made fascism possible (Reich, 1970).[10] His sweeping generalizations about the attitudes of the German masses without direct empirical data are themselves offensive to modern social science epistemology, let alone his assertions about the subconscious drives that caused them. The degree of inference from the identification of popular institutions like major religions that proscribe sexual enjoyment to varying degrees to the claim of mass sexual repression and frustration is astounding. People vary in the intensity of such drives and in the extent to which they will follow such institutional restraints. Furthermore, the conclusion that such repression, even if it were there, must necessarily lead to the psychological traits receptive to fascism is a clear *non sequitur*.

A more basic problem with this and other works purporting to offer an explanation of Naziism rather than a more generic authoritarianism is that one cannot construct explanations of idiosyncratic phenomena. It is not always clear in these works exactly what explicandum the authors had in mind. The authors of these studies speak of generic authoritarianism, but it is clear that Naziism is the phenomenon with which the authors were concerned, and this confusion forms the basis of some of their methodological vulnerability.

The work of Eric Fromm, although retaining a greater reputation of respectability in some intellectual circles, is essentially in the same vein of a modified Freudian analysis based upon sweeping generalizations founded in only the most vaguely defined, selective, and impressionistic data (Fromm, 1965). Fromm's thesis is based upon a posited innate basic human need of a sense of belonging to institutions or movements larger than oneself in order to give life meaning (as opposed to the basic need of sexuality that Freudians usually posit as the basic unconscious drive that ultimately causes most human behavior). According to Fromm, the end of the Middle Ages meant the breakdown of medieval institutions like the Church and feudalism, institutions that gave a sense of certainty about one's status and place in life. The ensuing Age of Reason and Enlightenment left the individual's status and place in life uncertain and largely to be determined by one's competitive efforts. The unbearable sense of aloneness and status uncertainty made man receptive to being subsumed by large social movements such as fascism. A further reaction to the status uncertainty that was particularly acute in the German lower middle class was what Fromm, using Freudian terminology, calls a *sado-masochistic personality*. This term refers to a personality that exhibits extreme submission to the point of self deprecation to any authoritative role and an equally extreme view of the lowliness and absence of rights or dignity of those below oneself in social roles.

Of course, the empirical content of such psychoanalytic concepts is so imprecise as to render the concepts scientifically useless. There are no widely accepted indicators by which any given person can be intersubjectively and unambiguously identified as either sado-masochistic or not. Not only are there insuperable difficulties involved in rendering such concepts empirical as applied to individuals, but the barriers to rendering them so empirical as applied to large, vaguely specified populations are compounded by the question of who is included in the population in question and the question of how widely the trait must be disseminated among the population and with what intensity for the population to be so characterized by that trait.

The inherent flaw in personality concepts that are based on the manifestation of putative unconscious drives and motivations is that such drives and motivations could be manifested in the sensory world in any one of several ways; hence, the manifestation of any one set of outlets cannot be either deterministically or even probably predicted from the assumption of these unconscious drives. If one observes a set of behaviors or expressed attitudes consistent with a presumed personality type, one can only say that those data support the conclusions about the personality type. The foregoing is what we call a *retrospective explanation*, or another version of what Blalock called "the fallacy of affirming the consequent" (Blalock, 1960); however, as was shown in Chapter 2, the epistemological imperatives of social science require prospective explanations, explanations with predictive power. Unless the personality type can be indicated by sensory data that are independent of the result it is supposed to explain, that personality concept becomes a residual concept—a kind of theoretical basket into which one can dump all the variation one cannot otherwise explain.

The Authoritarian Personality (Adorno, Brunswick, Levinson and Sanford, 1950) is, in contrast to the foregoing works that attempt to lay out the psychological requisites of fascism in an impressionistic manner, a landmark attempt to empirically establish that such a personality type exists and to measure its extent or development in selected individuals. Unlike Fromm, who insists his sado-masochistic personality type was a necessary but not sufficient condition for the emergence of the Third Reich, *The Authoritarian Personality* (or, as it is frequently called, the Berkeley study) makes no specific assertions about the relationship between the incidence of this personality type in a given cultural setting and the likelihood or persistence of authoritarian or fascist institutions.

The underlying logic of the project is that an underlying and more or less coherent personality structure that is not directly measurable will manifest itself in a variety of attitudes on different topics, attitudes that can be ascertained through the use of a survey instrument and from which the underlying personality can be inferred. Therefore, the authors try to demonstrate the existence of a personality type by the statistically significant joint occurrence of disparate attitudes such that a person's attitude on one question is highly predictive of his or her attitude on other substantively distinct questions. Beginning with a central tenet of Naziism, anti-Semitism, the authors set out to demonstrate that such an attitude does not occur in isolation from other cognitive orientations but, rather, is necessarily an integral part of a broader personality construct. In other words, they reject the famous null hypothesis offered by Jean Paul Sartre, "A man may be a good father and a good husband, a conscientious citizen, highly cultivated, philanthropic, and in addition, an anti-Semite" (Sartre, 1946 and 1948). The authors first succeeded in demonstrating that anti-Semitism is strongly correlated with "ethnocentrism" or prejudice in general and less strongly correlated with political and economic conservatism. They then extract a number of broader personality traits from unstructured interviews with high scorers on the anti-Semitism scale and use these traits to construct another attitudinal scale purporting to measure authoritarianism in general, the "F-Scale."

The authors of the Berkeley study, in seeking to demonstrate the existence of a putative personality type and to measure it from an attitudinal syndrome, were plowing new theoretical and methodological ground, ground that was later to yield numerous other personality constructs (Adorno, Brunswik, Levinson, and Sanford, 1950).[11] It is therefore a landmark study that provided a model or impetus for a considerable body of subsequent research. Like most innovative research, this study has been subject to a substantial body of critical comment, much of which is apparently quite justified.[12] The most significant of these criticisms is that the authors of the Berkeley study, in their clear demonstration that the observed covariation in attitudes is due to some underlying personality, appeared uninterested in and certainly unclear about the nature of that personality. There is, in particular, a confusion as to whether the F-Scale is intended to measure generalized authoritarianism or fascism. In the context of the times, the period immediately after World War II, the antidemocratic threat was perceived as equated with Naziism, an authoritarianism of the extreme right, while the Soviet Union had been a recent ally. The simplistic perception of the political spectrum as unidimensional, running from a liberal, tolerant, democratic left to an increasingly intolerant and antidemocratic right, is clearly untenable. The research by Inglehart and his associates discussed above constitutes a clear demonstration that there is more than one dimension to political orientations. H. J. Eysenck has similarly proposed two distinct dimensions to political orientations, a conclusion drawn from a factor analysis of some forty attitudinal questions, dimensions that he calls the R and T factors to represent a dimension running from radical to conservative and another running from tough minded to tender minded (Eysenck, 1954). Not all scholars agree with the way that Eysenck has identified the two dimensions, and one could certainly argue that even two dimensions do not adequately reflect the complexity of political reality. The explicit recognition of the multidimensionality of political orientations and values was a contribution that rendered the work of Eysenck important at that point in time.

The problem with the type of research in question on the cognitive receptivity to authoritarianism is to identify such a cognitive style that is independent of political content. Is there a way of thinking about problems and issues that is characteristic of the authoritarian and that is applicable to authoritarians of either the left or right and independent of content? After all, common sense tells us that there is such a phenomenon as authoritarianism of the left, even though many British and American Communists scored lower than average on the content-laden F Scale. Milton Rokeach has suggested that dogmatism may, in fact, describe that cognitive style by producing a scale to measure that trait for the political right and the political left (Rokeach, 1960). The idea that dogmatism may best characterize authoritarianism as a *cognitive style* that is independent of political content was supported by Roger Brown, who suggests that an "authoritarian is best characterized by the kind of information that will induce him to change his attitudes. The authoritarian will reverse his evaluations on the simple say so of an authority figure" (Brown, 1965). By implication, therefore, an authoritarian will *not* change his mind because of new information from outside his belief system. In other words, Rokeach may have hit on something by implicitly characterizing the authoritarian as closed minded.

Although one may argue that the distinction between authoritarianism of the left and of the right may be overblown and that the humanistic facade of the revolutionary left masks as much intolerance and even anti-Semitism as one finds on the fascist right, the criticism is still valid that the authors have not fully explored the theoretical nature and significance of that which they so elaborately undertook to measure. Yet, flawed and vulnerable though they be, the various attempts to find ways to render empirical and to measure this and other personality concepts have far more explanatory utility than all of the metaphysical speculation about the subconscious causes of imprecisely defined personality concepts.

PSYCHOLOGICAL EXPLANATIONS OF VIOLENCE

Dispositional concepts need not be devoid of empirical content. A literature on the causes of civil violence focused on psychological causes of that phenomenon and devoted a good deal of effort and a fair amount of ingenuity in devising plausible indirect indicators of some very soft concepts. This literature attempted to combine maximum geographical applicability with precise empirical indicators, thereby reconciling the inherently conflicting imperatives of generality and empiricism, of which much has already been written (Mayer, 1972).

Much of this literature accomplished this task by using aggregate data indicators to measure dispositional concepts. This data is relatively accessible and inexpensive to gather; hence, it renders the inclusion of the widest possible number and variety of cases logistically practical. The use of such aggregate data indicators also raises a troublesome array of methodological problems, especially the ecological fallacy and the questions about the validity of the indicators.

The work of Ivo and Rosa Feierabend and Betty Nesvold and

that of Ted R. Gurr typify and dominate this literature. The Feierabends and Nesvold attempt to explain the variation among political systems with respect to the level of civil violence in terms of the concept of *systemic frustration* (Feirabend and Nesvold, 1969; Feirabend and Feierabend, 1966). On the conceptual level, systemic frustration refers to a ratio between the formation of wants and the satisfaction of wants. These theoretical foundations of the empirical work of the Feierabends, Nesvold, and Gurr seem to flow logically from the then conjectural but creative insight of James Davies that revolution is most likely to occur not when material well-being is at its lowest point but after a period of significant improvement in such well-being (Davies, 1962). This, the so-called "J-Curve" hypothesis, holds that such a period of rising well-being generates a rise in expectations that continues after the ability of the political system to satisfy such expectations has begun to trail off. Wants will always rise faster than the capacity of the system to satisfy them. Violence becomes most likely when the gap between wants and satisfactions is the greatest, not when satisfactions alone are lowest.

Based upon this idea of violence producing frustration being the product of a ratio between want formation and want satisfaction, the Feierabends and Nesvold creatively devised criteria for measuring these soft concepts through a number of indirect indicators. For example, want formation is indicated by literacy and urbanization, based on the idea that want formation is a product of exposure to modernity. Want satisfaction is indicated by G.N.P., caloric intake per capita, and the number of physicians and telephones per unit of population, indicators chosen from among numerous possibilities on the basis of availability of data and economy of effort.

The validity of these indicators is merely based upon the fact that they are consistent with existing theoretical notions and with common sense; hence, their validity is, at least, open to challenge. This vulnerability is true of any attempt to apply indirect indicators to soft dispositional concepts; however, insofar as the indicators do not offend common sense (face validity) and are precisely specified, propositions based on such measurement techniques are falsifiable according the criteria of standard social science epistemology. As was discussed in Chapter 2, this criterion of falsifiability as propounded by Karl Popper is the key criterion of demarcation between scientific and nonscientific propositions; such epistemological standards do not require an absence of inference from the sensory data to the conclusion that the concepts are presumed present to a given extent.

The work of Ted Gurr offers the concept of relative deprivation as the key psychological variable, a concept that differs from systemic frustration in a couple of important respects. Instead of want formation, Gurr is measuring the perception of what one deserves, a conceptualization that adds the important element of justice without which no revolution can occur, as Crane Brinton warned many years ago (Brinton, 1952). Instead of want satisfaction, Gurr uses the concept of what one expects to get based on the idea that people act on their perceptions more than on objective reality. As with the case of systemic frustration, Gurr devotes a great deal of effort to suggest multiple indicators of these concepts.

While the Feierabends and Nesvold are content with statistically significant correlations between their indirectly measured conceptualization of systemic frustration and a concept of civil violence also based on multiple indicators qualified only by the level of coercion, Gurr builds a causal model that takes account of numerous structural, economic, and other psychological variables (Gurr, 1968). The remaining partial correlations after the introduction of numerous control variables indicate that short-term relative deprivation does not have a significant independent effect on the level of civil strife. The variables that seem to retain a significant correlation with violence after control variables have been partialed out are *persisting deprivation, legitimacy,* and *structural facilitation*. This last concept refers to the presence of institutions that can mobilize and organize anti-system activities, such as the strength of a Communist or other anti-system party. Coercive potential, the level of institutionalization, and the level of past strife are also significant predictors of the dependent variable. Legitimacy is the only variable that is more or less psychological. Hence, as Gurr himself says, ". . . the [inferred] psychological level can be ignored with relatively little loss of explanatory power" (Gurr, 1968).

Other quantitative studies of civil violence have, like Gurr and unlike the Feierabends, found system-level factors to be the best predictors of the level of civil violence. Douglas Hibbs, for example, focuses on such factors as ethnic and linguistic fractionalization, size of defense and internal security forces, elite accountability, and social mobilization, while ignoring the micro- or psychological, level component (Hibbs, 1973).

The literature on violence constitutes a demonstration that, with a little creative ingenuity, plausible indicators can be found for the softest of dispositional concepts even using aggregate data whose acessibility permits the inclusion of the widest geographical application of the propositions in question. Of course, the use of aggregate data raises the danger of the ecological fallacy, that unwarranted inference that presumes that what is true for the relationship between aggregates or social groups must necessarily be true for the relationship between individuals within those groups. Thus, although the nations with the higher aggregate index of systemic frustration may tend to have a higher level of violence, it does not necessarily follow that the individuals who contribute to that index are the ones who engage in the violence. However, what is not necessarily true may still be probably true. Once the inexorably tentative nature of social science conclusions is understood, the importance of the ecological fallacy does not loom as large. The deterministic necessity of the conclusions was never claimed by the scholars in question.

Complex theories of human behavior are never established or conclusively rejected by any one study. Each successful effort to render such theories falsifiable in terms of one sample of evidence contributes to the level of confidence or lack thereof that we have in any conjectural explanation. The validity of such indirect indicators is best established by the replication of the findings with a different set of indicators. The aforementioned violence literature by Gurr and the Feierabends remains an example of the possibility of translating soft dispositional concepts into sensory data applicable to a wide variety of cross-national contexts.

CONCLUSIONS: MICRO-LEVEL RESEARCH AND PSYCHOANALYTIC THEORY

Micro-level research is becoming increasingly relevant to political research, and the comparative field is no exception. It has already been suggested that the value-change research of Inglehart and his associates is one of the most significant bodies of research on postindustrial societies. Conceptual borrowing from other fields is not new to comparativists; indiscriminant transplanting of imposing and pretentious but methodologically shaky concepts and theoretic constructs has gotten the field off in nonproductive directions before. The love affair of the infamous Comparative Politics Committee of the S.S.R.C. with Parsonian theory throughout the 60s is a case in point. Comparativists must realize that, although other social sciences may have been involved in the enterprise of attempting to build explanatory theory longer than has most of political science, not all concepts or theoretic structures in such sister disciplines are equally worth co-opting.

Like the field of political science, psychology has long been fundamentally divided between those who collect data by rigorous empirical standards (usually in the study of animal behavior)—data of often trivial or unclear theoretic significance—and those who engage in grand speculative theorizing about the fundamental nature of man and the unconscious drives that motivate him, speculation of imprecise or, at least, unsystematic empirical content. For reasons that are not entirely clear to this author, political scientists have been particularly mesmerized by the offerings of this latter school of psychology. As we have seen in the case of Inglehart, even some of the best comparative research claims a basis in some of the most eggregiously speculative and unscientific personality theorizing.

Whether we are talking about a self-actualizing personality or a sado-masochistic character, we are engaging in the process of attaching labels without independent meaning to refer to the corpus of that which is inexplicable by accepted epistemological standards, much as did the purveyors of magical explanations for otherwise not understood phenomena not that many generations ago. There is an element of tautology in such reasoning. Why did the Germans behave that way? Because of their sado-masochistic personality. How do we know they had a sado-masochistic personality? In part, because of those behaviors.

The metaphysicians who utilize such conceptual tools generally adduce a body of background data, usually from the formative years of the individuals concerned or, in the case of collective or mass psychology, from putatively widely practiced patterns of child rearing, data that can be plausibly argued to account for the personality type in question. These are clearly retrospective explanations, however, in which the supportive data are selected to fit the already-known explicandum. Predictions of future personality traits from child-rearing patterns or other childhood data are exceedingly scarce.

The retrodictive and unscientific nature of psychoanalytic explanations can be seen with reference to the work of one of the canonized gurus of the field of political science in general, a scholar who has too often been cited by the leading writers in the comparative field as one who should be regarded as a guide and as one who points out fruitful directions for research (Eckstein, 1963; Almond and Powell, 1966; Chilcote, 1981; Easton, 1971). Among other things, the work of Harold Lasswell has focused on the psychoanalytic explanations of the quintessential political personality—the power seeker. Lasswell's basic theory might be summarized as follows: Public behavior consists of unconscious private needs displaced onto public objects, and the political orientation of power seeking is the public displacement of a need to compensate for severe ego deprivations in childhood (Laswell, 1948). Overlooking the problems in identifying power-seeking personalities with intersubjectivity and precision, it is, of course, easy to find some event in the lives of such power seekers that can be presented in retrospect as such an ego deprivation. All people have had such setbacks as they were growing up. In order to account for all of those individuals who suffered severe psychological blows without in any sense becoming power seekers, Lasswell offers the corollary that the ego deprivation must not be too severe so as to be overwhelming. How do we know when the severe ego deprivation was overwhelming? When the individual does not become a power seeker. This is of course a classic illustration of the "saving-the-hypothesis" fallacy against which epistemologists have warned us many times. With this corollary, Lasswell's "theory" is consistent with any conceivable set of findings. As such, it does not perform the critical scientific function of distinguishing between that which we should expect to see and that which we should not.

Lasswell's work has been more influential in the American field than in what is commonly identified as comparative politics. James David Barber's much acclaimed book on *Presidential Character* does not cite Lasswell but utilizes the same theoretic construct to "explain" the perceived behavior pattern of selected presidents. Lyndon Johnson, for instance, is described as a rather effeminate, violin-playing little boy who sought to retrieve the macho self image so important to a Texan through his intransigent policy in Vietnam, or as Barber puts it, refighting the battle of the Alamo in the jungles of Southeast Asia (Barber, 1977). Although these analyses seem to focus on American examples, the line between American and comparative politics is, as it should be, increasingly less clear and less rigid, and this technique is also applied to the analysis of political figures of principal interest to comparativists (Langer, 1972; Erikson, 1969; Davies, 1980).[13]

Psychoanalytic theory posits imprecisely defined and empirically ambiguous personality types that can account for patterns of behavior. The evidence for such types is sought in antecedent experience that could, in retrospect, be argued to have created cognitive conflicts and needs that can be resolved by the behavior that constitutes the explicandum. The process of displacing these cognitive needs onto public objects is a process of which the actor in question is unaware; hence, the relationship between the antecedent experiences and the behavior to be explained must be a matter of inference by some third party. Since the subject in question believes that he or she is acting for one set of reasons, and the analyst attributes a totally different interpretation, we have, at a minimum, more than one equally plausible interpretation of what is occurring. Such an explanation is scientifically inadequate.

The impact of the psychoanalytic tradition on micro-level research in comparative politics has been shown to be significant. The obvious cases include Lucien Pye's interpretation of the Burmese nation-building experience in terms of the ideas of Erik Erikson, Eric Fromm's explanation of twentieth century authoritarianism and implicitly Naziism in terms of the sado-masochistic character of the German lower middle class, and Ronald Inglehart's assumptions about the validity of Maslow's hierarchy of human needs. Less obviously, the use of dispositional concepts in micro-level research in general frequently means concepts of such weak empirical content that they become residual categories for that which is otherwise inexplicable.

When concepts lack precise empirical content, they tend to assume an implicit normative component.[14] This is clearly true of many of the dispositional concepts in political science, including most of those discussed in this chapter. It is clear that a "self-actualizing" person is one who possesses traits of which Maslow approves. On the other hand, Fromm is hardly speaking with admiration when he refers to the sado-masochistic character of the German lower middle class. When Barber assesses Lyndon Johnson and Bruce Mazlish assesses Richard Nixon as anal characters, they are not paying these presidents compliments (Mazlish, 1972; Barber, 1977). By the same token, Banfield's characterization of the culture of southern Italy as "amoral familism," another rather judgmental term without precise empirical indicators, also carries with it a pejorative connotation (Banfield, 1967).

It has been a theme of this book that comparative politics became a field in the postwar years that promised much in the way of becoming a truly explanatory discipline. Explanation in the normal scholarly sense of the term, carries certain imperatives. Chief among them, perhaps, is the imperative to produce concepts with both theoretic significance and empirical content. The meaning of empirical is clear and unyielding to anyone with an elementary understanding of scientific epistemology. It does not include selected and illustrative data adduced after the conclusions have been reached. As was shown by some of the violence literature, the task of assigning precise empirical indicators to dispositional concepts is not impossible. It is, however, a standard more researchers will have to accept.

NOTES

1. For a thorough discussion of this variable and of the concept of "political style" in general, see Spiro (1959), chapter 13.

2. See an updated version in Huntington (1968), chapter 2.

3. Dahrendorf (1980) posits Lipset's main criterion of legitimacy as a key determinant of the "governability of democracies."

4. Eckstein (1966, 1969, and 1973) constitutes a body of literature that illustrates an all-too-common practice among big-name scholars in the field of publishing—multiple rewrites of the same basic idea, an idea often of questionable scientific merit in the first place. Obviously, this practice contributes very little, if anything, to the enterprise of building explanatory theory.

5. See Dalton (1988), pp.225ff.

6. Lijphart claims that the selection's criteria are "beyond reproach." He regards the criteria as (1) being democratic and (2) stability. But Almond and Verba are clearly implying something beyond stability; they imply that the civic culture promotes stable and effective, or successful, democracy.

7. *Comparative Political Studies* 17(4, Jan.) 1965 devotes the entire issue to this topic. Dalton, Flanagan, and Beck (1980) is largely devoted to the electoral and party-system implication of the Inglehart thesis. Among countless other articles dealing with this topic are Marsh (1975) and Flanagan (1982).

8. This effort is typified by the functionalist school. Among the best known and impressively written statements of this perspective is Almond (1960). For the sociological source of this metaphysics, see Parsons, Bales, and Shils (1953). For an excellent critique of this school, see Gregor (1968).

9. See Almond (1970) for a collection of this seminal scholar's most famous articles on this topic. Pye (1966) was one of the earliest extended discussions of this theme. It was later more fully developed in Binder (1971) and Grew (1978).

10. Reich's "The Mass Psychology of Fascism" was originally published by The Orgone Institute Press in 1946.

11. Among other personality constructs gleaned from attitudinal syndromes, see Rokeach (1960) and McCloskey (1958).

12. Christie and Jahoda (1954) is a collection devoted to this topic. See especially the article therein by Herman Hyman and Paul Sheatsely, "The Authoritarian Personality: A Methodological Critique."

13. Davies (1980) is one of the most comprehensive and ambitious attempts to apply this perspective to a wide variety of notable political actors.

14. For a more complete development of this theme as applied to the use of the psychoanalytic perspective, see Mayer (1975).

REFERENCES

Adorno, T. W., Else Frenkel Brunswik, Daniel Levinson, and R. Nevitt Sanford. 1950. *The Authoritarian Personality*. New York: W. W. Norton.

Almond, Gabriel. 1960. "Introduction: A Functional Approach to Comparative Politics." In *The Politics of the Developing Areas*, edited by Gabriel Almond and James Coleman. Princeton, NJ: Princeton University Press.

Almond, Gabriel. 1965. "A Developmental Approach to Political Systems." *World Politics* XVII(2, Jan.):183–214.

Almond, Gabriel. 1970. *Political Development*. Boston: Little Brown.

Almond, Gabriel and G. Bingham Powell. 1966. *Comparative Politics: A Developmental Approach*. Boston: Little, Brown.

Almond, Gabriel and G. Bingham Powell. 1978. *Comparative Politics: System, Process and Policy*, 2nd ed. Boston: Little Brown.

Almond, Gabriel and Sidney Verba. 1965. *The Civic Culture*. Boston: Little, Brown.

Almond, Gabriel and Sidney Verba, eds. 1980. *The Civic Culture Revisited*. Boston: Little, Brown.

Apter, David. 1958. "A Comparative Method for the Study of Politics." *American Journal of Sociology* LXIV(4, Nov.):221–237.

Apter, David. 1965. *The Politics of Modernization*. Chicago: University of Chicago Press.

Banfield, Edward. 1967. *The Moral Basis of a Backward Society*. New York: The Free Press.

Barber, James David. 1977. *Presidential Character: Predicting Performance in the White House*, 2nd ed. Englewood Cliffs, NJ: Prentice Hall.

Beer, Samuel. 1962. "The Analysis of Political Systems." In *Patterns of Government*, 2nd ed., edited by Samuel Beer and Adam Ulam. New York: Random House.

Beer, Samuel. 1982. *Britain Against Itself: The Political Contradictions of Collectivism*. New York: W. W. Norton.

Bell, Daniel. 1962. *The End of Ideology*. New York: The Free Press.

Bell, Daniel. 1973. *The Coming of Post-Industrial Society*. New York: Basic Books.

Binder, Leonard. 1971. *Crises and Sequences in Political Development*. Princeton, NJ: Princeton University Press.

Blalock, Hubert M. 1960. *Social Statistics*. New York: McGraw Hill.

Brinton, Crane. 1952. *The Anatomy of Revolution*. Englewood Cliffs, NJ: Prentice Hall.

Brodbeck, May. 1968. "Explanation, Prediction and Imperfect Knowledge." In *Readings in the Philosophy of the Social Sciences*. New York: Macmillan.

Brown, Roger. 1965. *Social Psychology*. New York: The Free Press.

Chilcote, Ronald. 1981. *Theories of Comparative Politics: The Search for a Paradigm*. Boulder, CO: Westview Press.

Christie, Richard and Marie Jahoda. 1954. *Studies in the Scope and Method of the Authoritarian Personality*. Glencoe, IL: The Free Press.

Conradt, David. 1980. "Changing German Political Culture." In *The Civic Culture Revisited*, edited by Gabriel Almond and Sidney Verba. New York: New York University Press.

Cristolph, James. 1965. "Consensus and Cleavage in British Political Ideology." *American Political Science Review* LIX(3, Sept.):629–642.

Crozier, Michael, Samuel Huntington, and Joji Watanuki. 1975. *The Crisis of Democracy*. New York: New York University Press.

Dahrendorf, Ralf. 1980. "Effectiveness and Legitimacy: On the Governability of Democracies." *The Political Quarterly* (Oct.-Dec.):383–410.

Dalton, Russell. 1988. *Citizen Politics in Western Democracies: Public Opinion and Political Parties in the United States, Great Britain, West Germany and France*. Chatham, NJ: Chatham House.

Dalton, Russell, Scott Flanagan, and John Beck. 1984. *Electoral Change in Advanced Industrial Democracies*. Princeton, NJ: Princeton University Press.

Davies, A. D. 1980. *Skills, Outlooks, and Passions: A Psychoanalytic Approach to the Study of Politics*. Cambridge: Cambridge University Press.

Davies, James. 1962. "Toward a Theory of Revolution." *American Sociological Review* XXVII(1, Feb.):5–19.

Deutsch, Karl. 1961. "Social Mobilization and Political Development." *American Political Science Review* LV(3, Sept.):493–514.

DiPalma, Giuseppe. 1970. *Apathy and Participation: Mass Politics in Western Societies*. New York: The Free Press.

Easton, David. 1971. *The Political System: An Inquiry into the State of Political Science*, 2nd ed. New York: Knopf.

Eckstein, Harry. 1963. "A Perspective on Comparative Politics Past and Present." In *Comparative Politics: A Reader*, edited by Harry Eckstein and David Apter. New York: The Free Press.

Eckstein, Harry. 1966. "A Theory of Stable Democracy." In *Division and Cohesion in Democracy: A Study of Norway*. Princeton, NJ: Princeton University Press.

Eckstein, Harry. 1969. "Authority Relations and Governmental Performance: A Theoretical Framework." *Comparative Political Studies* 2(3, Oct.):269–326.

Eckstein, Harry. 1973. "Authority Patterns: A Structural Basis for Political Inquiry." *American Political Science Review* LXVII(4, Dec.):1142–1161.

Elder, Charles and Roger Cobb. 1983. *The Political Uses of Symbols*. New York: Longmans.

Erikson, Erik. 1950. *Childhood and Society*. New York: W. W. Norton.

Erikson, Erik. 1969. *Gandhi's Truth*. New York: W. W. Norton.

Eysenck, H. J. 1954. *The Psychology of Politics*. London: Routledge and Kegan Paul.
Feierabend, Ivo and Rosalind Feierabend. 1966. "Systemic Conditions of Political Violence: An Application of the Frustration-Aggression Theory." *Journal of Conflict Resolution* X(3, Sept.):249–271.
Feieraband, Ivo, Rosalind Feierabend, and Betty A. Nesvold. 1969. "Social Change and Political Violence: Cross-National Patterns." In *Violence in America*, Vol. II, A Report to the National Commission on the Causes and Prevention of Violence, edited by Hugh D. Graham and Ted Gurr. Washington, DC: U.S. Government Printing Office.
Flanagan, Scott, 1982. "Changing Values in Advanced Industrial Societies: The Silent Revolution from the Perspective of Japanese Findings." *Comparative Political Studies* 14(4, Jan.):403–444.
Fromm, Eric. 1965. *Escape From Freedom*. New York: Avon Books.
Gregor, James. 1968. "Political Science and the Uses of Functional Analysis." *American Political Science Review* LXII(2, June):425–439.
Grew, Raymond. 1978. *Crises of Political Development in Europe and the United States*. Princeton, NJ: Princeton University Press.
Gurr, Ted. 1968. "A Causal Model of Civil Strife: A Comparative Analysis Using New Indices." *American Political Science Review* LXII(4, Dec.):1104–1124.
Hibbs, Douglas A. 1973. *Mass Political Violence: A Cross-National Causal Analysis*. New York: John Wiley.
Huntington, Samuel. 1966. "Political Modernization: America vs. Europe." *World Politics* 18(1, April):373–414.
Huntington, Samuel. 1968. *Political Order in Changing Societies*. New Haven, CT: Yale University Press.
Huntington, Samuel. 1984. "Will Countries Become More Democratic?" *Political Science Quarterly* 99(2, Summer):193–218.
Huntington, Samuel. 1987. "The Goals of Development." In *Understanding Political Development*, edited by Myron Weiner and Samuel Huntington. Boston: Little, Brown.
Inglehart, Ronald. 1971. "The Silent Revolution in Europe: Intergenerational Change in Post-Industrial Society." *American Political Science Review* LXV(4, Dec.):991–1017.
Inglehart, Ronald. 1985. "New Perspectives on Value Change." *Comparative Political Studies* 17(4, Jan.):485–535.
Inkles, Alex and Daniel Levinson. 1954. "National Character." In *Handbook on Social Psychology*, edited by Gardner Lindzey. Cambridge, MA: Addison Wesley.
Kahan, George M., Guy Pauker, and Lucien Pye. 1955. "Comparative Politics of Non-Western Countries." *American Political Science Review* IL(4, Dec.):1022–1041.
Kaplan, Abraham. 1964. *The Conduct of Inquiry*. San Francisco: Chandler Publishing Company.
Kautsky, Karl. 1962. "An Essay in the Politics of Development." In *Political Change in Underdeveloped Countries: Nationalism and Communism*. New York: John Wiley.

Kavanaugh, Dennis. 1980. "Political Culture in Great Britain: The Decline of the Civic Culture." In *The Civic Culture Revisited*, edited by Gabriel Almond and Sidney Verba. New York: New York University Press.

Langer, Walter. 1972. *The Mind of Adolph Hitler*. New York: Basic Books.

LaPalombara, Joseph. 1966. "The Decline of Ideology: A Dissent and Interpretation." *American Political Science Review* LX(1, Mar.):5–16.

LaPalombara, Joseph. 1970. "Parsimony and Empiricism in Comparative Politics: An Anti-Scholastic View." In *The Methodology of Comparative Research*, edited by Robert Holt and John Turner. New York: The Free Press.

Lasswell, Harold. 1948. *Power and Personality*. New York: W. W. Norton.

Lerner, Daniel. 1958. *The Passing of Traditional Society*. Glencoe, IL: The Free Press.

Lijphart, Arend. 1980. "The Structure of Inference." In *The Civic Culture Revisited*, edited by Gabriel Almond and Sidney Verba, 37–56. Boston: Little, Brown.

Lipset, Seymour. 1959. "Some Social Requisites of Democracy." *American Political Science Review* LIII(1, Mar.):69–105.

Lipset, Seymour. 1963. "The End of Ideology: A Personal Postscript." In *Political Man*. New York: Doubleday.

Marsh, Alan. 1975. "The Silent Revolution, Value Priorities and the Quality of Life in Britain." *American Political Science Review* LXIX(1, Mar.):21–30.

Maslow, Abraham. 1970. *Motivation and Personality*, 2nd ed. New York: Harper and Row.

Mayer, Lawrence. 1972. *Comparative Political Inquiry*. Homewood, IL: The Dorsey Press.

Mayer, Lawrence. 1975. "Sub-Conscious Dispositions and Political Behavior: Normative or Explanatory." Paper prepared for delivery to the annual meeting of the Western Political Science Association.

Mazlish, Bruce. 1972. *In Search of Nixon: A Psychohistorical Inquiry*. Baltimore, MD: Penguin Books.

McClelland, David. 1961. *The Achieving Society*. New York: D. Van Nostrand.

McCloskey, Herbert. 1958. "Conservatism and Personality." *American Political Science Review* LII(1, Mar.):27–45.

Nie, Norman, G. Bingham Powell, and Kenneth Prewitt. 1969. "Social Structure and Political Participation: Developmental Relationships." *American Political Science Review* LXII(2 and 3, June and Sept.):361–378 and 808–832.

Parsons, Talcott, Robert Bales, and Edward Shils. 1953. *Working Papers in the Theory of Action*. New York: The Free Press.

Przeworski, Adam and Henry Teune. 1970. *The Logic of Comparative Social Inquiry*. New York: John Wiley.

Putnam, Robert. 1971. "Studying Elite Political Culture: The Case of Ideology." *American Political Science Review* LXV(3, Sept.):651–681.

Pye, Lucien. 1958. "The Non-Western Political Process." *Journal of Politics* 20(3, Aug.):468–486.

Pye, Lucien. 1962. *Politics, Personality and Nation Building: Burma's Search for Identity*. New Haven, CT: Yale University Press.

Pye, Lucien. 1966. *Aspects of Political Development*. Boston: Little, Brown.

Reich, Wilhelm. 1970. *The Mass Psychology of Fascism*. New York: Farrar, Strauss.

Rokeach, Milton. 1960. *The Open and Closed Mind*. New York: Basic Books.
Sartre, Jean Paul. 1946. *Anti-Semite and Jew (Reflections sur la question Juive)*, translated by G. J. Becker. New York: Schocken Books.
Schuech, Erwin K. 1969. "Social Context and Individual Behavior." In *Quantitative Ecological Analysis in the Social Sciences*, edited by Mattei Dogan and Stein Rokkan. Cambridge, MA: M.I.T. Press.
Skinner, B. F. 1972. *Beyond Freedom and Dignity*. New York: Knopf.
Smith, Donald. 1970. *Religion and Political Development*. Boston: Little Brown.
Spiro, Herbert. 1959. *Government by Constitution*. New York: Random House.
Verba, Sidney. 1965. "Comparative Political Culture." In *Political Culture and Political Development*, edited by Lucien Pye and Sydney Verba. Princeton, NJ: Princeton University Press.
Verba, Sidney, Norman Nie, and Jae On Kim. 1978. *Participation and Political Equality: A Seven Nation Comparison*. New York: The Free Press.
Wade, Mason. 1956. *The French Canadians*. London: Macmillan.
Wilson, Glenn. 1973. *The Psychology of Conservatism*. New York: Academic Press.

CHAPTER SEVEN

Kremlinology, Autocracies, and Comparative Politics

Comparativists have generally divided the world into three broad classes of political systems: the *first world* nations consisting of relatively industrialized democracies, the *third world* consisting of the less-industrialized nations, and the *relatively industrialized autocracies*, referring today to the Soviet bloc nations. As the earlier chapters have made clear, the behavioral revolution in political science was translated into a sociological orientation in the Parsonian tradition by the Comparative Politics Committee of The Social Science Research Council in the 1960s. Subsequently, the empirical methods of social science increasingly penetrated the comparative analysis of the first and second world nations with varying degrees of effectiveness and sophistication.

This penetration did not occur in the study of industrialized autocracies, however. As Paul Shoup (1968, pp. 185–204) has noted in his review of the study of Communist nations, this field has been "relatively neglected and certainly not enjoying the prestige of work with newly emerging nations or Western political systems." Clearly, scholars engaged in the study of Soviet bloc nations have, for the most part, eschewed the sociological paradigms and the quantitative methods that have increasingly characterized the mainstream of the comparative field. This assessment applies generally to scholars engaged in writing about the broader field of autocracies, including the phenomena of fascism. This eschewal of the methodological mainstream of the field had so dominated the study of autocracies that the enterprise had virtually become a distinct field. With the exception of a relatively few scholars, most notably the ubiquitous and omniscient renaissance man Sam Huntington (1970), scholars who publish in the mainstream of the field eschewed the second world nations as the Kremlinologists eschewed the comparative mainstream.

This epistemological isolation of the study of European Communist nations and, more generally, of the study of industrialized dictatorships seems to be a product of several attributes of this speciality that has tended to render it *sui generis*.

DATA PROBLEMS IN THE ANALYSIS OF AUTOCRACIES

The most obvious of these attributes is the lack of accessibility to the kinds of data that characterize the mainstream studies of the first and third world systems, data that make feasible a reasonable adherence to the epistemological standards of modern, explanatory social sciences.

Since these countries, by definition, do not operate competitive electoral systems, the voting and electoral behavior data that provide the basis of the kind of study that dominates empirical comparative analysis simply do not exist. Furthermore, the kinds of participation that are measured in their plethora of studies on that topic in Western domocracies are either suppressed—as in the case of protest activity, attending meetings, or organizing interests independently of the political system—or are meaningless—as in the case of voting behavior where no effective electoral choice is available. Therefore, this problem that cannot be remedied by overcoming political obstacles and obtaining access to data that does exist. The problem is systemic in that the data do not exist, and, moreover, they cannot meaningfully exist within the context of that type of system.

Many of the data used in empirical research on Western nations are based on the presumed legitimacy of subnational interests arising out of the stratification system of that society. Class-based cleavages, religious cleavages, ethnic cleavages, and cleavages based on various issues or causes generate attitudes about political issues and demands placed upon the political system. However, the difficult concept of *totalitarianism* aside for the present, industrialized autocracies generally aspire to be what Kornhouser called "mass societies," societies in which associational life that is independent of the remote political system is not accorded legitimacy (Kornhauser, 1959). Such societies adhere to the fiction that all citizens are so thoroughly assimilated into the mass movement that comprises the political system that the concept of private interests and attitudes independent of the movement or political system becomes unthinkable. Since it is not recognized that attitudes on political issues could exist independently of the official ideology or party line, meaningful attitudinal data cannot be obtained in such systems. We are dealing here with closed societies, societies that, by definition, do not accept the legitimacy of different perspectives on social, political, religious, or normative questions on which reasonable men inevitably disagree.

Some speculative work has been attempted on the impact of official ideologies on elite attitudes in the Soviet Union (Kelly and Flcron, 1971). Such work has, however, degenerated into speculative applications of metaphysical theories of motivation out of the psychoanalytic tradition. Lacking any data about the beliefs and values of the elites in question or any norms of correspondence between the concepts in question and the sensory world, the authors of such work have resorted to citing the works of psychoanalytic metaphysicians such as Maslow and Lasswell, the explanatory weakness of which was thoroughly explored in the preceding chapter.

Of course, beyond the systemic obstacles to attitudinal and behavioral data discussed above, it must be remembered that, in closed societies, the elites place political and administrative obstacles to the attempt to gather data that may conflict with the official image of a homogenous mass populace united in support of the system and the official ideology or policies. Such systems are not only not supportive of the efforts of social scientists to conduct sample surveys of their populations but do not even tolerate such projects on politically or socially sensitive issues. Paul Shoup suggests that surveys of refugees or expatriates from such nations go a long way toward remedying the unavailability of such data from the nations themselves (Shoup, 1968). Clearly, however, such refugee samples are likely to be highly unrepresentative of the populations to which they putatively refer. Alex Inkles and Raymond Bauer (1959) clearly imply such an inference by the title of their report of the best of these surveys, *The Soviet Citizen: Daily Life in a Totalitarian Society.*[1]

Survey data, of course, do not exhaust the type of empirical data utilized in comparative research. As the preceding chapters have made clear, some of the best cross-national research has been based upon aggregate data. Much of these data emanate from or are based upon government-supplied statistics and documents. One can rely on the accuracy and truthfulness of such data to an extent that varies from one government to another but even more so from one type of government to another. The data emanating from Western industrial democracies are, by and large, accurate, although not always as complete as one would like them to be. The data emanating from some of the less-developed systems, as was observed in Chapter 3, are less reliable. Lacking sophisticated data-gathering techniques, and sensitive about what the actual data might reveal about the capacities of their country relative to the both admired and resented West, officials in less-developed systems sometimes just invent the data that would actually be painstakingly gathered in the West.

The possibility of outright prevarication with regard to government-supplied data may be as great or even greater in the case of the industrialized autocracies. While it may be too much to assert, as do some of the most passionate critics of Soviet bloc systems, that truth to such systems is whatever serves that which the leaders perceive as the national interest, it would be difficult to deny that these systems have been occasionally caught stretching or modifying what we in the West know to be true. For example, the massive failures of agricultural production in the Soviet Union, failures that our own intelligence has reported have led to widespread hunger, have been routinely denied by Soviet authorities. The point is that one cannot use aggregate data supplied by the governments of industrialized autocracies (which, for the present, mean Soviet bloc nations) with some confidence that they are more or less accurate and true, as one would use similar data from Western systems.

This problem with aggregate data varies in degree from one Soviet bloc nation to another. In some of these systems—Yugoslavia, for instance—data are "relatively plentiful and reliable" (Shoup, 1968). This is more likely to be true, of course, on data that are not politically sensitive, data that are, unfortunately, less likely to be salient to the concerns of most political scientists.

In general, however, data from government documents and archives in Soviet bloc nations have been reserved for scholars from those systems and have been simply unavailable to investigators from the West (Shoup, 1968).[2] Access to data that are not politically sensitive has been opening up more in recent years. In fact, Western scholars have not taken advantage of the range of data that are available.

Since we are dealing with sociopolitical systems that are so fundamentally different from Western systems, and since these systems present unique impediments to the gathering of data, the data that are gathered from such systems may present grave questions of *equivalence,* in the sense that term is used by Przeworski and Teune (1970, pp. 106ff.), or of comparability. Even within the Communist bloc, similarly named political structures may not perform the same functions (Walsh, 1969). Problems of comparability are greatly exacerbated between Communist and non-Communist systems. Concepts such as representation or the structure of accountability take on a very different meaning outside the West, and measures of participation would not have the same significance in Communist bloc nations, where participation is co-opted by and managed under the aegis of the state or party, compared to the significance of such measures in the West. The problems of comparability or equivalence of data are, of course, related to the problems of conceptualization that are discussed more fully below.

Some scholars engaged in Communist studies point to the lack of a unifying conceptual framework to give their data comparability of equivalence. Functionalism or systems analysis are among those frameworks named as having that role in the rest of comparative politics. Such scholars misread the influence or importance of such frameworks in the rest of comparative politics, however. The analyses of the politics of the first world and the third world are as bereft of a single unifying paradigm as is the field of Communist studies. The distorted importance attributed by Kremlinologists to these neo-scholastic conceptual frameworks suggests that such scholars may have an imperfect comprehension of what the scientific study of political phenomena entails.

At this writing, Soviet politics is undergoing a transformation the depths and significance of which is under intense debate by informed observers of that system. Whether the the so-called "glasnost," or new openness, of the sociopolitical system under General Secretary Gorbachev signifies fundamental changes in the system is a matter on which reasonable and informed observors disagree; hence, it is too early to predict the extent to which the foregoing problems in the collection and analysis of data will be ameliorated by systemic changes in the Soviet Union. Given the resistance of such systems to fundamental change from within, in our limited experience with such systems, optimism on this score must remain guarded. But one can always hope.

CONCEPTUALIZATION: TOTALITARIANISM

With the rise and fall of the Third Reich in the 1940s and the subsequent revelations about the nature of Stalinism in the Soviet Union, the effort to comprehend these phenomena produced a plethora of literature dealing with the newly popular concept of totalitarianism from the late 1940s through the 1950s. The popularity of the concept both within and outside academia was accompanied by a lack of precision as to its exact empirical content. The scholars concerned with the study of Communist systems or engaged in a retrospective analysis of the Third Reich all freely used the term *totalitarianism*, but they were unable to reach a consensus as to whether a given system at a given point in time was or was not totalitarian. For example, most Kremlinologists regarded the Soviet Union during the Stalin years as a totalitarian state, but many have since concluded that the Soviet Union no longer fits that category. However, not only have they failed to reach a consensus on this point, but even those who agree that the Soviet Union has evolved away from totalitarianism are not clear as to when this transformation occurred. Thus, Seweryn Bialer in his widely discussed book, *The Soviet Paradox: External Expansion, Internal Decline*, eschews the term *totalitarian* in favor of the term *authoritarian* and suggests that the Soviet system is more predictable and rational than it once was, attributes that are inconsistent with totalitarian dictatorship, as it is commonly conceptualized (Bialer, 1987). Some scholars suggest that the technological and structural imperatives of a modern sociopolitical system are the major determinants of the actual nature of that system, irrespective of ideological or constitutional considerations. This so-called "convergence theory" becomes almost a technological determinism in arguing that the bureaucratizing (or, in the Weberian sense, rationalizing) of the political process is an inexorable concomitant of mature industrial societies.[3] Hence, according to this view, the Soviet Union is increasingly being dominated by a massive bureaucracy, a structure that is by definition nontotalitarian or even dictatorial. On the other hand, there are a few respected academic but passionate critics of the Soviet system, such as Nick Eberstadt, who argue that because of the system's attempt to totally politicize its communication system in order to control the thought of its own citizens and its interference in fundamental areas that we in the

West regard as private, for example religious practice, the system should still be regarded as totalitarian (Eberstadt, 1987). Eberstadt is apparently concerned that the concept of ordinary dictatorship or authoritarianism does not distinguish a system such as the Soviet Union from most of the remainder of the world's autocracies. Despite obvious significant changes since the Stalinist period, the Soviet Union is still different from these autocracies in the extent to which it penetrates the private lives of its citizens and, more importantly for political conservatives like Eberstadt, conducts an aggressive foreign policy relative to the West.

The disagreement among scholars over the question of whether the Soviet Union is still a totalitarian system is not over facts but over the interpretation of those facts, an argument that emanates from the imprecise empirical content of the concept in question. Totalitarianism has been conceptualized by Friedrich and Brzezinski (1956), Franz Neumann (1957), Hannah Arendt (1951 and 1973), and others with widely accepted common themes: the total subsumption of the individual personality in the idea of the state; the dominance of a single party that almost becomes coterminous with the state; an official, comprehensive, consumatory ideology; a monopoly of the use of force; and the use of terror to control dissent.

This conceptualization presents several difficulties for empirical analysis. First, these attributes are judgmental in nature; there are no accepted indicators to determine intersubjectively the extent to which such attributes are deemed to be present. Reasonable men equally aware of the relevant facts may still disagree on the extent to which individual personalities are subsumed in a given system or the extent to which terror is practiced in a system. The controversy over the meaningfulness of Gorbechev's putative "glasnost," or openness reforms, in the Soviet Union in 1987 illustrates the judgmental nature of these kinds of attributes.

Second, these attributes are, for the most part, matters of degree, and there are no theoretically defensible threshold levels of the extent to which such attributes must be present. It may be widely agreed, for instance, that some terror, in the sense of unpredictable punishment that is not meted out in accordance with preordained rules, is still practiced in the Soviet Union, but much less than was practiced in the Stalinist era. The unanswerable question then becomes, how much terror must be practiced by a state in order to fit the category of totalitarian? Clearly, the Soviet Union still invades areas that would normally be considered private and outside the bounds of permissable state activity by those of us in the West; yet, here again the state is considerably less intrusive in this way than it once was. How much invasion of the private sphere is required to qualify as a totalitarian state?

Third, the concept of totalitarianism is comprised of a number of distinct attributes. Yet, there is no standard for determining how many of these attributes must be present, not to mention to what degree, to qualify as a totalitarian state. Eberstadt is able to point to the continued practice of some of these attributes while not contesting that others no longer describe Soviet reality and, on that basis, suggest the system should still be regarded as totalitarian.

Given this disagreement as to precisely what qualifies a state to be included in the category totalitarian, the concept is seriously weakened as a tool for building explanatory theory. The insistence of people like Eberstadt on so labeling the Soviet Union is grounded in a normative purpose, the distinction of the Soviet Union as an evil and threatening system from other ordinary autocracies. The term clearly has pejorative connotations, especially since the Western world was mobilized to fight Nazi Germany, a system then perceived as the world's first great totalitarian dictatorship and one of the world's greatest evils. To so label any subsequent system is to implicitly attach to that system the same connotation of a threat to the basic values of Western civilization. The label *totalitarian* has thus become more of a normative judgment about the values that define that system's sense of national purpose than a description of the structure and processes by which the system operates.

The debate surrounding Karl Popper's labeling of Plato's *Re-*

public as a totalitarian society reflects this confusion (Popper, 1966). If one takes Nazi Germany (as it aspired to be) as the prototype of totalitarian society, one may note some similarities and some clear differences between it and the Republic. Popper never attempts to explicate the precise meaning of the concept of a totalitarian system; hence, one is never offered the criteria for accepting or rejecting Popper's categorization. His generally scathing critique of Plato's values, his ontology, and his methodology support the suspicion that Popper employs the term *totalitarianism* as a normative label rather than as an empirical description.

Fascism is a term that has been similarly used in a way that confuses empirical content and normative judgment. Although Ernst Nolte attempted a comprehensive definition of the term (Nolte, 1966), and although scholars such as James Gregor have argued that Mussolini's Italy constituted the prototype of the phenomenon (Gregor, 1974), the field is far from a consensus on the precise empirical content of the term. A wide range of systems have been so labeled by their critics, systems that have little in common with either Mussolini's Italy or Nazi Germany. Since the world, with the benefit of hindsight, has been able to reach a consensus that the defeated Axis powers constituted an immoral force, fascism (often with its convenient conceptual expanding prefix, "neo") has become a convenient label for whatever political force the labeler happens to oppose. A nation today never proudly refers to itself as fascist. It is clear that the term has acquired a negative moral content; it is not clear that the term has any clear empirical content.

The disagreements in the literature as to whether given regimes are fascist or not are the first clue about the imprecise empirical content of the term. While Gregor tends to regard fascism as virtually coterminous with its paradigmatic case of Mussolini's Italy, he tends to reject the notion of fascism as a generic term with a clearly defined reference class that can include National Socialism (Gregor, 1974). Yet others, such as Henry Ashby Turner, were able to link Italian Fascism, German National Socialism, and even the Soviet Union under Stalin as examples of a generic phenomenon that, with their growing dissatisfaction with the concept of totalitarianism, they chose to label as fascism (with a small case f) to cover what they regarded as the common properties of such systems (Turner, 1972). Even Turner's attempt to link such systems and thereby join the scholars that routinely refer to Nazi Germany as a quintessentially fascist system does not confront the question of whether to include such partially industrialized systems as Peronist Argentina and Franco's Spain.

The suggested attributes of the term create more confusion than clarity about the empirical reference points of the category. For example, one such distinguishing attribute of the term *fascism* is adherence to the leadership principle. Tucker (1961, pp. 281–289), for one, refers to fascism as an instrument "for acting out the [psychopathological] needs of the paranoid leader personality." Gregor observes that such a conceptualization raises the question of whether Castroism and Maoism, both clearly focused in the psychological drives of their particular leaders, are also fascist regimes (Gregor, 1974). If so, is fascism not distinguished from Communism, or is Communist dictatorship a subspecies of the broader category of fascism?

Fascism as a generic phenomenon has been characterized by a number of scholars as the expression of the mobilization of the atomized and amorphous masses. This characterization reflects a scholarly tradition on the dangers of excessive populism that goes back to the turn of the century with the writings of such scholars as Gustave Le Bon (1960). Populism itself is a political perspective that can be traced back to the work of Rousseau and his *le volonté general*, a perspective that seems to reflect the following properties or ideas: a claim by some leader or elite to speak for the unarticulated demands and feelings of the masses (or, in Nazi terminology, the *volk*); a claimed faith in the superior "common sense" wisdom of the masses, a claim that frequently degenerates into anti-intellectualism and that elicits perceptions of moral superiority for the masses; a claim or perception that there are knowable mass or communal interests distinguishable from particular or "special" interests and, hence, an innate hostility to pluralism; a claim or perception that those mass or communal interests are opposed by a conspiratorial elite; and a faith that simple solutions exist for the complex problems of the modern world, a faith that frequently is expressed by a yearning for a simpler but largely mythologized past.

This tradition of conceptualizing fascism as a movement emanating from the atomization of the masses varies from those scholars such as Ortega y Gasset (1932), who regard fascism as the very expression of the spirit of the masses in the tradition of Rousseau's leader embodying the general will, to others such as William Kornhouser who regard the masses as an instrument to be mobilized for the purposes of an elite. Hannah Arendt's work on totalitarianism identifies this phenomenon as resting on the atomized masses and what she calls "the mob," the residue of the breakdown of all classes (Arendt, 1951 and 1973). Arendt is totally unconcerned with empirical data of any systematic sort and, in this offhand journalistic style, eschews any attempt to precisely define the concept that is the central theme of her work. However, it is clear from her historical analysis and her focus on anti-Semitism that her work grew out of the attempt to explain the rise of National Socialism rather than generic fascism, not to mention generic totalitarianism.

While satisfying common sense impressions, the work in this tradition of explaining either fascism, Naziism, or totalitarianism as emanating from mass man violates most of the criteria of social science epistemology. The failure to clearly identify the phenomenon these scholars are purporting to explain has already been mentioned. The confusion between authoritarianism of the left and right discussed in the consideration of psychological explanations of these phenomena in the preceding chapter applies as well to the work on such phenomena as a product of the rise of the masses. Arendt is talking about totalitarianism while clearly discussing the historical context and attributes unique to National Socialism. Furthermore, in identifying mass man as the source of such movements, whatever they may be, these scholars are attributing an unspecified but apparently substantial and diverse array of psychological characteristics to whole populations without any hard evidence. William Kornhouser's work on mass society is a partial exception, in that he produces some evidence to show that nonjoiners—a convenient way of indicating atomized individuals—are more likely to have certain attitudes supportive of extremist movements (Kornhauser, 1959). Clearly, even if such atomized individuals could be effectively identified, individuals in this state of non-belonging are likely to have a variety of attitudinal reactions. Even though it is a positive step, the fragmentary evidence of Kornhouser does not provide an adequate basis for the sweeping assertions by scholars such as Arendt about the masses, the bourgeoisie, or the petite bourgeoisie.

The confusion about the phenomena of fascism and National Socialism is further illustrated by the characterization of fascism by some as a revolt against modernity and by others as a developmental dictatorship. Henry Turner and George Mosse, for example, both argue that the essence of National Socialist ideology was the glorification and preservation of *volkishness*, the folk culture (Turner, 1972; Mosse, 1981). Turner also points out the pervasive Nazi view of utopia as a mythical, tribal, and Wagnerian past and argues that their expansionist policies were primarily to acquire sufficient arable land to preserve peasant values and fight urban modernity. Others have argued that these apparent attributes of Naziism reflected not so much a revolt against modernity *per se* as a reflection of the fact that German nationalism was realized by a struggle against the West as epitomized by France and is, therefore, essentially anti-Western and antimodern only as the West connotes modernity.

Yet, others have conceptualized fascism as one subset of a broader category of what Tucker called "movement regimes" or what Gregor (1979, pp. 303ff.) calls "developmental dictatorships." The conceptualization of modernization or political development in terms of social mobilization has a well-established history in political science. *Social mobilization* refers to the process of inducting the population into the sociopolitical process and gathering the resources of society for the purposes of the sociopolitical system. Since development involves increasing the capacities of the system, including the advancement of technology and the building of industry, the imperatives of development include the diversion of resources from consumption to capital accumulation. Long-term gain necessitates short-term sacrifice. Yet, most populations appear to be more present-oriented than future-oriented, and market forces do not produce the requisite policies of austerity as individual and group interest prevail over community or systemic interests. Hence, as David Apter pointed out years ago, the early stages of modernization require an authoritarian system with the capacity to command the co-optation and allocation of the resources of society for long-range goals. In fact he called the paradigm of a developing system in the early stage of the modernization process a mobilization system (Apter, 1965). Therefore, dictatorships may be viewed as a response to the imperatives of the modernization process rather than a revolt against modernization.

This view of both fascist and Communist dictatorships as "developmental dictatorships" undercuts a promising conceptual distinction between the two major prototypes of totalitarian dictatorship, the fact that the official ideology of the Soviet Union posits a utopia of the future, based upon a basically optimistic view of the nature of man and an egalitarian ideological baggage, while National Socialism posits a utopia of the mystical, Wagnerian past, based upon a pessimistic view of the nature of man and a belief in the inherent inferiority of designated groups of people. While, as Friedrich and Brzezinski have shown, National Socialist Germany and the Soviet Union under Stalin shared a number of identifiable (if not measurable) attributes, the obliteration of distinctions between the two types of systems offends one's sense that the two phenomena are somehow different from one another. While these systems share some institutions and processes that allow one to speak of them both as cases of the same subset, totalitarian dictatorship, they do not share the same fundamental values.

This distinction between the sharing of institutions and process while diverging sharply on values underlies the controversy over *convergence theory*, the idea that mature industrial societies are becoming more similar as a function of economic and technological determinism, despite the constitutional and normative differences among them. It can be shown that postindustrial societies do, in fact, share similarities in institutions and processes, such as the dominating political role of the technocracy and, consequently, of the higher civil service and the growth, either formally or informally, of what are called neo-corporatist processes for the formulation of public policy. Such postindustrial societies have been shown to have very similar rates of social mobility, apparently as a function of the imperatives of the state of technology, despite great differences in the amount of egalitarian ideological baggage they may carry (Bendix and Lipset, 1959). Yet, those differences in ideological baggage do, in fact, exist and, despite similarities in the *processes and institutions* with which decisions are reached, these differences in values and sense of national purpose result in great differences in the *substantive content* of public policy.

The weakness of the distinctions in the literature between totalitarianism, generic fascism, National Socialism or Naziism, and other mobilizing dictatorships is illustrated in the work of Hannah Arendt, Freidrich and Brzezinski, and others who have attempted to stipulate the defining attributes of these phenomena. As noted above, Arendt gave considerable attention to the mass base of legitimacy for the category of systems under consideration, an attribute that not only applies to Nazi Germany and Stalin's Soviet Union but, to a greater or lesser extent, to a number of third world mobilizing dictatorships, such as Khomeini's Iran. It is usually argued that such nations cannot usefully be called totalitarian because they have been unsuccessful in co-opting all the elements of the society they ostensibly rule; they have not completely solved what Pye calls "the crisis of penetration." Yet, this crisis was incompletely solved in the two paradigmatic totalitarian powers. The imposition of the power of the state and the official values over the daily lives of residents was far less oppressive in, say, Siberia than it was in Russia. The mobilization of all aspects of society and the obliteration of the distinction between the public and private sector, a putative defining attribute of totalitarian dictatorship, was not only incompletely achieved by the Soviet and Nazi regimes but could also apply to a considerable extent to Iran's "Islamic Republic," where, at least in the major cities, the state more or less successfully controls what we in the West would consider completely private behaviors, such as the mode of dress and all aspects of moral behavior. Young people have been summarily executed for kissing in public. It thus appears that the distinction between a third world state like Iran and the two ostensibly totalitarian states is the degree of penetration of society achieved by the political system.

Arendt and others also focus on the concept of *terror* as a distinguishing attribute of totalitarian systems. *Terror* refers to the unpredictable or nonsystematic allocation of severe punishment by the state. Terror does not apply to punishment for "political crimes," however we may abhor the practice of meting out such punishment. Thus, the punishment of certain of the Soviet dissidents in recent years was not terror; one has a fair idea of the limits of permissable antistate activity in the present day Soviet Union. Yet, it is clear that under Stalin and under Hitler, countless people were seized, tortured, killed, or they simply disappeared without having engaged in any activity to which such punishment was probably attached. By not knowing what the limits of antistate activity might be, one avoids doing anything that might possibly anger the authorities; hence, terror is calculated to produce a more obsequiously compliant population than would a state that criminalizes political dissent in a predictable way under some form of due process of law.

Terror, thus defined, was clearly practiced in our two paradigmatic totalitarian dictatorships; however, degrees of terror were also seen in the Republic of Uganda under Idi Amin, in Cambodia under Pol Pot, and in China during the phase of the Great Cultural Revolution. Yet, one would probably not want to extend the concept of totalitarianism to such third world systems. The idea of degrees of terror is important. For example, it appears that the arrest and detention of a number of the perceived enemies of the regime, or of blacks and bystanders in the Union of South Africa, may be classified by some as instances of terror as defined above; yet, the degree and pervasiveness of the practice of terror in such a regime does not approach that which permeated the regimes of Hitler and Stalin. The point is that, without specific indicators for terror, reasonable men with equal access to the available evidence will still disagree as to whether and to what extent terror was present in any given context. Furthermore, even if agreement could be reached on the presence or extent of terror, there are no criteria for the determination of how much terror must be present to qualify the nation as totalitarian.

Concepts like totalitarianism, fascism, or National Socialism refer to a very few cases, far too few to afford enough data to form the basis of a conceptualization in which we have much confidence. Totalitarianism refers to perhaps two cases, neither of which perfectly fit the ideal type or model. It is not possible to confidently discern patterns of structures and processes on two cases with very much confidence; hence, any statement of the attributes shared by totalitarian systems must necessarily be very tentative at this point and any closure of the concept highly premature. Similarly, we know very little about the practice of some of the attributes of the totalitarian or fascist models. For example, we are not certain of the extent to which terror is actually practiced in a number of systems in which access to information by Western scholars is highly circumscribed.

Totalitarianism and fascism are complex models that, given the number of attributes they contain, very imperfectly describe any salient cases in the sensory world and refer to too few cases to be useful in the process of constructing explanatory theory. It may be more useful to attempt to develop indicators for some of the attributes or sub-concepts that these complex models contain. For example, it might be useful to develop cross-national propositions about the process of terror as either a dependent or independent variable, without worrying whether the states in question are actually totalitarian. Similarly, it may be more useful to know what the two otherwise quite different dictatorships, the Third Reich and Mussolini's Italy, have in common than trying to decide whether these systems can both be fitted under the same generic label of fascism.

The distinction between totalitarianism of the left and of the right has been observed by many critics to threaten the integrity of the concept of totalitarianism. Such critics suggest that this distinction is so fundamental that it is not meaningful to discuss totalitarianism as referring to a category of states sharing significant common attributes. Clearly, important distinctions can be made between Stalinism and the Third Reich. For example, fascism is ultra-nationalistic, while Marxism is, in theory, an international ideology that looks to the withering away of the state. However, the protection and enhancement of the state and its interests was as much a goal of Stalinism as in the Third Reich, since Stalin's revision of Marxism introduced the idea of "capitalistic encirclement" as a justification for reversing the antinationalistic imperatives of classical Marxism. Racism in general and anti-Semitism in particular was a key element in Nazi ideology, while Marxism preached the brotherhood of an entire economic class that presumably would ultimately comprise the great bulk of mankind. In fact, Jews were prominent among the early Bolsheviks. However, even this distinction is less compelling in practice as anti-Semitism becomes increasingly identified with the revolutionary left and the Soviet Union becomes one of the world's most vociferously anti-Semitic states.

The point is that, on a theoretic level, fascism, with its appeal to romantic emotionalism, its anti-modern imperatives, and its glorification of the folk and the nation is a very different phenomenon than Bolshevism, with its appeal to the economic interests of the industrial working class throughout the industrialized world and its vision of a future utopia based on a cooperative socioeconomic order. Yet, the fact remains that the Nazi and Bolshevik dictatorships did apparently share significant attributes. The concepts of totalitarianism and fascism have proven less than ideal for the delineation of such shared attributes while, at the same time, taking account of the significant distinctions. For this reason, scholars concerned with industrialized dictatorships have devoted less attention in recent years to the validity of the broad concepts of fascism and totalitarianism and more to an attempt to delineate the pattern and trends in existing dictatorships, especially to the question of whether the Soviet Union has been evolving into a more "open" system.

THE ANALYSIS OF TRENDS IN THE SOVIET DICTATORSHIP: GLASNOST AND PERESTROIKA

One of the dominant themes among Kremlinologists is the delineation of the evolution of the nature of that system from one to which the label *totalitarian* was frequently applied to one in which the role of the nominal elites has significantly changed and to which few scholars would apply that label today. Many of the most distinguished Kremlinologists had, until recently, perceived an evolution of the system from a dictatorship in which one or, at best, a very few individuals exercised virtually unchecked control over the system to a system governed by a massive and essentially immobilized bureaucracy (as bureaucracies are wont to be). In one of the earlier and most cited statements of this perspective, Milovan Djilas spoke of rule by *The New Class*, a class whose privileges and rewards emanate from the administrative role they occupy (Djilas, 1957) rather than as the result of some power struggle characteristic of the transition of power in dictatorships. Such a bureaucracy, an organization that, by definition, operates by a comprehensive and frequently onerous set of impersonal rules, is the very antithesis of totalitarian dictatorship, a system that is, by definition, unrestrained by any set of rules or other external check. Such a system would more closely resemble the concept of "bureaucratic authoritarianism" conceptualized by Guillermo O'Donnell with respect to Brazil and Argentina, a concept discussed in Chapter 3.

The Soviet state, these scholars report, has become a very conservative one, very fearful of innovation. Robert Byrnes identifies three major categories of impediments to change in the Soviet system: the primacy granted to the military and foreign policy as the basis of the legitimacy of the system, the stultifying impact of ideology on Soviet leaders, and the complexity of growing domestic problems, such that vigorous action to ameliorate one problem would have serious dysfunctional impacts on other problems (Byrnes, 1984). This line of analysis would account for the difficulty apparently faced by Soviet party chairman Gorbachev in his effort to institute significant and, perhaps, fundamental reforms of the Soviet system. In this analysis, Byrnes does not emphasize the inherently stultifying impact of overbearing bureaucratization itself, an impact that was discussed above with reference to the trends in postindustrial democracies. The dysfunctional effect of the politicization of the bureaucracy on creativity and innovation that Michel Crozier identified with respect to France would clearly apply to a state that scholars have suggested has developed the most extensive and overbearing bureaucratic apparatus in the world.

Yet, lacking hard data and clear criteria for measurement, this conclusion about the growing weight of the bureaucratic sector in the Soviet system must remain a judgmental one about which reasonable observers can and do disagree. That is why eminent Kremlinologists disagree as to whether the series of reforms that Gorbachev is attempting to impose upon the Soviet system at this writing, reforms popularly referred to as *glasnost* (openness or, more specifically, public debate) and *perestroika* (restructuring), amount to fundamental changes in the essence of the system or amount to what one observer likened to "a bandaid on a tumor" (Orlov, 1968).

There is one school of thought that the Soviet system has evolved toward one that is sometimes called "institutionalized pluralism" (Hough, 1972). In this model of the Soviet system, particular interests may be expressed within the confines and structure of the established institutions of the system, especially the vanguard party, as long as the legitimacy of such institutions is not challenged. The party itself acts as a broker of interests rather than its traditional role as the formulator and initiator of policy and controller of such interests. Jerry Hough, one of the proponents of this view, admits that other important scholars do not accept this conclusion that the directing role of the party has diminished and that there is a freer flow of information from society to the Soviet elite. While he correctly points out that the evidence for the continuing intolerance of the Soviet elite is inconclusive, the evidence of Hough's view is just as tentative, if not more so (Hough, 1972). Hough bases his conclusion that the Soviet elite is less rigid and more open to input from society on such things as the reduced average age of the elite, greater turnover rates among the elite, and social policies that "amount to a veritable war on poverty" and are leading toward a reduction of socioeconomic inequality (Hough, 1972). Aside from the massive and, perhaps, questionable inference involved in moving from such data to Hough's conclusion of a trend toward openness, other scholars dispute the data themselves.[4]

Hough's thesis reflects the broader debate, current at this writing, about the significance of *glasnost* and *perestroika* for the nature of the Soviet system. Hard data is absent, and a professional, academic literature on this question has yet to emerge. Rather, the debate is being engaged in the popular media and in serious but nonacademic journals of opinion (Orlov, 1988; Satter, 1988). On the question of whether these apparent efforts at reform, led by Secretary Gorbachev and resisted by numerous old-line Bosheviks like Yegor Ligachev as well as various *apparatchiki*, can or will transform the essence of the Soviet system, conclusions vary with the political orientation of the analyst. Conservatives, either among academic Kremlinologists, such as Robert Tucker of Princeton, or among emigrés from the Soviet bloc, such as Yuri Orlov, argue that the party can never permit these changes to threaten its fundamental control of the Soviet economy or its political processes, and, hence, these changes are unlikely to affect the essential nature of the system (Orlov, 1988). Meanwhile, equally prestigious but generally more liberal scholars, such as Steven Cohen of Princeton, argue that the changes that have occurred are unprecedented and, hence, constitute an essential transformation of that system. The open criticisms of past and present policies of the regime, the public rivalry between Gorbachev and Ligachev at the June 1988 All Party Conference, and the promised establishment of an institutionalized or permanently sitting representative assembly certainly constitute a break with the experience of the Soviet past as does a measured degree of autonomy for the managers of many of the system's major productive forces with instructions to show a profit within the confines of prices set by the *apparat*.

It appears that those who are disposed to regard the Soviet Union as a menacing and inherently expansionist power can reasonably interpret the available data to support their conclusion that the tightly controlled and threatening essence of the Soviet system is unreformed and perhaps unreformable, while those who are disposed to regard the nature of the Soviet regime as becoming considerably more "open," less expansionist, and less menacing can so interpret the data to support that conclusion as well. This debate is not a matter of identifying the facts as much as how one interprets the facts, facts of which Liberals and Conservatives are both aware. These scholars disagree as to whether the system is moving in a more democratic direction. If one conceptualizes democracy in terms of the degree to which dissent in general is permitted, then one must agree that the Soviet Union is relatively more tolerant of such dissent than in the past. However, if one conceptualizes democracy in terms of the Schumpterian definition discussed in Chapter 4 of the legitimacy of viable competition at more or less regular elections, one must agree that the system is not really closer to meeting this criterion. Here is another instance in which the soft and inevitably normative content of so many of our major concepts prevents a tentative consensus on the conclusion to an important question.

Another fact with ambiguous meaning and implication is that it is a matter of record that the Soviet elite did promise the establishment of a representative body with a fixed term of office, an institution that bears a structural resemblance to legislatures in the West. Yet it is unclear as to what functions this institution will perform and whether it will exert any decision-making power independent from the party elite.

Undoubtedly, over time, the precise role of such new or restructured institutions that emerge from whatever impact the concept of *perestroika* has on the system will become increasingly clear. The significance of such roles or functions will depend, however, on the meaning of some of the most often used and softest of concepts in the field. Much greater precision than is foreseeable would be required for concepts such as democratization before one could intersubjectively conclude whether any given case was moving toward either greater democratization or a more open society.

These concerns further emphasize the difficulty in obtaining data from the Soviet Union that constitute reliable and valid indicators of the concepts in which we are interested and the consequent judgmental and tentative nature of the conclusions we reach about trends in that system. Modern Kremlinologists, striving to bring their specialty into the mainstream of political science and unable to command the access to data sources enjoyed by their colleagues in most of the rest of the field, often resort to highly indirect indicators that demand a substantial inference from the observation of the sensory data to the conclusion that the concept is present.

For example, Milton Lodge conducted a study of the perceptions of Soviet elites on the effectiveness of their input into the policy process versus that of the party (Lodge, 1968). The results from such a study would reveal much about the extent to which that system has, in fact, evolved from the totalitarian dictatorship model toward one approaching "institutional pluralism." After all, the former model presumes that the policy is directed or dictated by the party elites and that what Lodge calls "specialist elites," such as economic, military, or legal elites, merely implement what has been decided by the party. Lodge claims to have found "evidence" of increasing specialist participation in the policy-making process in the post-Stalinist era. That evidence consisted of the content analysis of the lead articles in a selected group of published specialist journals for imagery of how much the party shapes policy decisions and how much the party should shape those decisions. Such inferences drawn from content analysis are perfectly acceptable from the standards of social science epistemology, as long as the methods are clearly stipulated and the inferential basis of the conclusions is clearly recognized. However, certain assumptions underlie the research method, assumptions that are not self-evidently valid. For example, it is assumed that these elites enjoy sufficient freedom to accurately express their perceptions in published articles. The method, therefore, assumes the essential findings, that there is greater openness in the system up to the point of challenging the ultimate authority of the party and its fundamental values. This assumption may be perfectly valid, but one can never verify it.

The underlying question in this literature on the evolution of the Soviet system is the extent to which the party maintains exclusive control over the policy-making process or whether other groups or interests are able to influence that process within clearly understood limits. The limits on the evidentiary basis for judgments on this question can be seen in the admittedly speculative inquiry into this topic by Joel Schwartz and William Keech. First, Schwartz and Keech conclude that the then leader, Krushchev, was isolated in the policy proposal in question from the other members of the party Presidium, thereby opening up the process for group influence. The evidence they cite for this putative disagreement among Krushchev's colleagues is their silence on the topic (Schwartz and Keech, 1969). The article is totally devoid of any hard evidence to support the claims made about Soviet politics. Even if one accepts the silence of the members of the Presidium as an indicator of internal disagreement with the leader, the fact of the silence is merely asserted; no evidence of it is offered. Neither do the authors address the question of how much silence indicates how much internal disagreement.

Hence, significant changes apparently have been occurring in the Soviet Union, but we are unsure of their extent because the literature on these changes either merely asserts them on the basis of an impressionistic familiarity with the system, concludes that they are a logically necessary concomitant of a mature industrial society, or relies on evidence of questionable validity. Thus, while we may agree with Barghoorn that the basic task or role of the C.P.S.U. is the maintenance of control over Soviet society, we also have to consider the functionalist judgment that, in a complex industrial society, interests do objectively exist, and their articulation will somehow be achieved in a healthy system, despite the official ideology that fundamentally denies the survival of such distinct interests. Pluralist tendencies, in this view, must be emerging in the Soviet Union because in a mature industrial society they would logically have to emerge; this conclusion has not been reached on the basis of compelling independent evidence. The evidence that is cited is often of questionable validity, as illustrated by Barghoorn, arguably one of the more behaviorally and sociologically oriented Kremlinologists, who bases his judgment on the rising salience of interests in the Soviet Union on the Inkles and Bauer refugee survey cited above (Barghoorn, 1972).

The soft nature of the evidence has produced a dissensus among Kremlinologists on this question of the extent to which the party has maintained an essentially monistic control over the Soviet policy-making process or whether a limited degree of pluralism has been inexorably emerging from the nature of an advanced industrial society, irrespective of the monistic ideological baggage of the system. Some scholars speculate that the newstanding representative assembly, assuming that it cannot function as a legislative body, may function as an unofficial conduit for the articulation of interests. Given the absence of conclusive intersubjective evidence such that any number of individuals viewing the evidence would have to reach the same conclusions regardless of their internal predispositions, the conclusions of the various scholars on this question appears to be a function of their own ideological dispositions. Scholars who are more politically and economically conservative perceive the collectivist values that the Soviet Union embodies as a threat to values that they hold. Such scholars are more likely to conclude that the essentially monistic and expansionistic nature of the Soviet system remains basically unchanged since the Stalinist era, that the party retains a firm control on the political process and effectively suppresses the articulation of interests and alternative points of view, and that the Soviet Union remains a serious military threat to the Western world (Janos, 1979; Bukovsky, 1986; Laquer, 1983).[5] Other scholars from a more liberal perspective conclude that the changes in the Soviet system are real and meaningful, that the party no longer retains the degree of monistic control that it once did, that the articulation of some interests is becoming more legitimate, and that the Soviet leadership is no longer committed to foreign policy expansionism that threatens the vital interests of the West (Kassoff, 1964; Sestanovich, 1987; Kennan, 1982). Thus, the degree and the meaningfulness of the evolutionary change in the Soviet system since the Stalinist period becomes more of a normative judgment than an empirical question that is resolvable by intersubjective, sensory data.

This is not to denigrate the usefulness of pointing out the vast normative differences between the two systems. The Soviet Union and the United States embody fundamentally different values and goals that have significantly different implications for the content of their respective public policies, and it is not only legitimate but important to say so. The point is that value-laden impressionistic judgments emanating from different normative perspectives are thinly disguised as putatively descriptive statements about empirical reality. Thus, as Skilling himself (1966), one of the leading proponents of the qualified pluralism school of Kremlinology, points out with respect to the critics of his interest group perspective on Soviet politics, these critics largely focused on the claim that the input and legitimacy of such groups were logically incompatible with the Marxist, totalitarian character that they *assumed* still describes the Soviet system (Skilling, 1986, pp. 224–225).

Clearly, it is dangerous to reason from the imperatives of Marxist-Leninist ideology to conclusions about what individual Soviet leaders may do in response to problems of their system as such problems develop. The Soviet Union and its satellite nations are clearly in the throes of serious economic problems that are producing an unprecedented degree of unrest among their populations. The challenges to the authorities in Yugoslavia in the fall of 1988 and the several challenges to authority by the

"Solidarity" movement in Poland in the 1980s illustrate this unrest. In addition, partly encouraged or made possible by *glasnost*, the Soviet system is experiencing an unprecedented expression of a heretofore suppressed cultural defense among the "nations" that comprise the Soviet Union, as illustrated by the fall 1980 Armenian uprising in Azerbaijan as well as similar events in the Baltic republics. Normally, there is an official "ideologist" in the Politburo whose responsibility it is to give out the official line, a line that is designed to justify the policy choices made by the current leadership on generally pragmatic or *realpolitik* grounds. For many years, the old Bolshevik, Mikhail Suslov, performed this function. More recently, Ligachev, the prinicipal opponent of Gorbachev's reformist policies, had filled this role. Accordingly, Ligachev was replaced by Medvedev, an ally of Gorbachev. The point is that this role is going to be filled by someone who will interpret Marxism-Leninism in line with the political purposes of the Soviet leader, and any analysis of the entailments of that ideology is virtually useless as a predictor or explanation of Soviet political behavior.

POLITICAL PARTIES IN INDUSTRIALIZED AUTOCRACIES

Because of the long-standing and widespread assumption that modern dictatorships were tightly and effectively controlled from the top by the political party that embodied the movement and the state, much of the research effort of Kremlinologists has been focused on the elites of these parties. These include studies of the background and attributes of these elites, such as their education, previous occupations, and their age. Presumably, such data are relatively accessible to American researchers; however, these data are frequently not integrated in any theoretic context that suggests how such data are related to expectations of how these elites will behave. Michael Gehlen and Michael McBride, for example, produced a study of the attributes of members of the Soviet Central Committee, including such factors as age, educational background, previous party status, gender, and region of origin (Gehlen and McBride, 1971). While it is interesting to know more about those who occupy the roles from which authoritative policy is made for the Soviet system, the authors never make clear why we really need to know these things. They never integrate their data into a rigorous theoretic context. Thus, the finding of a correlation between age and education does not afford us greater understanding of the Soviet Union as a political system unless it can also be shown that the younger, better-educated members of the target group behave significantly differently from their older, less-educated colleagues in their political roles. As William Walsh has noted in an excellent survey of the literature on Communist elites, many of these studies simply assume a causal nexus between changes in the individual attributes of these elites and changes in the socioeconomic or political attributes of the systems in question (Walsh, 1969). A more fundamental problem in such studies may be the identification of the elites themselves. They are commonly identified as in the Gehlen-McBride study by the institutional roles they occupy. It is by no means clear that membership on the Central Committee, for example, automatically conveys the same political influence on all such individuals in all Communist systems. Walsh suggests a functionalist perspective may be a more realistic way of identifying elites; however, he does not tell us how such functional elites might actually be identified in a closed system in which institutional membership may be the only reliable information available. Given such data limitations, institutional roles are not an unreasonable indicator of elite status. The more important research problem is to inquire into and hopefully test rather than merely assume relationships between changes in elite attributes and changes in elite behavior or policy trends.

Elite studies have provided support for the identification of one trend in the Soviet system, that of *co-optation* as a means of adapting to the imperatives of a postindustrial society (Fleron, 1971). The term has become one of the *au courant* concepts in the analysis of Communist systems, referring to the practice of such systems to recruit into party or governmental leadership positions those individuals that possess the knowledge and expertise of the technocracy required to run an advanced industrial society rather than to place party ideologues into such roles. Party elite studies have found an increasing number of individuals with technical or other professional backgrounds, what Fleron and others call "the specialized elites," compared to the domination of elite roles by party faithful in the past. Thus, the Soviet Union has avoided the dilemma of choosing between the political elite, who are faithful to party principles, and the technical elites, who could perform the functions required by a complex industrial order, by recruiting such technical elites into party roles once they have been selected for the technical skills.

The evolutionary trends that we have been discussing in this section were anticipated, to a large extent, by the ubiquitous and always insightful professor Huntington in the introductory essay to the book that he edited with Clement Moore, *Authoritarian Politics in Modern Society*, with his concept of an "established one-party system" as opposed to a "revolutionary one-party system" (Huntington, 1970). Established one-party systems are a way of adapting to the challenges of modernization in which the importance of ideology diminishes, a more bureaucratic and institutionalized oligarchy replaces the personalistic and charismatic leadership, specialized or technocratic elites acquire more initiative in policy formation, and a plurality of interests can legitimately articulate their demands within the structure of the ruling party (Huntington, 1970). This insight anticipated the empirical findings on the co-optation of technocratic elites by the ruling party and the finding that the party ideologues no longer dominate the policy-making process to the extent that it was assumed they did in the Stalinist era.

Thus, the trends of a modern authoritarian dictatorship almost follow the path suggested by Max Weber in the early part of this century when he spoke of the inexorable bureaucratization of society as an ineluctable concomitant of the modernization process and the "routinization of charisma" to describe the evolution of leadership in that modernization process (Weber, 1947). The identification of these trends in the Soviet system raises the question of whether these trends are ineluctable for all authoritarian dictatorships in mature industrial societies. Logic would suggest that they are, inasmuch as they are entailments of the imperatives of such societies; yet, we lack the data to establish such patterns empirically. Thus far, the Soviet system is our single example of an advanced industrial dictatorship persisting over a considerable period of time and enjoying a period of peace. The Third Reich did not persist beyond its participation in world war and, hence, did not offer another case to adequately test the anticipated trends. However, as some of the third world dictatorships mature and develop a more technologically advanced industrial order, a test of this theory may yet become possible, providing that the major concepts involved become sufficiently operationalized to integrate them into empirical propositions. An empirical test of the theory of Huntington and others of the inevitability of stipulated trends in the structure and process of authoritarian dictatorships in technologically modern societies may be one of the important research tasks for scholars in this field in the years ahead and an important link with the modernization paradigm that has become a dominant force in the broader field of comparative politics.

CONCLUSIONS: KREMLINOLOGY JOINS THE FIELD?

It has been shown that, until recent years, the analysis of industrialized dictatorships and of Communist studies in particular has been isolated from the broad stream of comparative political inquiry as that broader discipline has been described in this book. While it has been shown that comparativists in general had been among the leaders in the attempt to transform political science from a descriptive and normative enterprise to an explanatory one by attempting to adopt the epistemological criteria of the scientific method to their discipline, these criteria had been eschewed or simply ignored by the preponderant number of Kremlinologists as the world of the industrialized dictatorships were reciprocally ignored by the leading scholars in the mainstream of comparative analysis.

For some of the same reasons that led to the effort to transform the broader field of comparative analysis, many of the leading Kremlinologists have been attempting to generate their own "behavioral revolution" and thereby integrate their specialty into the broader comparative field. As with the broader field of comparative analysis and with political science in general before the behavioral revolution, the focus on description without explanation and on normative proselytizing brought diminishing prestige and research support to the enterprise of Kremlinology compared to the more explanatory oriented social sciences. This effort to transform the field of Kremlinology has proceeded to the point where several volumes of articles purporting to represent collections of behaviorally oriented Communist studies have appeared (Kanet, 1971; Fleron, 1969; White and Nelson, 1986).

Yet, the conclusion of this review of the effort to integrate Kremlinology and the study of industrialized dictatorships into the modern comparative analysis is that the success of this effort has been muted by several factors that work toward keeping the Kremlinology enterprise *sui generis*. The first factor is the data problem. While a number of advocates of the behavioral approach to Communist studies claim that these problems have been overstated and that access to data has been opened up considerably, such data problems still beset Kremlinologists to an extent not faced by scholars concerned with industrialized democracies and even more than scholars studying the less-developed or so-called third world systems. More data is now available as is indicated by the appearance of volumes such as Mickiewicz's *Handbook of Soviet Social Science Data* (1973), a volume that would have been virtually unthinkable during Stalin's reign.

However, as noted above, the available data are limited to areas that are not politically sensitive in the sense of threatening the image, let alone the legitimacy, of the Soviet system. Hence, much of the data in the Mickiewicz volume is of the census type or detailing such information as agricultural production, demographic figures, labor statistics, and so forth. However, one would have a difficult time obtaining accurate information from which one could infer the degree of alienation of segments of the Soviet population from their political system. In particular, we have seen how the intersubjective analysis and interpretation of important trends in the Soviet Union is hampered by the lack of access to information on what is actually happening with respect to *glasnost* and *perestroika*.

Therefore, it seems fair to suggest that the amount and variety of available data is increasing in the field of Soviet studies; however, the range of such data is significantly more circumscribed by political limitations than it would be in less-closed societies.

The study of Communist dictatorships is *sui generis* in the manner and extent to which it is beset with problems of normative considerations. David Ricci, in his powerful critique of the behavioral and scientific movement in political science, is far from alone in arguing that a primary task of the discipline is to "inspire pride and enthusiasm in democracy" and to teach the connotations of the attendent values that a democratic community must share (Ricci, 1984, p. 302). The implicit moral equivalence of political values in the scientific study of politics forms the basis of a recurring theme in the critique of that epistemological orientation. The inescapable fact is that most people in the Western world regard the idea of democracy as good and the idea of totalitarian dictatorship as evil. The latter term can never be merely a term to label a class of systems with certain shared attributes but ineluctably becomes a term expressing moral condemnation affixed to phenomena that we do not like. Thus, we have seen that it was important to some strongly anti-Communist scholars that the name *totalitarian* be retained for the Soviet Union, even though the commonly understood empirical content of that term, in the judgment of many, no longer applied to that system. Similarly *fascism* (sometimes with its magically expanding prefix, *neo*) has become a generic term applied to an impossibly diverse array of political systems, the only common thread in such applications being that the system in question was intensely disliked by the user of the term. These terms probably have some potential scientific utility. Clearly, for example, those two systems to which we commonly affix the term *totalitarian* both weaken the distinction between the public sector and a private sector that is none of the government's business and subsume the integrity of human personality into the organic community to an extent unprecedented in human history. However, the different values implied by the respective Communist and fascist millenaristic views of the future constitute an important distinction between these two types of systems. Moreover, aside from the problems of measurement, whatever empirical content and explanatory utility these terms might have had has been lost in their indiscriminant use as generic terms of approbation. The normative values entailed by the concepts in this chapter are so powerful that it has been more difficult to separate the normative and explanatory modes of analysis in this field than in the other aspects of comparative analysis.

Although the terms *fascist* and *totalitarian* may be irrevocably damaged in terms of their utility for explanatory analysis by their misappropriation for normative purposes, these terms do entail specific properties that scholars may find it useful to consider. Properties such as the use of terror and the encroachment of the state on the private sector, including the increasing subsumption of the individual personality by the spirit of the community or state, are matters of degree rather than discrete, either-or variables, and such properties present difficult problems of measurement. Yet, such problems are not inherently insuperable, and it remains useful to know the extent to which a system rewards and punishes according to predictable rules (however oppressive those rules may be) and the extent to which a system respects a private sector that should be beyond the business, if not the reach, of the state.

It is, therefore, being suggested that, rather than engage in polemics surrounding the impossibly broad and normatively infected terms *fascism* and *totalitarianism*, it may be more profitable to concentrate on the operationalization of concepts referring to putative aspects of these broad types, concepts such as the presence or absence of terror, the encroachment of the state on the private sector, and the degree of legitimation of associations and interests independent of the state. It is not unthinkable that patterns may eventually be discerned in these more narrowly circumscribed phenomena, while avoiding the impossible question of whether or not a given system is totalitarian, fascist, or whatever.

All areas of political science are beset with significant lacunae in their data deriving, in part, from the inaccessibility of some critical facts and, in part, from the inability to assign precise empirical content to key concepts. These problems of accessibility and measurability have been more pronounced in the study of industrialized dictatorships, however. The greatest danger in the enterprise of building explanatory theory in the Kremlinology field is that research will be limited to the generally nonpolitical and, in some cases, trivial data that such a closed society chooses to make available to Western researchers. Furthermore, the paucity of the most desirable kinds of data results in dangerously tenuous degrees of inference from the data that are available and the conclusions one feels compelled to make

For example, as the previous chapter on micro-analysis points out, attitudes, feelings, and beliefs constitute some of the most important kinds of data in modern comparative analysis. These are precisely the kinds of data that cannot be directly obtained on politically sensitive matters in a closed society. Sample surveys by Western social scientists in the Soviet Union do not seem to be likely in the foreseeable future. Attempts to circumvent this particular lacuna in directly obtained data include content analysis of published speeches and documents by members of the Soviet elite (Lodge, 1968; Blough and Stewart, 1987). Clearly, there is a level of inference from such published reports to the actual attitudes of such elite members. There is a question about the extent to which the actual salient attitudes are accurately represented in published reports in a closed society in which there may be real consequences for the open expression of dissent from the official or the leader's policy position. For this reason, findings like those of Blough and Stewart of the published expression of more dissensus than the putative policy of consensus on economic policies would like to acknowledge are rather remarkable and hold out significant promise that significant information may still be gleaned from this procedure on certain questions. Obviously, attitudes on other more politically sensitive questions cannot be expected to be reflected in published reports. Moreover, such data can refer only to members of the elites; however, as the previous chapter made clear, knowledge of the attitudes of the ordinary citizen is important for any reasonably complete explanation of the operation of a political system. While it is true that the input of nonelites in an autocratic setting is, by definition, presumptively less effective than it would be in a democratic setting, the impact of nonelites in the former setting is by no means negligible. Thus far, attitudinal research in Communist studies has been confined to those of elites as inferred from the analysis of published reports, the analysis of personnel changes, and the analysis of elite backgrounds, while mass attitudes have had to be inferred from the analysis of the attitudes of inherently unrepresentative groups of emigres and refugees.

Clearly, much has been accomplished in reversing the situation described earlier by Paul Shoup in the integration of the previously isolated study of dictatorships and Communist systems into the mainstream of modern comparative analysis. It has been argued throughout this book that the entire field of comparative political inquiry still faces serious problems in its proclaimed task of building explanatory and empirical theory. It is equally clear that Kremlinology faces greater obstacles to the goal of building empirical explanatory theory than does the rest of the field, obstacles that, to this point, have only been imperfectly overcome.

NOTES

1. For an example of the continued use of refugee or emigre surveys, see White (1978).

2. See Walsh (1969) for the argument that these problems are overstated and that relevant data are becoming increasingly accessible, especially in Warsaw Pact nations outside the USSR.

3. See Crozier (1973a) for the perspective that mature industrial society ineluctably entails the heavy weight of bureaucratic power. Brzezinski and Huntington (1965) consider and ultimately reject convergence theory. For an argument that convergence theory has qualified validity, see Mayer and Burnett (1977).

4. See Echols (1981) for the argument that socialist regimes with directed economies do not substantially reduce inequalities variously measured across several dimensions. Skilling (1986, pp. 221–242) rejects Hough's interpretation of the data as not "eras(ing) the authoritarian character of such systems."

5. This theme of the unchanged, expansionist, monistic Soviet Union is a recurring one in the pages of *Commentary*.

REFERENCES

Apter, David. 1965. *The Politics of Modernization*. Chicago: University of Chicago Press.

Arendt, Hannah. 1951 and 1973. *The Origins of Totalitarianism*, New Edition. New York: Harcourt, Brace, Jovanovich.

Barghoorn, Frederick C. 1972. *Politics in the U.S.S.R.*, 2nd ed. Boston: Little, Brown.

Bendix, Richard and Seymour Lipset. 1959. *Social Mobility in Industrial Societies*. Berkeley: University of California Press.

Bialer, Seweryn. 1987. *The Soviet Paradox: External Expansion, Internal Decline*. New York: Knopf.

Blough, Roger and Philip Stewart. 1987. "Political Obstacles to Reform and Innovation in Soviet Economic Policy: Brezhnev's Political Legacy." *Comparative Political Studies* 20(1, April):72–97.

Brzezinski, Zbigniew and Samuel Huntington. 1965. *Political Power, U.S.A./U.S.S.R.* New York: The Viking Press.

Bukovsky, Vladimir. 1986. "Will Gorbachev Reform the Soviet Union." *Commentary* 82(3, Sept.):19–24.

Byrnes, Robert F. 1984. "Changes in the Soviet Political System: Limits and Likelihoods." *The Review of Politics* 46(4, Oct.):502–515.

Crozier, Michael. 1973a. *The Stalled Society*. New York: The Viking Press.

Crozier, Michael. 1973b. "Europe." In *The Crisis of Democracy*, edited by Michael Crozier, Samuel Huntington, and Joji Watanuki. New York: New York University Press.

Djilas, Milovan. 1957. *The New Class*. New York: Praeger.

Eberstadt, Nick. 1987. "The Latest Myths About the Soviet Union." *Commentary* 83(5, May):19–27.

Echols, John. 1981. "Does Socialism Mean Greater Equality: A Comparison of

East and West Along Several Major Dimensions." *American Journal of Political Science* 25(1, Feb.):1–31.

Fleron, Frederic. 1971. "Co-optation as a Mechanism of Adaptation to Change: The Soviet Political Leadership System." In *The Behavioral Revolution and Communist Studies*, edited by Roger Kanet. New York: The Free Press.

Friedrich, Carl and Zbigniew Brzezinski. 1956. *Totalitarian Dictatorship and Autocracy*. Cambridge, MA: Harvard University Press.

Gehlen, Michael and Michael McBride. 1971. "The Soviet Central Committee: An Elite Analysis." In *The Behavioral Revolution and Communist Studies*, edited by Roger Kanet. New York: The Free Press.

Gregor, James. 1974. *Interpretations of Fascism*. Morristown, NJ: General Learning Press.

Gregor, James. 1979. *Italian Fascism and Developmental Dictatorship*. Princeton, NJ: Princeton University Press.

Hough, Jerry F. 1972. "The Soviet System: Petrification or Pluralism." *Problems of Communism* 21(2, Mar.-April):25–45.

Huntington, Samuel. 1970. "Social and Institutional Dynamics of One-Party Systems." In *Authoritarian Politics in Modern Society: The Dynamics of Established One-Party Systems*, edited by Samuel Huntington and Clement Moore. New York: Basic Books.

Inkles, Allen and Raymond Bauer. 1959. *The Soviet Citizen: Daily Life in a Totalitarian Society*. Cambridge, MA: Harvard University Press.

Janos, Andrew. 1979. "Interest Groups and the Structure of Power: Critique and Comparisons." *Studies in Comparative Communism* 12(1, Spring):6–20.

Kanet, Roger. 1971. *The Behavioral Revolution and Communist Studies*. New York: The Free Press.

Kassoff, Allen. 1964. "The Administered Society: Totalitarianism Without Terror." *World Politics* XVI(4, July):558–575.

Kelly, Rita Mae and Frederic Fleron. 1971. "Motivation, Methodology and Communist Ideology." In *The Behavioral Revolution and Communist Studies*, edited by Roger Kanet. New York: The Free Press.

Kennan, George F. 1982. *The Nuclear Delusion*. New York: Pantheon Books.

Kornhouser, William. 1959. *The Politics of Mass Society*. New York: The Free Press.

Lacquer, Walter. 1983. "What We Know About the Soviet Union." *Commentary* 75(2, Feb.):13–21.

LeBon, Gustav. 1960. *The Crowd*. New York: The Viking Press.

Lodge, Milton. 1968. "Groupism in the Post-Stalin Period." *Midwest Journal of Political Science* XII(3, Aug.):330–351.

Mayer, Lawrence and John Burnett. 1977. *Politics in Industrial Societies*. New York: John Wiley.

Mickiewicz, Ellen. 1973. *Handbook on Soviet Social Science Data*. New York: The Free Press.

Mosse, George. 1981. *The Crisis of German Ideology: Intellectual Origins of the Third Reich*. New York: Schocken Books.

Neumann, Franz. 1957. "Notes on the Theory of Dictatorship." In *The Democratic and Authoritarian State*. New York: The Free Press.

Nolte, Ernst. 1966. *Three Faces of Fascism*. New York: Holt, Rinehart, and Winston.

Orlov, Yuri. 1988. "Before and After Glasnost." *Commentary* 86(4,Oct.):24–34.

Ortega y Gasset, Jose. 1932. *The Revolt of the Masses*. New York: W. W. Norton.

Popper, Karl. 1966. *The Open Society and its Enemies*, Volume 1, *The Spell of Plato*. New York: Harper and Row.

Przeworski, Adam and Henry Teune. 1970. *The Logic of Comparative Social Inquiry*. New York: John Wiley.

Ricci, David. 1984. *The Tragedy of Political Science*. New Haven: Yale University Press.

Satter, David. 1988. "Why Glasnost Can't Work." *The New Republic* 198(24, June 13):18–22.

Schwartz, Joel and William Keech. 1969. "Group Influence and the Policy Process in the Soviet Union." In *Communist Studies in the Social Sciences*, edited by Frederic Fleron. Chicago: Rand McNally.

Sestanovich, Stephen. 1987. "What Gorbachev Wants." *The New Republic* 196(May 25):20–23.

Shoup, Paul. 1968. "Comparing Communist Nations: Prospects for an Empirical Approach." *American Political Science Review* LXII(1, Mar.):185–204.

Skilling, H. Gordon. 1966. "Interest Groups and Communist Politics." *World Politics* 18(3, April):435–451.

Skilling, H. Gordon. 1986. "Interest Groups and Soviet Politics Revisited." Reprinted in *Communist Politics: A Reader*, edited by Stephen White and Daniel Nelson. New York: New York University Press.

Tucker, Richard. 1961. "Toward a Comparative Politics of Movement Regimes." *American Political Science Review* LV(2, June):281–289.

Turner, Henry Ashby. 1972. "Fascism and Modernization." *World Politics* 24(4, June):547–564.

Walsh, William. 1969. "Toward a Multiple Strategy Approach to Research on Comparative Communist Elites." In *Communist Studies in the Social Sciences*, edited by Frederic Fleron. Chicago: Rand McNally.

Weber, Max. 1947. *The Theory of Social and Economic Organization*, edited by Talcott Parsons. New York: The Free Press.

White, Stephen. 1978. "Continuity and Change in Soviet Political Culture." *Comparative Political Studies* 11(3, Oct.):381–396.

White, Stephen and Daniel Nelson (Eds.). 1986. *Communist Politics: A Reader*. New York: New York University Press.

CHAPTER EIGHT

Conclusions: Whither Comparative Politics?

Revolutions rarely achieve their envisioned millenium. With goals derived from an idealized model rather than formulated independently of existing reality, questions of achievability are often ignored. Moreover, the revolutionaries themselves are seldom united behind a single clear and coherent view of the millenium for which they are putatively striving.

The data presented in Chapter 1 do not indicate a completely failed revolution; the ensuing chapters have shown how the field has been transformed to too great an extent to reach that conclusion. However, those data do seem to indicate that the revolution has far from completely penetrated the field. The fact that so many academic practitioners of comparative political analysis have not enthusiastically jumped on the bandwagon of the modern social science revolution in comparative politics in the way that they teach the course or even in the way they conduct their "research" or scholarly activities may be taken to indicate either a skepticism or a disillusionment about the possibilities and achievements of the revolution in their field.

Here in approximately the fourth decade of the revolution in comparative politics, one finds the practitioners of the field badly divided over whether the revolution was a good idea in the first place. This survey of the state of the field leads to the inescapable conclusion that comparative politics is in a state of conceptual disarray, with little consensus on the nature or purpose of the field, and, hence, no consensus on the criteria for determining what constitutes valid or acceptable research, let alone distinguishing good from bad scholarship. This absence of consensus can put graduate students and aspiring scholars whose scholarship must satisfy a panel of their peers (i.e., dissertation committees and manuscript referees) in a very difficult position when those peers profoundly disagree on what constitutes good scholarship. Among said practitioners, there is one broad area of agreement. Most of them are profoundly dissatisfied with the state of the field, although for different reasons.

It was shown in Chapter 1 that a significant although diminishing fraction of comparativists reject the idea that the construction of cross-nationally applicable explanatory theory is feasible in the study of politics and that it is meaningless to analyze an aspect of political systems such as their party system, the role of interest groups, or some attribute of their political culture in isolation from the whole configuration of elements that comprise the political system. This orientation, known as the configurationist school, focuses on the undeniably idiosyncratic nature of each political system. Clearly, the character of any institution and how it functions derives, in part, from configuration of the context in which the institution is located.

It is not the intent of this book to deny the idiosyncratic nature of political systems, nor is such a denial necessary in order to argue the utility of the comparative method as it was conceptualized in Chapter 2. The underlying assumption of the comparative method is that, despite the idiosyncratic nature of each political system, patterns or regularities can be discerned among such otherwise unique systems, patterns that undeniably affect how institutions function and individuals behave within those systems. This assumption seems self-evidently valid; hence, the rejectionist position that scholars should eschew the attempt to construct cross-national generalizations does not concern us in this book. *Rather the concern is to understand why the combined effort of so many able scholars over more than four decades, scholars who seem fully committed to the goal of cross-nationally valid explanatory theory, has produced so little of such theory.*

The survey of work in the field of comparative politics over the preceding seven chapters reveals substantial successes in producing a growing corpus of creative theories that account for a continually unfolding body of phenomena and events that we wish to explain. Simplistic explanations have been discarded or substantially revised in favor of more complex or sophisticated theories that account for a greater variety of factors and that more accurately predict occurrences of their explicanda. For example, the simplistic causal nexus between electoral systems and stable democracy in parliamentary systems has been substantially modified by subsequent scholarship, and we have seen how the consensual conclusions about the cultural foundations of effective democracy have been reassessed and modified several times. Indeed, our understanding of the actual nature of modern industrial democracy from a descriptive perspective has been substantially modified by the move from normatively or impressionistically derived models to the use of modern research techniques and the acquisition and interpretation of sensory data on trends in the actual structures and processes of such systems. The work of such people as Nordlinger, Crozier, Schmitter, and Inglehart has made possible major strides in moving from a traditional civics-textbook view of democratic systems to a much more sophisticated knowledge of how modern industrial democracies actually do operate and of trends and prospects in the operation of such systems (Nordlinger, 1981; Crozier 1975; Schmitter, 1977).

Some of the impressive theoretic advances in which conventional wisdom has been discarded or modified have been in the formulation of creative but essentially conjectural theory that has not been rendered susceptible to rigorous empirical testing. Huntington's work on the dysfunctional impact of rapid social mobilization suggests reasons for the failure of the Marshall

Plan, Point Four, and Alliance for Progress mentality to have produced much stable democracy in the non-Western world, work that has been reinforced by the logical analysis of scholars such as Mancur Olsen and James Davies (Olsen, 1963; Davies, 1962). This genre of work is distinguished from a class of speculative theory epitomized by Harry Eckstein's congruence theory in that the former body of work on the destabilizing impact of rapid mobilization was formulated with an awareness of the need to measure the principal concepts, and, indeed, the basic tenets of this theory have been subjected to some empirical testing by the Feierabends, while Eckstein offers no conceivable way that his theory could be measured, nor does he indicate any awareness that such possibility of empirical content is ultimately necessary to give his work scientific value.

Much progress has, in fact, been made in assigning empirical content to an increasing fraction of our heretofore soft concepts through the creative use of indirect indicators. The discussion of the attempts to measure such psychological determinants of civil violence as systemic frustration and relative deprivation exemplified this creativity (Feierabend and Feierabend, 1972; Gurr, 1968). The measures of various other personality orientations such as the achievement motivation of McClelland and his associates, of conservatism, of authoritarianism, and dogmatism also, to varying degrees, illustrate this kind of creativity (McClelland, 1961 and 1967). Such creativity in devising ways to measure the inherently soft concepts with which political scientists must deal is one of the urgent tasks in further transforming the discipline into an explanatory and predictive one. Since the kinds of indirect measures that must be used in most comparative political analyses inherently raise questions of validity that cannot in any given study be definitively answered, the necessity of replicative studies for building a body of knowledge in which we can have confidence becomes obvious. By reexamining the same research questions numerous times, using independently derived sets of indicators, one can tentatively gain greater confidence that one is measuring approximately that which one is purporting to measure. Unfortunately, academic prestige appears to accrue to those who are the first to paint with the broad theoretic brush, to suggest the salient questions, and to, perhaps, identify the salient concepts. These theoretic trailblazers usually pay scant attention to the imperatives of rigorous empirical testability in theorizing at a level of abstraction that obscures any rules of correspondence between the concepts in question and the sensory world and, thereby, render the task of replication exceedingly difficult, if not impossible.

WHAT NEEDS TO BE DONE TO BUILD EXPLANATORY THEORY?

It is being argued here that the greatest promise of advancing knowledge in the field of comparative political analysis lies not in the prospect of a major theoretic breakthrough in which a symbolic light bulb suddenly illuminates over the head of some Ivy League scholar as he or she leans back in the executive chair in his or her office, but rather in the dull and academically less pretigious task of wallowing about in the data—measuring, reconceptualizing, replicating, and, on that basis, incrementally modifying the theoretic insights that already exist. The abdication of responsibility for the empirical content of one's theoretic insights has been far too widespread among the leading comparativists—often accomplished with a qualifying disclaimer to the actual theoretic status of one's work, such as using the prefix to a title, "Toward a Theory of . . ." or as Leonard Binder somewhat more pretentiously put it, "Prolegomena to a Theory of . . . ." (Binder, 1957). This practice exemplifies what Lee Sigelman (1971, p. 302) sarcastically refers to as

> the strategy of presenting your research as a tentative first step toward some new frontier, a tactic that will allow you to deflect unsympathetic criticism with an exasperated, "What did you expect? I told you it's only an exploratory study."

These disclaimers are frequently presented as a subtitle following a colon; hence, Sigelman, in the same essay refers to them as the "Colonial Corollary."

Although the revolution in comparative politics brought forth an avalanche of this kind of nonempirical, highly abstract, and conjectural theorizing, much of it from the Comparative Politics Committee of the Social Science Research Council that played such as prominent role in the field in the 60s and 70s, work in the field has increasingly been characterized by creative and often difficult efforts to measure the concepts under consideration to the point where one rarely encounters essays on the wonders of functional analysis or armchair theorizing, such as Eckstein's "A Theory of Stable Democracy" or his "On the Etiology of Internal Wars" (Eckstein, 1966 and 1972). The contrast between such work of those who demonstrate a lack of concern with the problems of measurement and testability, on the one hand, and the work of someone like Ted Gurr, who devotes extensive effort and space to the problem of selecting indicators for each of the concepts in his rather elaborate causal model, is a startling one in the literature on violence and internal war (Gurr, 1968).

Given that they profess an intention to engage in social science research, it is not possible to know whether scholars like Eckstein lacked a good undergraduate comprehension of the imperatives of that kind of research or whether they envisioned a division of labor in which a group of elite scholars (presumably at the prestigious universities) would have the primary responsibility for theory construction, while the countless other academics would be more or less confined to the task of devising ways of imparting empirical content to the theoretic insights of the former group of superior minds. This theorizing produced what Carl Hempel called "explanation sketches" fulfilling what Abraham Kaplan called the "heuristic function" of explanation (Kaplan, 1964). That is, they produced the broad outlines of the direction that a real explanation will take. The flaw in this division-of-labor strategy is that when concepts are created without concern to how they can be measured, they are frequently created without the precision necessary to make such measurement eventually possible. It has been argued, for example, with respect to Eckstein's congruence theory, that there is no conceivable way to measure the precise degree of congruence between social and governmental authority patterns, nor are there any criteria for logically stipulating the threshold levels of congruence below which instability would logically be expected. The conclusion that is being suggested here is that the field has progressed to the point that explanatory theory created without the suggestion of how the relevant concepts can be measured is not very useful for the goal of building a body of verifiable knowledge. Although some of the most prominent theorists in the field, such as David Easton and Gabriel Almond, have also produced sound bodies of empirical research (the former in socialization studies and the latter in the *Civic Culture* studies, among others), the sociological theorizing for which they are most famous has not produced any testable hypotheses (Easton and Dennis, 1965; Easton, 1951; Almond and Verba, 1965; Almond, 1960 and 1965).

THE INTEGRATION OF THEORY AND DATA

The foregoing critique of some of the empirically empty, speculative theorizing that characterized too much of the field a decade or two ago presumes that a primary goal of the revolution in comparative politics is a body of empirically falsifiable explanatory theory. The literature surveyed in this book reveals a distinct trend toward greater attention to the problems of measurement and, consequently, the identification and measurement of numerous significant and interesting trends, such as the dealignment and realignment thesis regarding parties and cleavages or Inglehart's "Silent Revolution" in values.

Progress in the task of measurement has been uneven, however, and has been concentrated in the literature on parties and, to some extent, manifested in the literature on micro-analysis to the exclusion of most of the remainder of the field. The major impediment to substantial progress in measurement in much of the remainder of the discipline of comparative politics is the lack of consensus and the imprecision in the definition of the key concepts. It was shown, for example, that widespread disagreement remains in the discipline as to the essential meaning of such key concepts as democracy, modernization, conservatism (or its converse, liberalism), ideology, or fascism, among many others. It will, of course, not be possible to establish measures of concepts that are consensually valid unless widespread agreement can be reached on precisely what one is purporting to measure.

This absence of consensus on the meaning of key concepts is related to an absence of consensus on the purposes for which the concepts will be used. In particular, the choices between explanatory purposes on the one hand and polemical or descriptive purposes on the other have not been resolved to the satisfaction of all scholars in the field.

With regard to the former choice between explanatory and polemical purposes, the concept of *imperialism* provides a case in point. The classic, long-standing, and widely understood meaning of that term is the extension of the political authority of a nation over people and territory outside of that nation's political boundaries. It referred to the actual political control of such territory—i.e., the acquisition of colonies. As is well known, in the first decades after World War II, such imperialism by Western powers over their colonial possessions in the Afro-Asian world was reduced to an insignificant level.

Recent decades have witnessed the emergence of a school of polemicists seeking to characterize the overall relationship of the Western world in general and of the United States in particular with the nations of Latin America, Africa, Asia, and the Near East as one of exploitation of these Latin and Afro-Asian peoples. The dependency theorists epitomize this assignment of blame for the real problems and miseries of many of these less-developed nations on the policies and on the very economic structure of the Western nations. In doing so, they have co-opted the term *imperialism* and, frequently, with the aid of that ubiquitous *neo* prefix discussed above, applied it to nations that no longer possess or politically control colonies and even to the United States, a classically isolationist power that was only minimally involved in the colonial enterprise. By taking the *purpose* of imperialism or colonialism in the Leninist perspective, a perspective apparently shared by many such dependency polemicists, and confusing it with the essential *meaning* of the term, even to Lenin, those who charge the United States and its Western allies of imperialism or neo-imperialism distort the meaning of that term as it has been traditionally understood.

This is a case of distorting or rendering imprecise the meaning of a concept for polemical purposes, whereas an explanatory purpose requires precision in conceptualization, as argued at length throughout this book. The term *imperialism* carries with it a negative symbolism. It, therefore, becomes a term that one seeks to apply to objects one dislikes, thus implicitly attacking them. Calling the United States imperialist entails a negative judgment about that nation's foreign policies.

Other cases of conceptual distortion may not reflect polemical purposes. For example, we have seen how the concept of *corporatism* has been lifted out of its widely understood context of fascist Italy by Schmitter, Lembruch, and others and applied to the vastly different context of Western democracy. The radically different meaning given to the term is handled by one of the cure-all prefixes that serve to modify the meaning of corporatism in its new setting.

In any event, the goal of building a body of falsifiable explanatory theory—assuming that is the goal of comparative political inquiry—cannot proceed until a consensus is reached on the need for precise conceptualization. That consensus, of course, presumes a prior consensus on the goals of the field. The need for precise conceptualization follows from the goal of empirically falsifiable theory. Falsifiability, as was shown in Chapter 2, implies measurement. However, measurement is useless unless we agree on the validity of the measures used. That, in turn, requires that we agree on the meaning of precisely what it is that we seek to measure. That imprecise conceptualization can lead to questions about the validity of elaborate measures was illustrated in the discussion of the literature on authoritarian and other personality types. In the Berkeley study, we saw how elaborate and carefully developed questionnaires and analyses of open-ended interviews masked an ambiguity with regard to the meaning of the concepts being measured.

One may be tempted to conclude from this discussion that theory, which should specify the meaning of the concepts being used as well as the logical entailments of the relationships among such concepts, should precede data analysis. This message is not what this book intends to convey. Quite to the contrary, the foregoing chapters are intended to convey the conclusion that formulation of theory that is unaccompanied by and unintegrated with at least some empirical application is not likely to further the explanatory and predictive goals of social science as they were discussed in Chapter 2.

It appears that scholars formulate their concepts with sufficient precision to permit measurement only when they themselves accept responsibility for applying and testing their theories in the sensory world. Theories formulated independently of an attempt to apply such theories to the empirical world frequently consist of concepts so imprecise that they cannot be assigned empirical content.

If Lasswell, for example, had actually tried to present his essential proposition from *Power and Personality* in the form of a testable hypothesis, it would have become apparent that concepts such as "power-wielding personality" or "deprivations severe enough to cause compensatory behavior but not severe enough to be overwhelming" cannot by their nature be assigned precise indicators (Lasswell, 1948).

Despite the efforts of Huntington to suggest ways in which his key concept of institutionalization might be measured, efforts discussed in Chapter 3, numerous critics of Huntington's work in this area focus on the persisting imprecision in this concept (Ben-Dor, 1975; Baxter, 1972; Kesselman, 1970). Moreover, Sigelman raises the fundamental question of whether vaguely stipulated social psychological processes can validly be translated into structural indicators (Sigelman, 1978). Hence, one of the most frequently cited propositions in the field[1] cannot be falsified by any conceivable set of findings. The similar weakness of Eckstein's congruence theory was noted above.

This book raises the question of whether a field that aspires to build a body of explanatory theory consistent with the criteria of social science epistemology ought to be devoting so much of its creative energy to the formulation, discussion, and dissemination of what we called in Chapter 2 "explanation sketches:" creative and theoretic insights not precise enough to be rigorously tested against empirical data. A continuing theme of this book is that the authors of theoretic principles ought to assume the responsibility of demonstrating the actual application of such theory to the sensory or empirical world, a responsibility that will not only encourage the formulation of new insights in terms as precise as possible, but should also act as a filtering or selective criterion for determining which new ideas will be useful for the broader goal of a cumulative body of explanatory theory and which are not likely to contribute to that goal.

Therefore, more vexing than dissensus on the meaning of concepts for the goal of widely accepted sets of indicators is the vagueness of the meaning of those concepts. It is one thing to understand the essence of what a concept means for the purposes of discussing it in conversational, nonscientific settings; the requirements for precision in building a replicative and cumulative body of testable theory are much more rigorous. This level of precision is too often not reached with regard to the key concepts in the literature. With regard to Nordlinger's central concept of autonomy, for example, in his insightful *On the Autonomy of the Democratic State,* key elements of that broad concept are such things as societal preferences, state preferences, or societal influence on public policy (Nordlinger, 1981). We are not told, however, of any criteria for determining the extent to which and the strength with which preferences must be held among citizenry to be labeled as "societal preferences" or which aspects of a non-monolithic elite determine "state preferences." Since the relationship between state preferences and policy outcomes is one of the key questions in the book, the two are presumably not coterminous.

In the Weberian tradition of conceptualizing *modernization* as *rationalization*, meaning essentially the bureaucratization of authority and social structure, scholars such as Apter define *modernization* in terms of increasing role specificity and social complexity (Apter, 1965). While this definition may make logical sense, it is hard to see how it can be translated into measurable indicators. It has been argued extensively elsewhere how the functional categories of Almond and others present the same difficulty.[2] The neo-corporatist literature presents this difficulty as well, since influence and its direction have proven extremely resistant to translation into unambiguous indicators (Schmitter, 1979 and 1977; Lembruch, 1977).[3] For this reason, equally informed experts on this phenomena disagree as to whether neo-corporatism is, in fact, increasingly characterizing the politics of the Western world (Panitch, 1980; Cox, 1981). It was argued in Chapter 6 that the concept of *authoritarianism* epitomizes this difficulty of vagueness and imprecision in meaning, despite the great effort to develop measures of it. *Fascism* and *totalitarianism* similarly lack precision in meaning.

Despite the experience of persisting imprecision in the concept of authoritarianism after the Herculean efforts to develop survey instruments and scales and coding criteria for open-ended interviews, efforts to specify indicators for soft concepts may contribute to the specification of the meaning of such concepts. The specification of indicators leads to efforts to justify their validity; however, their validity would be difficult to establish unless the essence of that which they measure is clearly delineated. The continued practice of conceptualization without taking responsibility for the empirical content of those concepts reduces the need for precision in the specification of their meaning.

This conclusion is not intended to mean that political scientists should not discuss anything they cannot measure. The danger that the discipline may thereby confine itself to trivia and irrelevancy is real. One of the lessons to emerge from the survey of the parties literature is that the fact that something is measurable does not necessarily mean it is worth measuring. The amount of effort devoted to both legislative and electoral voting must not be justified by the impact of such voting on political outcomes. Thus, despite efforts to justify it, an early study by the present author utilizing legislative roll call data from Australia and Canada may exemplify this point of measuring the irrelevant in the light of the fact that the level of actual dissent or controversy surrounding any government policy proposal is not ordinarily reflected in such roll call votes in Great Britain and the Older Commonwealth (Mayer, 1970).

Clearly, theoretic constructs or concepts that are not imbued with precise empirical content at the time of their formulation may nevertheless possess suggestive or "heuristic" value. This term *heuristic*—the offering of a direction toward the solution to a problem without being able to justify a solution itself—has become one of the standard cliches used by scholars to defend the value of work that falls short of the criteria of social science epistemology and, as such, has been one of the more misused terms in the discipline. Despite its abuse, *heuristic* does describe some nonempirical work that did seem to point the way to later empirical work. For example, the "J-Curve" thesis of Davies and Crane Brinton's work did presage the later empirical work of scholars such as the Feierabends and Gurr, who demonstrated that political violence tends to occur following a period of rising material well-being rather than the previous conventional wisdom of political violence arising out of conditions of abject misery.

Despite the criticisms noted above on the work of Huntington on political order and stability in modernizing societies, his work possibly exemplifies this *genre* of material that stimulates and redirects our thinking on a matter of major concern for the discipline without directly generating rigorously falsifiable propositions. The crusade in the spring of 1987 by mathematics professor Serge Lange to deny Samuel Huntington, an Eaton Professor at Harvard and the President of the American Political Science Association, membership in the National Academy of Science because his work was judged by his detractors to be scientifically worthless ("smokescreen pseudoscience . . . no general conclusions . . . full of nonsense"),[4] strikes at the heart of the academic respect of the discipline. This work of Huntington, geared to the formulation of creative insights, is widely respected, judging from the extreme frequency with which it is cited in the literature of the field; yet, even this work, formulated without a serious attempt to render its theoretic propositions rigorously falsifiable, renders the discipline vulnerable to this kind of attack.

The point is that the volume of such heuristic theorizing far exceeds that of rigorously empirical work. Under pressures to publish regularly, and considering the greater difficulty and expense in obtaining and processing relevant data, scholars have come to view empirically empty theorizing as an attractive enterprise. Often resorting to what others view as "pretentious language" (Lange's term) or jargon to distract attention from this lack of empirical content, scholars continue to publish these broad, ambitious, empirically empty propositions.

The frequently used disclaimers that their work should not be criticized from the perspective of social science epistemology because theirs was only "an exploratory study" (Sigelman, 1971) or that the study was not intended to be empirically rigorous will not do if we are serious about our stated intentions to build an empirical body of explanatory theory. The question remains as to why the study was not so intended. We have had three decades of exploratory studies and prolegomenas to theories. It is not clear that the goals of the discipline are brought closer to realization by most of this work. The discipline might be better served by moving away from the division of labor between theorizing and the collection and processing of the relevant data, even if were not true that only a fraction of such heuristic theorizing is translated into empirical propositions and tested by other scholars.

EXPLANATION VERSUS EXHORTATION: THE NORMATIVE DIMENSION

The social sciences in general and, perhaps, political science in particular are inexorably infected with a normative dimension that distinguishes them from the physical and biological sciences. While it is increasingly true in this day of advanced technology that the latter group of hard sciences do confront questions about the impact of the knowledge they create on fundamental human values, the more rigorous empirical basis of these disciplines and, perhaps, the more morally neutral nature of their subject matter allows them to conceptualize more intersubjectively than is possible in the former group of soft sciences. Given the growing normative implications of the work of physical and biological scientists (e.g., advances in nuclear weapons technology, genetic engineering, *in vitro* fertilization), it seems reasonable to argue that the differences between the hard and soft sciences are differences of degree in this respect, as well as with respect to the tentative and ultimately incomplete nature of their respective explanations. In political science, however, the problem of normative considerations affecting the enterprise of constructing explanations is a more pressing and extensive problem than in most other disciplines.

This author, together with a research collaborator, encountered the phenomenon of normative considerations clouding the willingness and ability to analyze the data at hand in some research on the cross-national patterns of voting by women (Mayer and Smith, 1985 and 1983). This research found from an analysis of voting patterns in several Western democracies that gender, even when controlled for likely "feminist" attributes, such as being head of household, being employed outside the home, or possessing an advanced formal education, did not predict a left-oriented voting pattern as the feminist "gender gap" literature has suggested the trend to be. In fact, to the extent that gender was predictive of voting behavior at all, it was distinctly in a conservative direction.

The outraged reaction of a number of feminists at the panel in which these results were presented led them to attack the validity of the conclusions. The point here is that this response illustrates how normatively derived conclusions can create a perceptual screen that filters out data that do not support such conclusions. Much of the criticism seemed to emanate from the perspective that since it is known that the feminist movement is succeeding, any findings that appear to contradict this conclusion must be flawed. The authors of this research share the values and hopes of feminists for greater participation of women in public and professional life, for overwhelming support among women for feminist attitudes and values, and for choices by women of those political alternatives that support and maximize such values. However, one's hopes and preferences should not determine the selection of data or the inferences drawn from these data.

The normative dimension in comparative politics is not invariably a bad thing. It was argued in Chapter 7 that the critical differences between autocratic or dictatorial states and democratic ones at a given state of technology may lie less in structure and process and more in the underlying values that define these respective groups of systems. One may accept the theory of certain structural imperatives to an advanced state of technology that are manifested in all postindustrial systems without accepting a moral neutrality between the Soviet and Western blocs of nations.

Indeed, the explication of the normative premises of one's work can be positive by giving direction and purpose to that work, by providing what A. D. Lindsey calls "ends in view" (Lindsay, 1962). The work of Huntington, Lipset, Easton, and others in the institutionalist and systems schools unabashedly values political order and pattern maintenance. Their work is concerned with how these values or goals may be reached or maximized without a great deal of direct concern for such potentially conflicting goals as socioeconomic equality, social change, or some conception of justice. Once the value premise is revealed, one does not have to accept it to understand and profit from reading the work.

The difficulty and, indeed, the danger of the normative dimension is when normatively laden concepts are presented as morally neutral and when polemic is thinly disguised as analysis. It was argued in Chapter 3 that much of the dependency literature exemplifies this confusion. A concept such as *neoimperialism* takes on the character of a term of approbation rather than a class of consistent and intersubjectively defined indicators. The "infrastructure of dependency" becomes any third world elites that are pro-Western, and the diametric incompatibility between Western interests and those of the third world nation in question is assumed rather than established. Data are selected and marshalled to support the predetermined conclusion that some conception of socialism is the only avenue to progress in that part of the world, and alternative explanations of or cures for underdevelopment are not seriously considered.

The explanation of third world underdevelopment in terms of the ineluctable imperatives of monopoly capitalism is hardly a new idea. As was pointed out in Chapter 3, J. A. Hobson, around the turn of the century, and V. I. Lenin, a few years later, constructed explanations along the same lines. Many critics of dependency theory argue that it is merely a slightly modified restatement of Lenin's theory of imperialism with the unstated understanding that Marxism-Leninism has a highly negative symbolic content for most people in the West. Others argue that dependency theory is distinct in significant ways from Leninism. It is not necessary to resolve that discussion here. It is enough to note that, like Lenin's theory of imperialism, dependency theory is a non-theory, in the scientific sense of the term. Although some of its logical entailments have been subject to empirical examination (with negative results; see Vengroff, 1977), the essence of the theory itself remains unaccountable to any conceivable body of data. Moreover, alternative theories can do as good a job or better in accounting for the explicandum, as was pointed out in Chapter 3.

The epistemological weakness and normative character of dependency theory is illustrative of a persisting tendency in the field to disguise polemic purposes as academically respectable analysis. Political activists and ideologues of one type or another seem to gravitate toward the discipline in order to acquire a cloak of legitimacy for their particular crusade, a trend that has not abated in political science despite the passage of the politically passionate and idealistic 60s from the consciousness of the general public. The continued outpouring of new-left invective in the guise of academic respectability by political scientists such as Michael Parenti illustrates the persistence of this trend (Parenti, 1989). It is, therefore, important for serious scholars to be vigilant for the blurring of the distinction between empirical and normative concepts and propositions. A concept either is translatable into a valid or widely accepted set of indicators, or it is not. A proposition entails and can thereby be falsified by some conceivable findings or data, or it does not. Propositions that can be so falsified are considered empirical and scientific; the others are not.

The continuing insistence by so many comparativists that there are alternative types of scientific explanation and alternative methods for constructing such explanations reflects a persisting failure of too many scholars to come to terms with and actually understand the epistemology of social and political science and, more generally, of science itself. The tremendous body of what LaPalombara called "neo-scholastic" metaphysics (LaPalombara, 1970) produced by some of the leading advocates of a scientific approach, and the widespread adulation given Kuhn's *The Structure of Scientific Revolutions* (Kuhn, 1962), a work that not only produced a highly misleading model of "normal science" as dominated by a single paradigm, but seems to deny the very possibility of modern science with its untenable argument that theories cannot, by their nature, be objectively accountable to the data,[5] both seem to raise disturbing questions about the extent to which many of a our leading scholars, including some of the foremost advocates of a more scientific comparative politics, really understand the enterprise they are advocating and purporting to lead.

WHERE DO WE GO FROM HERE? THE RELEVANCE OF KUHN'S MODEL FOR POLITICAL SCIENCE

Not only does the field of comparative political analysis remain badly divided over whether we ought to pursue the transformation of the discipline into a more scientific and explanatory enterprise but among those who agree that the field ought to be so transformed and indeed are among the foremost advocates of such a transformation, there is no common understanding of the essence of scientific epistemology and, therefore, what kinds of activities contribute to the goals of that enterprise. It was stated at the outset of this chapter that revolutions rarely achieve their millenia. This failure is, in part, due to the fact that the leaders of such revolutions are rarely united behind a clear and coherent vision of that millenium. This analogy can be applied to the field of comparative political analysis by pointing out the absence of a clear vision of a scientific discipline among the scholars who have been leading the move toward that enterprise.

The aforementioned reception given to Kuhn's misleading perception of science is a case in point. This favorable reception indicates a failure to understand what is involved in the cumulative building of knowledge that actually characterizes the scientific enterprise. Knowledge is not advanced by the symbolic light bulb over some scholar's head suddenly revealing an entire general theory of his or her discipline, as with Kuhn's image of Einstein's theory of relativity supplanting Newtonian mechanics. Rather, knowledge is incrementally advanced by the modification of existing theories in such a way as to account for deviant cases and thereby explain a greater percentage of the heretofore unexplained variation. The identification of another variable to render an existing explanatory theory at the same time more complex and more complete, or the modification or conceptualization of a variable, constitutes the normal way to reduce the unexplained residuals.[6] Yet, this kind of refinement of existing causal models is not nearly as glamorous as the claim to have broken new theoretical ground. Moreover, such a less-glamorous refinement of existing theory is much more difficult to get accepted for publication in the major journals of the field than a claim to have conceived of a new theoretic breakthrough with the pious but insincere hope this preface to or prolegomena to a new quasi-theory will stimulate further research to give that breakthrough empirical content.

Therefore, Kuhn's model of "normal science," a period in which scholars are busily engaged in the task of "paradigm articulation," the gathering of data to support the conventionally accepted dominant parradigm, is as misleading as is his image of scientific revolutions. Natural science is not dominated by a single paradigm, and new theory modifies but does not entirely supplant the old. Newtonian mechanics is not dead in physics, and Einstein's theory grew out of the need to account for anomolies in the existing theory. Normal science is not necessarily theoretically static, as is implied by the Kuhn model, but, rather, is frequently characterized by incremental reductions in the unexplained residuals and refinement of existing theory.

This is not to imply that new theoretic insights never occur or are without value when they do. Clearly, this book has examined many such major advances or changes in the ways we think about aspects of politics. Among them are Inglehart's "Silent Revolution," Schmitter's neo-corporatism in Europe, or the realignment and dealignment literature on parties. However, such efforts fall considerably short of what Kuhn meant by a scientific revolution but, rather, constitute much more modest advances in accounting for a greater portion of those phenomena we seek to understand. These more modest objectives hold much greater promise of success and are consistent with a clearer understanding of the scientific enterprise than the rather fruitless search for bold new theoretic breakthroughs.

EQUIVALENT MEASUREMENT AS A KEY PRIORITY

The enterprise of constructing scientific explanations of social or political phenomena is beset with the difficulty of rendering empirical content to the inherently soft concepts with which scholars in these disciplines must contend. The specification of indirect indicators for such concepts inexorably raises questions of the validity of such indicators, questions that cannot be conclusively resolved. Such questions must necessarily cloud the confidence that we have in the results of any given study and thereby impede the process of building a cumulative body of knowledge.

That process assumes, after all, that one can resolve some research questions with a fair amount of confidence and agreement in order to build on those results.

The standard mechanisms for justifying implicit claims for the validity of one's indicators are well known and have been fully described in countless books on research methods. These mechanisms are variously named and classified by different authors; however, certain terms appear to be recurring in discussions of validity, such as *face validity, construct validity,* and *predictive validity*. These mechanisms afford greater confidence in and a measure of justification for claims of validity for measures of soft concepts, but again it must be stressed that they do not conclusively establish such validity.

The problem of validity is particularly acute in cross-cultural analysis, the heart of comparative politics, because the meaning of indicators is specific to each cultural context. The standard mechanisms, such as face validity or construct validity, may be less useful when dealing with studies emanating from vastly different cultural settings.

One way of addressing this problem is through the replication of existing studies in a range of spacio-temporal settings utilizing different indicators, indicators that the scholar familiar with that setting judges to be appropriate to the concepts in question. Hence, the replication of existing theoretic insights becomes one of the important tasks ahead for advancing the goals of the discipline, a task that also lacks the glamor of the creation of new theory. Here again, the major journals, in their publication decisions, are not as encouraging to this mundane kind of wallowing about in the data as they are to claims of new theoretic breakthroughs. Yet, it may be argued that such replication is far more valuable in the task of the cumulative building of a corpus of empirically verifiable propositions in which we at least tentatively have confidence than are the grandiose claims of the grand theorizers.

What all of this discussion seems to imply is that the task of building a more scientific discipline requires an army of scholars that have a less distorted view of the nature of such an academic enterprise. Perhaps many of those who have set the direction for the field in this revolution and have produced some of its most influential work were educated before training in scientific epistemology was routinely included in the curriculum of political scientists. Probably some of those mentors engaged in such training were themselves poorly trained or untrained and have a distorted view of social science epistemology that they pass along to their students. In any event, much of the work purporting to contribute to the goal of building scientific knowledge of politics betrays a poor comprehension by its authors of the imperatives of that goal. We will not succeed in "doing science" until more of us understand what that entails and until more of us agree that this goal should be the basic purpose of the field. Until the discipline is more successful in producing a body of intersubjectively justifiable knowledge in which there is widespread confidence, a significant fraction of the scholars in the field of comparative politics will retain lingering doubts about the wisdom and possibilities of that enterprise, and the revolution in comparative politics will remain incomplete.

NOTES

1. Sigelman finds *Political Order in Changing Societies* cited over 250 times between 1975 and 1977, while the average work is cited 3.5 times in its lifetime.

2. For one of the best and most scathing critiques of functionalism in general in political science, see Gregor (1968).

3. See also the concept of "liberal corporatism" as developed by Lembruch (1977).

4. Quoted from *The New Republic*, July 27, 1987, p. 17.

5. See the excellent critique of Kuhn as his book relates to political science in Landau (1972).

6. By adding another factor to and modifying Taylor and Hudson's concept of party system (1971), Mayer (1980) was able to explain a significantly higher percentage of variation in the explicandum *cabinet stability in European democracies* than were Taylor and Hudson.

REFERENCES

Almond, Gabriel. 1960. "A Functional Approach to Comparative Politics." In *The Politics of Developing Areas*, edited by Gabriel Almond and James Coleman. Princeton, NJ: Princeton University Press.

Almond, Gabriel. 1965. "A Developmental Approach to Political Systems." *World Politics* XVII(2, Jan.):183–214.

Almond, Gabriel and Sidney Verba. 1965. *The Civic Culture*. Boston: Little, Brown.

Apter, David. 1965. *The Politics of Modernization*. Chicago: University of Chicago Press.

Baxter, Donald. 1972. "The Notion of Institutionalization in Political Development: A Concept Mauled." Paper delivered to the annual meeting of the Southern Political Science Association.

Ben-Dor, Gabriel. 1975. "Institutionalization and Political Development: A Conceptual and Theoretical Analysis." *Comparative Studies in History and Society* 17(3, July):309–325.

Binder, Leonard. 1957. "Prolegomena to the Comparative Study of Middle East Governments." *American Political Science Review* LI(3, Sept.):651–668.

Cox, Andrew. 1981. "Corporatism as Reductionism: The Analytic Limits of the Corporate Thesis." *Government and Opposition* 16(1, Winter):78–95.

Crozier, Michael. 1975. "Western Europe." In *The Crisis of Democracy*, edited by Michael Crozier, Sam Huntington, and Joji Watanuki. New York: New York University Press.

Davies, James. 1962. "Toward a Theory of Revolution." *American Sociological Review* XXVII(1, Feb.):5–18.

Easton, David. 1951. *The Political System*. New York: Knopf.

Easton, David and Jack Dennis. 1965. "The Child's Image of Government." *The Annals of the American Academy of Political and Social Science* 361(3, Sept.):40–57.

Eckstein, Harry. 1966. "A Theory of Stable Democracy." Appendix B to *Division and Cohesion in Democracy: A Study of Norway*. Princeton, NJ: Princeton University Press.

Eckstein, Harry. 1972. "On the Etiology of Internal Wars." In *Anger, Violence, and Politics*, edited by Ivo Feierabend, Rosalind Feierabend, and Ted Gurr. Englewood Cliffs, NJ: Prentice Hall.

Feierabend, Ivo and Rosalind Feierabend. (1972). "Systemic Conditions of Political Aggression: An Application of Frustration-Aggression Theory." In *Anger, Violence, and Politics*, edited by the Feierabends and Ted Gurr. Englewood Cliffs, NJ: Prentice-Hall.

Gregor, James. 1968. "Political Science and the Uses of Functional Analysis." *American Political Science Review* LXII(4, Dec.):425–439.

Gurr, Ted. 1968. "A Causal Model of Civil Strife: A Comparative Analysis Using New Indices." *American Political Science Review* LXII(4, Dec.):1104–1124.

Kaplan, Abraham. 1964. *The Conduct of Inquiry*. San Francisco: Chandler.

Kesselman, Mark. 1970. "Overinstitutionalization and Political Constraint: The Case of France." *Comparative Politics* 3(1, Oct.):21–44.

Kuhn, Thomas. 1962. *The Structure of Scientific Revolutions*. Chicago: University of Chicago Press.

Landau, Martin. 1972. *Political Theory and Political Science*. New York: Macmillan.

LaPalombara, Joseph. 1970. "Parsimony and Empiricism in Comparative Politics: An Anti-Scholastic View." In *The Methodology of Comparative Research*, edited by Robert Holt and John Turner. New York: The Free Press.

Lasswell, Harold. 1948. *Power and Personality*. New York: W. W. Norton.

Lembruch, Gerhard. 1977. "Liberal Corporatism and Party Government." *Comparative Political Studies* 10(1, April):91–124.

Lindsay, A. D. 1962. *The Modern Democratic State.* New York: Oxford Galaxy Books.
Mayer, Lawrence. 1970. "Federalism and Party Behavior in Australia and Canada." *Western Political Quarterly* 23(4, Dec.):795–807.
Mayer, Lawrence. 1972. *Comparative Political Inquiry.* Homewood, IL: The Dorsey Press.
Mayer, Lawrence. 1980. "Party Systems and Cabinet Stability." In *Western European Party Systems,* edited by Peter Merkl. New York: The Free Press.
Mayer, Lawrence and Roland Smith. 1983. "The Changing Political Behavior of Women in Western Democracies." Paper delivered to the annual meeting of the American Political Science Association.
Mayer, Lawrence and Roland Smith. 1985. "Feminism and Religiosity: Female Electoral Behaviour in Western Europe." *West Eurupean Politics* 8(4, Oct.):38–50.
McClelland, David. 1961 and 1967. *The Achieving Society.* New York: The Free Press.
Nordlinger, Eric. 1981. *On the Autonomy of the Democratic State.* Cambridge: Harvard University Press.
Olsen, Mancur. 1963. "Rapid Growth as a Destabilizing Force." *Journal of Economic History* 3(4, Dec.):529–552.
Panitch, Leo. 1980. "Recent Theorizations of Corporatism: Reflections on a Growth Industry." *British Journal of Sociology* 31(2, June):159–187.
Parenti, Michael. 1980. *The Sword and the Dollar: Imperialism, Revolution, and the Arms Race.* New York: St. Martin's Press.
Schmitter, Phillipe. 1977. "Modes of Interest Mediation and Models of Societal Change in Western Europe." *Comparative Political Studies* 10(1, April):7–35.
Schmitter, Phillipe. 1979. "Still the Century of Corporatism?" In *Trends Toward Corporatists Intermediation,* edited by Phillipe Schmitter and Gerhard Lembruch, pp. 6–52. Beverly Hills, CA: Sage Publications.
Sigelman, Lee. 1971. "How to Succeed in Political Science by Being Very Trying: A Methodological Sampler." *PS* 10(3, Summer):302.
Sigelman, Lee. 1978. "Understanding Political Instability: An Evaluation of the Social Mobilization Approach." Paper delivered to the annual meeting of the Midwest Political Science Association.
Taylor, Michael and V. M. Hudson. 1971. "Party Systems and Cabinet Stability." *American Political Science Review* LXV(1, Mar.):28–37.
Vengroff, Richard. 1977. "Dependence, Development, and Inequality in Black Africa." *African Studies Review* 20(2, Sept.):17–26.

Index

Adorno, T. W., 218
alienation, 190
The Alliance [Social Democratic and Liberal Parties in Britain], 148
Almond, Gabriel, 16, 61, 64, 65, 67, 68, 84, 96, 105, 132, 196–199, 206, 213, 225, 278, 283
Amery, L. S., 117
Apter, David, 72, 83, 96, 207, 247, 283
Aquino, Corazon, 108
Arendt, Hannah, 241, 245, 248
authority, attitudes toward, 184
Authoritarian Personality, 217–219
Ayer, A. J., 34, 56

Banfield, Edward, 87, 227
Barber, James David, 226
Barghoorn, Frederick, 257–258
Bauer, Raymond, 237, 258
Bauer, P. T., 84
Baxter, Donald, 281
Beck, John, 148
Beer, Samuel, 136, 162–163, 184
Bell, Daniel, 120–121, 124, 144, 188–189
Bendix, Richard, 248

Ben-Dor, Gabriel, 281
Berg-Schlosser, Dirk, 92
Bialer, Seweryn, 240
Binder, Leonard, 51, 52, 275
Bodenheimer, Susan, 80, 85, 86, 91–92, 95, 97
Blalock, Hubert, 41, 86, 217
Blough, Roger, 267
Bollen, Kenneth, 84
Brinton, Crane, 16, 132, 222, 284
Brodbeck, May, 32, 194
Brown, Roger, 219
Brunswik, Else, 218
Brzezinski, Zbigniew, 241, 247, 248
Buddhism, 213–214
Budge, Ivan, 162
Bukovsky, Vladimir, 259
bureaucracy, 69; separation of politics and . . . , 118; heavy weight of bureaucratic power, 118–119; in post-industrial societies, 210; classic . . . , 121–122; representative, 122ff
bureaucratic authoritarian regimes, 69, 72
Burnett, John, 120, 123, 132–133
Byrnes, Robert, 252–253

297

Campbell, Angus, 162
Campbell, Harold, 166, 169
capabilities of a system, 68
Cardozo, Fernando, 97
Castroism, 244
Catholic Church, 91, 214
Causon, Allen, 128
ceteris paribus qualifier in scientific propositions, 37–38
Chalet, Monica, 161
Chapell, Henry, 164
Chilcote, Ronald, 225
Christian Democratic Appeal [Netherlands], 170
Civic Culture, The, 196–199
concepts: in scientific explanations, 30, 281; empirical vs. normative, 289; inferential and indirect indicators, 54, 221; softness of . . . , 179, 283; dispositional, 180, 281; transendent or Platonic essentialism, 182; validity of indicators . . . , 182, 221, 279, 292; equivalence of . . . , 183, 238, 291–292; psychoanalytic, 216ff; generality vs. empiricism, 220; refers to too few cases, 250; heuristic value of . . . , 284; polemical purposes, 279–280
Cnudde, Charles, 70
Cobb, Roger, 190
Cohen, Steven, 254
comparative method, 42ff
configurative approach, 15, 273
congruence theory, 194–196, 278, 282
Conradt, David, 200–201
convergence theory, 128, 240, 247
comparative politics, defined, 12, 18–19, 57
Converse, Phillip, 162
co-optation, 261
corporatism, neo, 124ff., 280, 291
correlation, 40–41
Cox, Andrew, 128, 129, 283
Crewe, Ivor, 162
Crick, Bernard, 117
Cristolph, James, 185

Crozier, Michael, 121–122, 130, 131, 199, 253, 274
cultural defense, 147–148
Cutwright, Phillips, 70–71, 73
cybernetics, 130

Dahl, Robert, 104
Dahrendorf, Ralf, 130, 134, 193
Dalton, Russell, 145, 148, 164, 166, 167, 198
Davies, A.D., 226
Davies, James, 221, 275, 284
dealignment [from party identification], 166–170, 278, 291
democracy: and stability, 71; defining 71, 102ff
Democraten 66 [Netherlands], 148
Dennis, Jack, 278
dependency theory, 23–24, 79–95
Deutsch, Karl, 69, 130, 134, 206
development, political, defined, 213
Diamant, Alfred, 68, 120
Di Palma, Giuseppe, 191
Dittrich, Karl, 170, 171
Djilas, Milovan, 252
Dos Santos, Theotonio, 80
Down, Anthony, 163–164, 170
Duran, Charles, 95
Duverger, Maurice, 48, 157

Easton, David, 21, 22, 51, 131, 225, 278, 287
Eberstadt, Nick, 240–242
Eckstein, Harry, 19, 194–196, 225, 277–278, 282
ecological fallacy, 54, 223
Ehrman, Henry, 120
Eisenstadt, S. N., 68
Elder, Charles, 190
empiricism: and generality, 8, 55; and falsifiability, 34
equality: between West and Third World, 76; inequality and dependency, 79ff; political, 104–105; as criterion for democracy, 115

Index

Erikson, Eric, 208, 210, 227
Evans, Peter, 94
experimental method, 38ff
explanation: as the purpose of the new comparative politics, 14–15; scientific, defined, 30; post-hoc, 70
Eysenck, H. J., 219

Fairlie, Dennis, 162
fascism, 243, 245, 250, 266
Feierabend, Ivo and Rosalind, 55, 221, 224, 275, 284
Flanagan, Scott, 148
Fleron, Frederic, 236, 261–262, 264
Frank, Andre Gunder, 80, 95
Free Quebec Party [Canada], 147
free will, 36
Freud, Sigmund, 180, 209
Friedrich, Carl, 241, 247, 248
Fromm, Eric, 215–216, 227

Gadbois, George, 8, 18, 19
Gasioworski, Mark, 84–85
Gehlen, Michael, 260–261
glasnost, 239, 241, 252ff., 260, 265
Gorbachev, Mikhail, General Secretary of C.P.S.U. and President of U.S.S.R., 239, 241, 253, 254
Green Party [West Germany], 148
Gregor, A. James, 243–244, 246
Grew, Raymond, 188
Grofman, Bernard, 39, 150
Gurr, Ted, 55, 132, 221–224, 275, 277, 284

Harding, Steve, 145
Hegel, George, 22–23
hegomonic party system, 109, 113
Hempel, Carl, 32, 277
Herman, V. A., 158
Hermans, F. A., 48–49, 150–151, 155, 156, 157
Hibbs, Douglas, 223

Hill, Keith, 157
historicism, 22
Hobson, J. A., 79, 80, 288
Holbert, Ann, 50
Hough, Jerry, 253–254
Huntington, Samuel, 63, 68, 70, 74, 96, 130, 131, 133, 188, 192, 199, 206, 213, 235, 262, 274, 281, 284–285, 287

Ideology: end of . . . , 144, 159, 186; ideological style vs. pragmatism, 185–188; and tolerance, 186
imperialism, 79–83, 279–280
Inglehart, Ronald, 145, 146, 147, 161, 202–206, 219, 224, 227, 274, 291
Inkles, Alex, 180, 237, 258
institutionlization and political development, 68, 133
Irwin, Gale, 170, 171
Islam, 82, 212
Islamic fundamentalism, 64

Janos, Andrew, 259
Jews, 53, 79; and anti-Semitism, 218–220; and the Soviet Union, 250
justice, 63

Kahan, George M., 189
Kalleberg, Arthur, 65
Kanet, Roger, 264
Kaplan, Abraham, 33, 209, 277
Kassof, Allen, 259
Kautsky, Karl, 206
Kavanaugh, Dennis, 135, 200–201
Keech, William, 164, 257
Kelly, Rita Mae, 236
Kennan, George, 259
Kesselman, Mark, 281
Khomeini, the Ayatollah, 248
King, Anthony, 149, 162
Kingsly, Donald, 122
Kirchheimer, Otto, 159–160, 169, 172

Kornhouser, William, 236, 245, 246
Kuhn, Thomas, 97, 289–291

Labour Party [Britain], 169
Lacquer, Walter, 259
Lakeman, Enid, 151, 156
Lange, Serge, 284–285
Langer, Walter, 226
La Palombara, Joseph, 144, 186, 196, 289
Lasswell, Harold, 69, 225–226, 236, 281
Le Bon, Gustave, 244
legitimacy: crisis of . . . , 129ff; defined, 131–132; significance for stability, 131–132
Lembruch, Gerhard, 126, 283
Lenin, V. I., 79–83
Lerner, Daniel, 68, 70, 76, 207
Levinson, Daniel, 180, 218
Levitin, Teresa, 145
Ligachev, Yegor, 254, 260
Lijphart, Arend, 102–103, 116, 156, 200
Lindsey, A. D., 287
Lipset, Seymour, 104
Lipsitz, Lewis, 104
Livingston, William S., 116
Lodge, Milton, 256, 267
Lorwin, Val, 157

March, James, 120
Macridis, Ray, 13, 19, 67
Marcos, Ferdinand, 108
Marxism: and historicism, 23; and dependency, 64, 80–83, 97, 288; and ideologism, 212; internationalist implications, 250; and Soviet Union, 259
Maslow, Abraham, 35, 202–203, 227, 236
mass societies, 236
Mayer, Lawrence, 8, 18, 20, 65, 120, 123, 132–133, 179, 220, 284, 286
Mazlish, Bruce, 227

McBride, Michael, 260–261
McClelland, David, 88, 209–210, 275
McCloskey, Herbert, 182
McCrone, Donald, 70
McKenzie, Robert, 162–163
McQuillan, Will, 129
measurement: validity of, 54–55; equivalence of, 55; contextual relativity of, 57; of responsiveness, 105
Meehan, Eugene, 39
Metcalf, Les, 129
Mickiewicz, Ellen, 264
Miller, Warren, 145, 162
Milnor, Andrew, 150, 155
mobilization, social, 68, 69, 70, 73–74, 76
Muller, Edward, 39
Moore, Clement, 262

Nagel, Ernest, 31
Naziism, 214ff. 242, 243
Nelson, Daniel, 264
Nelson, Joan, 73
Nesvold, Betty, 55, 221–224
Neumann, Franz, 106, 241
Nie, Norman, 191
N'Krumah, Kwame, 110
Nolte Ernst, 243
Nordlinger, Eric, 111, 274, 282
Nyerere, Julius, President of Tanzania, 83

O'Donnell, Guillermo, 69, 252
Olsen Mancur, 275
operational definitions, 54, 57
order, as a political value, 63
Organski, Kenneth, 23
Orlov, Yuri, 254
Ortega y Gasset, Jose, 245

Packenham, Robert, 94, 95
Palmer, Monte, 87
Pahl, R. E., 128

Index

Panetch Leo, 125, 283
Parenti, Michael, 83, 89, 289
parsimony, as a value in theory, 47–48
Parsons, Talcott, 51, 224
participation, 73–74, 103–106
parties, political, relevance of, 170–171
Paulker, Guy, 189
perestroika [in the U.S.S.R.], 252ff., 265
planning or planned economy, 127
Popper, Karl, 22, 56, 222, 242
populism, 244
positivism, 30–31
post-behavioralism, 21
post-industrial society, 120–121, 248
Powell, Bingham, 16, 105, 191, 225
prediction in science, 28–34, 225
Prewitt, Kenneth, 191
proportional representation, 48, 49
Przeworski, Adam, 32, 42, 43, 46, 168, 179, 238
psychoanalytic perspective, 108ff
psychological representation, 123
Putnam, Robert, 122, 144, 164, 186, 188
Pye, Lucien, 66, 73, 96, 189, 206, 207, 208, 226, 248

Rapoport, Anatol, 33
Rawls, John, 115
Reich, Wilhelm, 215
religion and political development, 212–213
revolution, 16, 75, 272
Ricci, David, 265
Riggs, Fred, 118–120
Robertson, David, 161
Robinson, W. S., 54
Rokeach, Milton, 219–220
Rose, Richard, 149, 161, 166, 172
Rostow, Walt Whitman, 23
Rousseau, Jean Jacques, 244, 245

Salisbury, Robert, 126
Sanford, R. Nevitt, 218

Sankiaho, Risto, 147
Sartori, Giovani, 154, 168
Sartre, Jean Paul, 218
Schuech, Erwin, 201
Schlessinger, Joseph, 169
Schmitter, Phillipe, 124–126, 274, 283, 291
Schumpeter, Joseph, 103, 109
Schwartz, Joel, 257
scientific method, 21, 28, 35; and falsifiability, 34; and non-western nations, 62
Scottish National Party, 147
secularization of society, 211
Sestanovich, Stephen, 259
Shamir, Michael, 160
Shoup, Paul, 234, 237, 238, 268
Sigelmann, Lee, 8, 18, 19, 106, 119, 275, 282, 285
Simon, Herbert, 120
Skilling, H. Gordon, 259
Skinner, B. F., 30, 35, 179
Smith, Donald, 212
Smith, Roland, 123, 286
Social Democratic Party [Britain], 169
Social Democratic Party [Germany], 160
sociological representation, 122
Solidarity [movement in Poland], 260
Sowell, Thomas, 93
Spiro, Herbert, 132, 151, 188
stability: constitutional and cabinet distinguished, 151; indicators of, 152–153; cabinet explained, 149ff; constitutional and legitimacy, 114, 129–137
statistical method, 40
Stewart, Mariane, 166, 169
Stewart, Phillip, 267
Stokes, Donald, 162
Strauss, Leo, 35
Suslov, Mikhail, 260

Talman, Joseph, 106
Tate, Neale, 168
Tawney, R. H., 88

Taylor, Michael, 158
technology: transfer of and development, 93; mobilizing imperatives of, 133; and policy making, 136
technocracy, 124, 136, 211, 262
Teune, Henry, 32, 42, 43, 46, 168, 179, 238
terror [in a totalitarian system], 241, 242, 249–250
Thatcher, Margaret, 164
theory, scientific, 30, 31
totalitarianism, 236, 240–243, 252; distinguish t . . . of the left and right, 250; as a normative term, 265–266
Toure, Sekou, 110
Toynbee, Arnold, 69
Tucker, Richard, 244, 246, 254
Turner, Henry Ashby, 243–244, 246

Union for the New Republic [France-Gaullist], 160
understanding, as distinguished from explanation, 15

Vengroff, Richard, 86, 288
Verba, Sydney, 196–199, 210, 278
violence, 30; psychological explanations of . . . , 220ff; contrasting empirical and non empirical work on, 277; validity of indicators in violence literature, 220–222
Volksunie [Flemish party in Belgium], 147

Wade, Mason, 190
Walloon Assembly [party in Belgium], 147
Walsh, William, 238, 261
Watanuki, Joji, 130, 131, 199
Weber, Max, 66, 88, 283
White, Stephen, 264
Wiarda, Howard, 7
Williams, Phillip, 117
Wilson, Glenn, 182
Wilson, Woodrow, 118
Winkler, J. T., 128

Yough, Syung Nam, 106

zero—sum society, 134

About the Author

Lawrence Mayer received his A.B. *cum laude* from the University of Florida. He received an M.A. from the University of California at Berkeley and was awarded his Ph.D. from the University of Texas in 1969. He has taught at the University of Texas, California State University at Fullerton, and the University of Miami at Coral Gables before joining the faculty at Texas Tech University, where he has been a full Professor of Political Science since 1981.

Mayer is the author of *Comparative Political Inquiry* (The Dorsey Press, 1972), principal author of *Politics in Industrial Societies* (with John Burnett, John Wiley, 1977), and coauthor of all three editions of *American Public Policy* (1980, 1984, and 1989). He has also published a number of articles appearing in such sources as *West European Party Systems*, ed. Peter Merkl; *Comparative Political Studies*; *The Western Political Quarterly*; and *West European Politics*, as well as numerous book reviews and convention papers.

The courses he has taught on the graduate and undergraduate levels include the politics of industrial democracies, the politics of developing societies, comparative political analysis, the scope and methods of political inquiry, research design, political psychology, and American public policy. His current research interests are focused on feminist attitudes and values and the impact of such factors on partisan political choice in Western Europe.

Of Related Interest...

THE ELUSIVE STATE
International and Comparative Perspectives
edited by **JAMES A. CAPORASO**, *University of Washington*

After decades of neglect, the concept of the state is once again a central object of empirical research, theory, and debate. In turn, this has brought to the surface the differing approaches and perspectives of international relations scholars and comparativists. The importance of the state as a political unit, its relationships vis-à-vis social structures, and even its definition are disputed between the two groups. In **The Elusive State: International and Comparative Perspectives**, James A. Caporaso and a distinguished group of contributors examine the state and offer penetrating analyses on such topics as the political culture and institutions of police states, the historical perspective of sovereignty, the relationships between interest group power and state power in "strong" versus "weak" states, and the influence of the marketplace on state authority.

ISBN: 0-8039-3381-9 cloth / ISBN: 0-8039-3382-7 paper

CONTEMPORARY POLITICAL CULTURE
Politics in a Postmodern Age
edited by **JOHN R. GIBBINS**, *Teesside Polytechnic, Middlesbrough, UK*

Many dramatic changes have taken place recently in European politics—changes which have neither been predicted nor successfully explained. These changes include the widespread popular reception of new right ideas, the success of conservative parties, the decline of consensus politics and corporatist cooperation, and the increasing power of the new media and information systems. **Contemporary Political Culture: Politics in a Postmodern Age** explores these phenomena and concludes that fundamental long-term changes in the contours of European political culture explain the rise of the new politics and recent political events. The contributors reexamine and reevaluate the concepts of political culture and cultural changes in a pioneering application of the theory of postmodernism to Western political behavior and political science.

Sage Modern Politics Series, Volume 23
ISBN: 0-8039-8176-7 cloth / ISBN: 0-8039-8177-5 paper

SAGE PUBLICATIONS
The Publishers of Professional Social Science
Newbury Park   London   New Delhi